W9-AEX-638

English university life
in the Middle Ages

English university life
in the Middle Ages

Alan B. Cobban

Ohio State University Press
Columbus

Copyright © 1999 by Alan B. Cobban

Published in the United States by the Ohio State University Press.
Published simultaneously in the United Kingdom by UCL Press.

Library of Congress Cataloging-in-Publication Data available from the
Ohio State University Press.

ISBN 0–8142–0826–6 (cloth); 0–8142–5028–9 (paperback)

Type set in Mono Bembo by Graphicraft Limited, Hong Kong.
Printed and bound by T. J. International Ltd., Padstow.

The paper used in this publication meets the minimum requirements of the
American National Standard for Information Sciences—Permanence of Paper
for Printed Library Materials. ANSI Z39.48–1992.

9 8 7 6 5 4 3 2 1

For Jo

Contents

Preface

The aim of this book is to give as rounded an appraisal of life in the medieval universities of Oxford and Cambridge in so far as the evidence will allow. The materials for this ambitious endeavour include the varied and extensive contents of university and college archives, formal university and collegiate statutes, model letters contained in formularies that pertain to university life, educational treatises, royal charters and writs, municipal records, coroners' rolls, and the many miscellaneous extra-university records that are concerned with university events and personnel. Because nothing akin to personal diaries or memoirs of students or teaching masters have survived from pre-1500, it is not possible to reconstruct with precision a typical day in the lives of undergraduates or masters or chancellors or other university officials, whether academic or non-academic. Nevertheless, using a wide diversity of sources, some kind of composite view of each section of the English academic community may be assembled even if the extant evidence does not permit uniform insights across the whole university spectrum. Not only does this study embrace the social and economic conditions of undergraduates, their teaching masters, college fellows and commoners who lived in colleges, halls or hostels, but due weight is also afforded to those groupings on the academic periphery who made such an important contribution to the functioning of the English universities. College founders, benefactors, women in a variety of supportive roles, university and college servants, master-craftsmen and their workforces and teachers of "university extension" courses all added to the vigour and rich heterogeneity of the academic community.

Knowledge of the methods of teaching and of the texts used for each discipline, whether in arts or in the superior faculties of theology, law and medicine, has to be derived largely from statutory materials, although these can be fleshed out with the aid of less formal sources. This is not altogether ideal because statutory material, being inherently static, is not always an accurate guide as to the evolving nature of teaching and learning. However, enough may be discerned to give a fair representation of the essentials of the educative process. Turning to another area of this book, it is a notable feature of the relations between the English universities and the citizenry of Oxford and Cambridge that, amid all the violent affrays and criminal misdeeds of university members and townspeople alike, there was preserved a tenuous framework of co-operation concerning issues of mutual benefit. As to whether co-operation or violent conflict was the norm is an intriguing question to which there is no easy answer.

Another matter of considerable interest is the repressive attitude adopted by the universities towards many types of recreations and entertainments. This may be explicable in terms of both disciplinary problems and lingering monastic influences that stressed the denial of bodily pleasure and promoted the ideal of the model student who lived a moral and sober life free from trivial distractions. Even so, university, college and hall prohibitions did not cover all amusements, and the entertainments of scholars, whether legitimate or illicit, are given attention in this study as a critical aspect of student life. One point that is strongly emphasized in this book is that the medieval English universities were essentially masters' guilds that were governed by the teaching masters solely in the academic interests of their own members, free from the restraints of external paymasters and with only a sparse reliance on non-academic administrators. This form of university organization can only have had a salutary impact on teaching, learning and scholarship, and is an interesting model for serious consideration in the modern age.

At the close of the nineteenth and in the early-twentieth centuries historians such as Hastings Rashdall, Robert S. Rait and Charles H. Haskins laid the pioneering groundwork for the study of medieval student life. Since 1961 I have researched many different facets of medieval university history, both English and continental. Using my own cumulative researches in combination with the work of a galaxy of other historians, it is hoped that this book will make a tangible contribution to the field of study that was opened up by these early pioneers.

I wish to thank the Marc Fitch Fund for a generous grant towards the costs of the illustrations used in this book.

University of Liverpool 1998

List of illustrations

List of abbreviations

BA	Bachelor of arts
BCL	Bachelor of civil law
BCnL	Bachelor of canon law
BIHR	*Bulletin of the Institute of Historical Research*
BJRL	*Bulletin of the John Rylands University Library of Manchester*
BRUC	A. B. Emden, *A biographical register of the University of Cambridge to 1500* (Cambridge, Cambridge University Press, 1963)
BRUO	A. B. Emden, *A biographical register of the University of Oxford to AD 1500* (3 vols) (Oxford, Clarendon Press, 1957–9)
Camb. Docs	Queen's Commissioners (ed.), *Documents relating to the university and colleges of Cambridge* (3 vols) (London, Longman, 1852)
EHR	*English Historical Review*
HUO	J. I. Catto (ed.), *The history of the University of Oxford*, I (Oxford, Clarendon Press, 1984); J. I. Catto & T. A. R. Evans (eds), II (1992); J. McConica (ed.), III (1986)
MA	Master of arts
MGram	Master of grammar
PRO	Public Record Office
Statutes	Queen's Commissioners (ed.), *Statutes of the colleges of Oxford* (3 vols) (Oxford & London, Parker & Longman, 1853)
TRHS	*Transactions of the Royal Historical Society*

CHAPTER ONE

The undergraduate experience

The undergraduate experience in the medieval English universities was intended to be exclusively male. This remained the situation in England until the nineteenth century. In 1832, at the newly-founded University of London, University College took the first steps that, later in the century, were to make it an important pioneering force in the realm of women's university education.[1] It was not until the 1870s and 1880s, however, that women students began to infiltrate the hallowed portals of Oxford and Cambridge. The first women's institutions that were established for their reception were Girton and Newnham at Cambridge and Lady Margaret Hall and Somerville at Oxford.[2] In late-medieval England women in the middling and upper echelons of society could acquire varying degrees of education through parents and guardians, nurses, domestic chaplains, parish priests and, less frequently, through male tutors or mistresses, their female equivalents. Women's education could be furthered by girls being boarded out for a period in a household of similar or higher social standing or by undergoing a spell of residence in a nunnery where educational facilities were often

---

1. See S. Rothblatt, "London: a metropolitan university?", in *The university and the city: from medieval origins to the present*, T. Bender (ed.) (New York & Oxford, Oxford University Press, 1988), p. 129.
2. C. N. L. Brooke & R. Highfield, *Oxford and Cambridge* (Cambridge, Cambridge University Press, 1988), pp. 310–19; V. H. H. Green, *Oxford University* (London, Batsford, 1974), pp. 185–6; M. Sanderson, *The universities in the nineteenth century* (London & Boston, Routledge & Kegan Paul, 1975), pp. 173–7.

provided for young laity of both sexes.[3] Apart from elements of formal education, young women were also trained in religion, deportment, music and dance, and in other appropriate social graces. It has to be stressed, however, that while women of means might well accumulate an array of educational and social accomplishments, they were firmly excluded from the world of formal education, from the world of the universities and, with a few minor exceptions, from the schools.[4]

The masculine character of university life in medieval England was reinforced by other considerations. In common with many continental universities, Oxford and Cambridge had inherited a remnant of the monastic ethos that for centuries had so permeated education. This monastic influence was much diluted in the eleventh and twelfth centuries following the rise of the cathedral and other types of urban schools that were the immediate precursors of the university age.[5] The monastic legacy found expression in the communal mode of living prescribed for the academic halls of Oxford, the hostels of Cambridge and for the colleges of both universities. Monastic influence is also manifest in the denial of bodily pleasures that is inherent in so many of the university and collegiate statutory prohibitions relating to non-academic activities.[6] Moreover, the commanding presence at medieval Oxford and Cambridge of communities of monks, regular canons and the four orders of friars served to emphasize to the undergraduate population that university education was a male corporate enterprise that was in a state of continuous interaction with the prevailing religious culture.

3. N. Orme, *Education and society in medieval and renaissance England* (London & Ronceverte, West Virginia, Hambledon, 1989), pp. 153–75, 224–42; see also H. Leyser, *Medieval women: a social history of women in England 450–1500* (London, Weidenfeld & Nicolson, 1995), p. 138.
4. See the examples cited by N. Orme, *English schools in the Middle Ages* (London, Methuen, 1973), pp. 54–5; see also J. A. H. Moran, *The growth of English schooling 1340–1548* (Princeton, NJ, Princeton University Press, 1985), pp. 69–70.
5. For the cathedral schools see G. Paré, A. Brunet, P. Tremblay, *La renaissance du xiiᵉ siècle: les écoles et l'enseignement* (Paris, Vrin, 1933); E. Lesne, "Les écoles de la fin du viiiᵉ siècle à la fin du xiiᵉ", in *Histoire de la propriété ecclésiastique en France* (Lille, Facultés Catholiques de Lille, 1940); S. d'Irsay, *Moyen âge et renaissance*, vol. 1 of *Histoire des universités françaises et étrangères des origines à nos jours* (Paris, Picard, 1933). See also J. Verger, "les écoles cathédrales méridionales. Etat de la question", *Cahiers de Fanjeaux* **30**, 1995, pp. 245–68.
6. See below, Chapter 6, pp. 198–211: "Recreations and entertainments".

In addition to monastic influences, English undergraduates were to some degree aligned to the secular clergy. Although the English universities strove from an early date to define themselves as essentially lay corporations, their members, in company with students and teaching masters throughout Europe, had acquired the coveted privilege of clerical status.[7] In parallel with the secular clergy, English scholars were recognized as clerks, even if many of them were so only by virtue of having the first tonsure, the lowest of the minor orders.[8] Clerical status brought with it the claim that undergraduates and all genuine scholars of whatever degree were immune from the normal processes of secular jurisdiction. This implied that English scholars were subject to the ecclesiastical courts. In the university arena this signified, for most purposes, the chancellors' courts that were deemed to be of ecclesiastical derivation. From this point of view, and also because the career prospects of so many university members were focused on the church, English scholars could be seen as almost forming a branch of the ecclesiastical order. Indeed, in the eyes of the citizens of Oxford and Cambridge the scholars were viewed as constituting elitist fraternities that had a lot in common with the mystique of ecclesiastical corporations and had arrogated to themselves unwarranted privileges.[9] This broad association between university members and the army of the church ran counter to the idealized self-image of the English universities as a separate estate in society that was independent of ecclesiastical controls. Nevertheless, the ambiguity remains that English undergraduates and their graduate colleagues comprised, in a tenuous sense, a kind of ecclesiastical sodality. As such, they would have readily acquiesced in the church's

---

7. Oxford's scholars received clerical immunity in the award of the papal legate of June 1214. Versions of this award, which was in essence Oxford University's first charter of privileges, are printed by H. E. Salter (ed.), *The medieval archives of the University of Oxford* (2 vols), Oxford Historical Society **70, 73** (Oxford, Clarendon Press, 1917–19), I, pp. 2–4, and by H. Anstey (ed.), *Munimenta academica: documents illustrative of academical life and studies at Oxford* (2 vols) (London, Longman, 1868), I, pp. 1–4. There is no comparable papal award for Cambridge, but it may be assumed that Cambridge scholars had acquired clerical status not later than 1225, the year in which there is the first definite evidence for the Cambridge chancellorship: see A. B. Cobban, *The medieval English universities: Oxford and Cambridge to c.1500* (Berkeley, Calif. & Aldershot, England, University of California Press & Scolar Press, 1988), p. 258.
8. On the difficulties associated with the issue of the first tonsure see R. N. Swanson, *Church and society in late-medieval England* (Oxford, Basil Blackwell, 1989), pp. 41–2.
9. See below, Chapter 6, pp. 183–97: "Relations with the town".

perspective on university education as an essentially male preserve from which women were excluded by dint of their sex and character.

English undergraduates were led to believe that they were privileged members of universities of remarkable antiquity. By the late-medieval period the mythological origins of Oxford and Cambridge had been set in place.[10] Students were doubtless enthralled by tales that Oxford University had been founded either by King Alfred in c.873 or by Greek philosophers in the company of King Brutus and those exiles from Troy who had supposedly instituted British society. Cambridge students thrilled to the myth that their university had been established by a group of Athenian philosophers brought to Cambridge by Prince Cantaber, an exile from Spain who had become the son-in-law of a British king. Charters had been allegedly granted to the university by King Arthur in 531, by King Cadwallader in 681 and by King Edward the Elder in 951.[11] An alternative claim was that the university had been established by Sigebert, king of the East Angles, in the seventh century.[12] Such fables, which were further elaborated by antiquarians between the sixteenth and eighteenth centuries, were designed not only to argue the competing entitlements to prior antiquity of Oxford and Cambridge but also to convince that both universities were as venerable as any in European history. Indeed, the *Historiola*, an account of the origins of Oxford University that was compiled *a.*1313, goes so far as to assert that Oxford was the oldest university in the Christian world.[13] Propaganda of this nature coloured and enlivened the environment of English undergraduates and their seniors and gave them a sense of belonging to a glorious tradition of learning that was allegedly unsurpassed anywhere in Europe.

The reality was very different. Oxford was recognized as a fully-fledged university or *studium generale* only towards the close of the twelfth century. Initially, it specialized in arts, civil and canon law, and

10. For the mythological origins of Oxford and Cambridge see Cobban, *Medieval English universities*, pp. 20–6 and notes; J. Parker, *The early history of Oxford 727–1100* (Oxford, Clarendon Press, 1885); C. H. Cooper (ed.), *Annals of Cambridge* (4 vols) (Cambridge, Warwick, 1842–53), I, pp. 1–3.

11. These spurious charters are printed by G. Dyer (ed.), *The privileges of the University of Cambridge* (2 vols) (London, Longman, 1824), I, pp. 55–8.

12. Cobban, *Medieval English universities*, p. 24; Cooper, *Annals of Cambridge*, I, p. 2.

13. The *Historiola* is printed by Anstey, *Munimenta academica*, II, pp. 367–9 and by S. Gibson (ed.), *Statuta antiqua universitatis oxoniensis* (Oxford, Clarendon Press, 1931), pp. 17–19.

theology, and seems to have incorporated medicine as a formal discipline in the late-thirteenth century.[14] As such, Oxford belonged to the primary band of European universities of which Bologna, Paris and Montpellier were the leading luminaries. Cambridge evolved into a university at some point between an exodus from Oxford to Cambridge in 1209 and the early 1220s.[15] Originally, Cambridge concentrated on arts, canon law and theology, faculties of civil law and medicine being added later in the century. Cambridge was ranged with the secondary wave of universities that included Palencia in Castile and the Italian universities of Reggio, Vicenza, Arezzo, Padua and Naples. The University of Naples was founded in 1224 by the Emperor Frederick II and was apparently the first university in Europe to be erected by a specific deed of foundation that did not follow a period of evolutionary growth.[16] It is notable that a country of England's modest size and population had produced two of Europe's early universities. This was insufficient, however, to slake England's patriotic thirst for a dazzling academic heritage. In the fourteenth and fifteenth centuries the Hundred Years' War had generated nationalist feelings that found a variety of outlets. Universities across Europe became important founts of either national or regional sentiment. In England the propagandist origins of Oxford and Cambridge made a contribution to a developing sense of national consciousness that is not always acknowledged. Through academic mythology English students were given a fictive historical past that was as prestigious as that for any race in Latin Christendom.

The experience of medieval students depended to some extent on where they lay within the socio-economic spectrum. In the absence of

14. On the evolutionary origins of Oxford see Cobban, *Medieval English universities*, ch. 2; R. W. Southern, "From schools to university", in *The early Oxford schools*, J. I. Catto (ed.), vol. 1 of *The history of the University of Oxford* (Oxford, Clarendon Press, 1984), pp. 1–36; G. Leff, *Paris and Oxford Universities in the thirteenth and fourteenth centuries* (New York, John Wiley, 1968), pp. 76–82; H. Rashdall, *The universities of Europe in the Middle Ages* (3 vols), 2nd edn, F. M. Powicke & A. B. Emden (eds) (Oxford, Oxford University Press, 1936), III, pp. 5–48.
15. See Cobban, *Medieval English universities*, ch. 2; D. R. L. Leader, *The university to 1546*, vol. 1 of *The history of the University of Cambridge* (Cambridge, Cambridge University Press, 1988), ch. 1; M. B. Hackett, *The original statutes of Cambridge University: the text and its history* (Cambridge, Cambridge University Press, 1970); J. A. Brundage, "The Cambridge faculty of canon law and the ecclesiastical courts of Ely", in *Medieval Cambridge: essays on the pre-Reformation university*, P. Zutshi (ed.) (Woodbridge, Suffolk, Boydell Press, 1993), pp. 21–45.
16. Rashdall, *Universities*, II, p. 22.

state grants, students had to raise the necessary funding for maintenance and tuition fees from private sources, usually from a parent or
other relative, or from a guardian or a patron, whether ecclesiastical
or lay, who was prepared to act as an academic sponsor. Before the
sixteenth century it seems that most students, both in England and in
northern Europe, were of middling to lower social condition, although
it has to be conceded that the family background of so many students
has gone unrecorded. Typically, English undergraduates were the sons
of lesser gentry, merchants, artisans, government employees of high
and low degree, lawyers, schoolmasters, physicians, and village officials
and manorial office-holders such as stewards, bailiffs and reeves. They
were also recruited from the more affluent peasant and yeoman families, from the numerous nephews and wards of ecclesiastics, and from
the families of urban property-holders of varying wealth and status.[17] If
able sons of poor families could not find a local patron, there was the
possibility of reaching university as a member of one of the orders of
friars. It was not until the late-fifteenth and sixteenth centuries that
students of noble birth infiltrated the English universities in sizeable
numbers. In the thirteenth, fourteenth and fifteenth centuries sons of
the nobility were only a minority presence, and this stands in marked
contrast to the substantial colonies of nobles to be found in the academic
populations of many of the Italian, French provincial, Spanish and
German universities of the medieval period.[18]

The relative paucity of English students of noble birth prior to the
late-fifteenth century had important implications for the generality of
undergraduates. It meant that their working environment was com-
paratively innocent of the kind of aristocratic privilege that was such a
prevalent feature of Oxford and Cambridge from the Tudor age to the
early-twentieth century. Although the medieval student had to con-
front natural divisions within the university community arising from

17. See Cobban, *Medieval English universities*, p. 302; T. H. Aston, G. D. Duncan &
T. A. R. Evans, "The medieval alumni of the University of Cambridge", *Past & Present*
86, 1980, pp. 50–1.
18. See, for example, A. B. Cobban, *The medieval universities: their development and organization* (London, Methuen, 1975), pp. 62, 169, 201–2; J. Verger, *Les universités au moyen
âge* (Vendôme, Presses universitaires de France, 1973), pp. 176–87. For the nobility in
German universities see J. M. Fletcher, "Wealth and poverty in the medieval German
universities", in *Europe in the late Middle Ages*, J. R. Hale, J. R. L. Highfield &
B. Smalley (eds) (London, Faber & Faber, 1965), pp. 410–13.

differences of age and intellectual capacity, the hierarchical levels of structure that did exist were not based overmuch upon class. It is true that the companies of friars and monks occupied an elevated position by virtue of their religious calling, maturity and learning, and those few members of the upper gentry and nobility who were in residence represented an obviously privileged element. Generally speaking, however, the world of the English medieval undergraduate was somewhat removed from the rigid class structures that obtained in society at large. To that extent the English universities of pre-sixteenth-century vintage were open-access communities that were designed to accommodate students of ability irrespective of social origins. As long as prospective students were male, had at least minimal finances and a grasp of Latin grammar sufficient to cope with the exigencies of instruction in that language, they would satisfy the vague and unofficial criteria for university entry.[19]

This general accessibility had much to do with the fact that for long decisions about the admission of students were made at the individual level and not by the university as a corporate body. That is to say, in the thirteenth century the acceptance of a student was largely a matter of negotiation with a selected teaching master who would assess the candidate's aptitude for study. If accepted, students would have their names inscribed on the *matricula* or roll of a teaching master. This was in the nature of a contract whereby the undergraduate had to attend the master's ordinary (formal) lectures in the university schools, and in return the master undertook to protect and be responsible for the behaviour of the student.

The earliest English evidence for this form of undergraduate contract or matriculation is found at Oxford in a statute of *a*.1231 and at Cambridge in a similar statute of between 1236 and 1254.[20] In the case

---

19. See the discussion by Cobban, *Medieval English universities*, pp. 352–5; R. C. Schwinges, "Admission", in *A history of the university in Europe*, H. de Ridder-Symoens (ed.) (Cambridge, Cambridge University Press, 1992), I, pp. 171–7.
20. For matriculation arrangements at Oxford see the statute of *a*.1231 in Gibson, *Statuta antiqua*, p. 82, and for later legislation on this subject, pp. 60–1, 83. For matriculation legislation at Cambridge see Hackett, *The original statutes of Cambridge University*, pp. 210–11, with discussion, pp. 72–4; see also *Liber procuratoris antiquus*, Cambridge University Archives, Coll. Admin. 3, fol. 25, and Queen's Commissioners (ed.), *Documents relating to the university and colleges of Cambridge* (3 vols) (London, Longman, 1852), I, p. 332–3 (cited hereafter as *Camb. Docs*).

of Oxford the undergraduate is to be registered with a regent (teaching) master from whom at least one ordinary lecture each day must be heard. At Cambridge the new student is to attend at least three lectures a week given by the regent master on whose roll the undergraduate's name has been inscribed. These two statutes seem to contain the first references to actual matriculation rolls (*rotulus* or *matricula*) within a university context, although the system of matriculation is clearly indicated in the statutes of 1215 granted to Paris University by the papal legate, Robert of Courçon.[21]

An important difference between the two English statutes is that the Cambridge students were allowed the latitude of 15 days from their arrival to enrol with a particular master. The Oxford statute is silent on this point. The Cambridge provision was paralleled at the University of Bologna where new entrants to the joint guild of arts and medicine were empowered, by the statutes of 1405, to experience the teaching of their lecturers for 15 days, without charge, before committing themselves to the courses of specific teaching doctors.[22] In this case, the lecturing staff had to submit to a competitive trial to win the custom of their fee-paying consumers. At Bologna, teaching was viewed as a commodity like any other, and it was logical that new students should sample lecture courses before making their academic purchases. It is unlikely that the sampling process was so closely systematized at Cambridge as at Bologna where students were generally older, more mature and punctilious in defining the contractual obligations of their lecturers. Nevertheless, the generous time allowed to register with a teaching master at Cambridge emphasizes the importance attached to this procedure. Only through matriculation were undergraduates at Oxford and Cambridge recognized as genuine as opposed to false scholars and entitled to enjoy the protective privileges of the university. The inscription of the undergraduate's name in the roll of a specific teaching master was the official proof of affiliation to the university community. This system

21. J. Paquet, *Les matricules universitaires* (Turnhout, Belgium, Brepols, 1992), p. 14. For the Paris statute of 1215 see H. Denifle & E. Chatelain (eds), *Chartularium universitatis Parisiensis* (4 vols) (Paris, Delalain, 1889–97), I, pp. 178–9, trans. in L. Thorndike (ed.), *University records and life in the Middle Ages* (New York, Octagon, 1971), pp. 27–30.
22. C. Malagola (ed.), *Statuti delle università et dei collegi dello studio bolognese* (Bologna, N. Zanichelli, 1888), p. 248. See also A. B. Cobban, "Elective salaried lectureships in the universities of southern Europe in the pre-Reformation era", *Bulletin of the John Rylands University Library of Manchester* **67**, 1985, p. 684.

was broadly similar throughout continental universities, although there are instances of discrepancy between the statutory provision and actual practice. For example, at the University of Avignon there were law students in the fifteenth century who matriculated only upon taking their bachelor degrees whereas the statutes of 1441 stipulated that students were to matriculate within 30 days of their settlement in the town.[23]

As indicated, the master to whom the English undergraduate was assigned was to serve as teacher, trusted mentor, defender of the student if embroiled in a legal dispute and, before halls, hostels and colleges came into being, probably as supervisor of financial and moral issues as well. Although each registered student attended the lectures of the selected regent master, this did not prevent attendance at the lecture courses of other masters.[24] Moreover, it seems that it was possible for undergraduates, at a later stage in the degree course, to change the masters with whom they were initially registered.[25] The process of selection of these particular masters is unclear, but it is likely that the student's relatives or patrons took soundings and played a part in determining the final choice. An instance of this is contained in the letters of the Paston family of Norfolk. When Walter Paston first went up to Oxford, probably early in 1473, Walter's mother, Margaret, arranged that their domestic chaplain should accompany the youth to ensure that the new student was "set in good and sad rule" and that all necessary items were bought.[26] The Oxford chancellor's register of the fifteenth century refers to *tueators* or *creditors* who were mature companions who were sometimes sent to university to keep watch over the affairs of youthful charges from easy social backgrounds.[27] Such companions would ensure that these youths were registered with an appropriate regent master and were suitably accommodated. Clearly, the Paston family's chaplain fits this category exactly.

---

23. M. Fournier (ed.), *Les statuts et privilèges des universités françaises depuis leur fondation jusqu'en 1789* (3 vols) (Paris, Larose & Forcel, 1890–2), II, p. 424.
24. See the remarks of J. M. Fletcher, "The faculty of arts", in *HUO*, I, p. 373.
25. *ibid.*
26. N. Davis (ed.), *Paston letters and papers of the fifteenth century* (2 vols) (Oxford, Clarendon Press, 1971–6), I, p. 370; H. S. Bennett, *The Pastons and their England* (Cambridge, Cambridge University Press, 1951), p. 106.
27. H. E. Salter (ed.), *Registrum cancellarii oxoniensis 1434–1469* (2 vols), Oxford Historical Society **93**, **94** (Oxford, Clarendon Press, 1932), I, pp. xxx, 321; II, p. 43.

The responsibility of regent masters to maintain their own rolls of *bona fide* students, apparently as their personal property, absolved the English university chancellors from compiling centralized registers for more than three hundred years. An Oxford statute of *a*.1275 required regent masters to read out the names on their rolls publicly in their schools at the beginning of each term, and to do so a further three times within each term.[28] These rolls have not survived with the possible exception of what may be a roll of a Cambridge regent master of *a*.1268 that is preserved among the manuscripts of Gonville and Caius College, Cambridge.[29] By a royal statute of 1420 Oxford undergraduates had to appear before the chancellor within a month of entry to swear an oath to observe the statutes relating to keeping the peace.[30] There is here still no mention of a general university register, although by this date principals of halls presumably kept lists of their members. It was not until 1544 at Cambridge and 1565 at Oxford that centralized university matriculation was instituted by statute.[31]

In the fourteenth and fifteenth centuries when endowed halls at Oxford and the equivalent hostels at Cambridge became the usual mode of residence for undergraduates, decisions about admissions were transferred to the principals of these establishments. During the late-fifteenth and sixteenth centuries the endowed secular college came to absorb most English students, although, exceptionally, the royal College of the King's Hall, Cambridge, and New College, Oxford, had admitted undergraduates as fellows from the fourteenth century.[32] With

---

28. Gibson, *Statuta antiqua*, pp. 60–1.
29. Hackett, *Original statutes of Cambridge University*, p. 167.
30. Gibson, *Statuta antiqua*, pp. 226–7.
31. For the Cambridge matriculation registers see H. E. Peek & C. P. Hall, *The archives of the University of Cambridge* (Cambridge, Cambridge University Press, 1962), pp. 30–1. For Oxford's first matriculation register, extending from 1565 to 1615, see W. A. Pantin, *Oxford life in Oxford archives* (Oxford, Clarendon Press, 1972), pp. 3–4. For a discussion of the value of the Oxford matriculation registers as historical sources see L. Stone, "The size and composition of the Oxford student body 1580–1910", in *The university in society* (2 vols), L. Stone (ed.) (Princeton, NJ, Princeton University Press, 1975), I, pp. 12–15.
32. For English colleges, halls and hostels, see, for example, Cobban, *Medieval English universities*, ch. 4, and Cobban, "Colleges and halls 1380–1500", in *Late medieval Oxford*, J. I. Catto & T. A. R. Evans (eds), vol. 2 of *HUO* (Oxford, Clarendon Press, 1992), pp. 581–633. For the King's Hall see A. B. Cobban, *The King's Hall within the University of Cambridge in the later Middle Ages* (Cambridge, Cambridge University Press, 1969).

the general supersession of halls and hostels by secular colleges, it was a logical progression that collegiate heads would have the lion's share in admissions. Candidates who had influential friends or patrons or contacts at either Oxford or Cambridge would more easily gain access to the hall or hostel or college of first choice. Strong connections developed between many families and particular colleges. For example, a family of college tenants at Newton Longueville, Buckinghamshire, sent members to New College in 1480, 1510, 1525 and 1528.[33] There are several examples of fathers and sons who attended Queens' College, Cambridge, in the sixteenth century.[34] Moreover, certain Oxford colleges gave first preference for entry to founder's kin.[35] This preferential system for kinsmen was originated by Walter of Merton at Merton College in *c.*1262–4. It was imitated in the fourteenth century by Robert of Eglesfield and William of Wykeham, founders of Queen's College and New College in 1341 and 1379 respectively, and by Archbishop Chichele, founder of All Souls in 1437.[36] Although members of founder's kin were present in some profusion at Merton College, they were far less in evidence at the other colleges where the concept of founder's kinsmen had been introduced. At New College, for instance, there were only six admissions under founder's kin by the time of Wykeham's

---

For New College see R. L. Storey, "The foundation and the medieval college 1379–1530", in *New College 1379–1979*, J. Buxton & P. Williams (eds) (Oxford, Warden & Fellows of New College, 1979), pp. 3–43, and G. F. Lytle, "The social origins of Oxford students in the late Middle Ages: New College, *c.*1380–*c.*1510", in *The universities in the late Middle Ages*, J. Isewijn & J. Paquet (eds) (Louvain, Belgium, Louvain University Press, 1978), pp. 426–54.

33. G. F. Lytle, *Oxford students and English society c.1300–c.1510* (PhD thesis, Department of History, Princeton University, 1975), p. 42. See also A. B. Emden, *A biographical register of the University of Oxford to AD 1500* (3 vols) (Oxford, Clarendon Press, 1957–9), III, p. 2135 (cited hereafter as *BRUO*); A. B. Emden, *A biographical register of the University of Oxford AD 1501 to 1540* (Oxford, Clarendon Press, 1974), p. 652.
34. J. Twigg, *A history of Queens' College, Cambridge, 1448–1986* (Woodbridge, Suffolk, Boydell Press, 1987), p. 87.
35. The main study of founder's kin is by G. D. Squibb, *Founder's kin: privilege and pedigree* (Oxford, Clarendon Press, 1972). See also Cobban, *Medieval English universities*, pp. 135–7.
36. For founder's kin at Merton see the statutes in Queen's Commissioners (ed.), *Statutes of the colleges of Oxford* (3 vols) (Oxford & London, Parker & Longmans, 1853), I, ch. 2, p. 6 (code of 1264), p. 17 (code of 1270), p. 36 (code of 1274); for Queen's see *ibid.*, I, ch. 4, p. 12; for New College see *ibid.*, I, ch. 5, p. 5; for All Souls see *ibid.*, I, ch. 7, pp. 21–2 (cited hereafter as *Statutes*).

11

death in 1404, and only six more were admitted in the next half century.[37]

The system of founder's kin was not reproduced as such at Cambridge. This is rather surprising, but many colleges at both Oxford and Cambridge were the recipients of "engrafted" places. That is to say, benefactors founded scholarships or fellowships in an existing college, and these were wholly or partially for the benefit of kinsmen. The earliest instance of "engrafting" is to be found at Merton College where John Wylliot, Chancellor of Exeter Cathedral, provided endowments in c.1370–80 for several poor scholars or portionists, later called postmasters.[38] In selecting the portionists, who were to study arts, first preference was to be given to Wylliot's kinsmen. "Engrafting" in colleges was only sparingly resorted to before 1500 but became common from the sixteenth century onwards. For example, at St John's College, Cambridge, five scholarships were founded by John Dowman, Archdeacon of Suffolk, in 1526, preference being accorded to kinsmen born in Yorkshire and having the same surname.[39] At the same college Roger Lupton, Provost of Eton, founded six scholarships in 1527 with first preference assigned to kinsmen bearing the Lupton name.[40]

Just as many colleges had close contacts with particular dioceses or counties where they owned land or from where they received benefactions, so several unendowed Oxford halls had links with ethnic groupings or geographical areas. It seems that Welsh students were much in evidence at Brend, Gloucester, Haberdash, Hincksey (Hinxey), St Edward, St George, Stock and Trillmill Halls. Aristotle Hall in Logic Lane was perhaps most popular with Irish scholars but they also frequented, among others, Heron (Eagle), Vine, Coventry and Beef Halls. In the early fourteenth century scholars from southwest England favoured St Edmund Hall, and scholars from Kent probably had an attachment to Great Lion Hall in the late-fourteenth century.[41] There is no comparable

---

37. Squibb, *Founder's kin*, p. 35; Storey, "The foundation and the medieval college", p. 31; G. F. Lytle, "Patronage and the election of Winchester scholars during the late Middle Ages and Renaissance", in *Winchester College: sixth-centenary essays*, R. Custance (ed.) (Oxford, Oxford University Press, 1982), p. 169.
38. Squibb, *Founder's kin*, pp. 14, 136.
39. *ibid.*, p. 150.
40. *ibid.*
41. See R. W. Hays, "Welsh students at Oxford and Cambridge universities in the Middle Ages", *Welsh Historical Review* 4, 1968–9, p. 330; J. I. Catto, "Citizens, scholars and

evidence of special links with the Cambridge hostels. Welsh, Irish and Scottish students were much less numerous at Cambridge than at Oxford, and no hostel has been particularly connected with racial groupings.

The King's Hall, Cambridge, and New College, Oxford, were the only colleges to admit significant numbers of undergraduates as foundation members before the mid-fifteenth century.[42] It is true that several other colleges had a few incorporated undergraduate members as distinct from poor grammar boys. These included, at Oxford, Balliol, Exeter and All Souls. Merton College had special categories of scholars in the form of the boys of Walter of Merton's kin, the poor secondary scholars and Wylliot's portionists. In some respects these groups were similar to undergraduates who were foundation members, although they lived in premises external to the college and they were eligible for election as scholars only after acquiring the status of bachelor of arts. Moreover, the Benedictine establishment, Canterbury College, founded at Oxford in 1363, had, by 1384, made arrangements for the maintenance of five poor, secular undergraduates who were to be supported for a minimum of seven years. During that time they were to study arts, with one or two being permitted to go on to study civil law. They were also to give assistance in the chapel and to the monk-fellows. It was assumed that they would eventually enter the secular clergy or join a religious order. It is of considerable interest that several colleges had a small undergraduate presence at a time when colleges were mainly postgraduate institutions.[43] There is, however, no doubt that of the English colleges only the King's Hall and New College had substantial colonies of undergraduate fellows or probationary fellows before c.1450. This pattern was radically altered with the foundation of King's College, Cambridge, in 1441, and Magdalen College, Oxford, established in 1458.

The founder of King's College, Henry VI, arranged for a complement of 70 fellows and undergraduate scholars. The scholars were to

masters", in *HUO*, I, p. 179; M. H. Somers, *Irish scholars in the universities at Paris and Oxford before 1500* (PhD thesis, Department of History, City University of New York, 1979), p. 24.

42. Cobban, *The King's Hall*, ch. 2; Cobban, *Medieval English universities*, pp. 118–19; Storey, "The foundation and the medieval college", pp. 6–7.

43. For undergraduates at Balliol, Exeter, All Souls, Merton and Canterbury College see A. B. Cobban, "Colleges and halls 1380–1500", in *HUO*, II, pp. 591–2 and notes.

be admitted from the twin foundation, Eton College, and they were to be aged between 15 and 20 years. After three years of probation the undergraduate scholars could be received as fellows.[44] William Waynflete, the founder of Magdalen College, made provision in the statutes of c.1480–2 for 30 undergraduate members who were called demies because they were granted only half of the fellows' allowance in commons. The demies could properly be termed undergraduates. They were to be at least 12 years of age, could continue until the age of 25 and were to be taught grammar, logic and sophistry, although they had to prove their competence in grammar before advancing to their other subjects. The demies were neither fellows nor probationary fellows as were the incorporated undergraduates at the King's Hall and New College. It was possible, however, for demies to be promoted to fellowships, a practice that was very sparingly exercised before 1500.[45] Following the example of King's and Magdalen, most of the English colleges, both the old-established and the new, gradually came to admit undergraduates. In the sixteenth century the colleges emerged as the natural venues for undergraduates as a result of the phased decline and eventual disappearance of most of the halls and hostels.

Although New College and the King's Hall were comparable in terms of their large undergraduate constituencies, they had diametrically opposed recruitment policies. At New College undergraduates were to be selected from scholars who had been at the twin foundation of Winchester College for at least a year. They were to be admitted for a probationary period of two years, after which they would normally proceed to full fellowships. Preference was given first to founder's kin, secondly to inhabitants of the parishes where New College and Winchester had property, and thirdly to natives of the counties of Oxfordshire, Berkshire, Wiltshire, Somerset, Buckinghamshire, Essex, Middlesex, Dorset, Kent, Sussex and Cambridgeshire in that order. If the complement of scholars could not be filled from these preferred categories, they

---

44. J. Saltmarsh, "King's College", in *Victoria history of the county of Cambridge and the Isle of Ely. Volume 3*, J. P. C. Roach (ed.) (London, Oxford University Press, 1959), pp. 382–3; *Camb. Docs*, II, pp. 482–3.
45. *Statutes*, II, ch. 8, pp. 5–6, 15–17; N. Denholm-Young, "Magdalen College", in *Victoria history of the county of Oxford. Volume 3*, H. E. Salter & M. Lobel (eds) (London, Oxford University Press, 1954), p. 194; V. Davis, *William Waynflete: bishop and educationalist* (Woodbridge, Suffolk, Boydell Press, 1993), pp. 82–3.

could be recruited from other parts of the kingdom.[46] Of the 804 under-graduates who are known to have proceeded to New College between c.1390 and c.1510, 238 were recruited from Winchester diocese, 220 from Salisbury diocese, 140 from Lincoln diocese, 79 from the dioceses of Bath and Wells and 63 from London diocese. The remaining dioceses in England and Wales furnished a total of 64 scholars.[47] Clearly, New College relied heavily upon the southern half of England for its undergraduate admissions. This is in broad accord with what is imperfectly known of Oxford University's overall recruitment. Oxford's main intake seems to have derived from the counties of the southwest, the northern dioceses of Carlisle, Durham and York, and the region of the west Midlands.

In contrast, the statutes of the King's Hall, Cambridge, of 1380 did not stipulate preferred areas of recruitment for its undergraduate fellows. Uniquely, this college had its origins as an offshoot of the royal household of Edward II when the king sent a clerk and 12 children of the chapel royal to be educated at Cambridge. At first they lived in rented premises as the Society of the King's Scholars. In 1337 Edward III converted this Society into the endowed College of the King's Hall. Both the Society of the King's Scholars and the later King's Hall were designed to an appreciable degree to provide trained personnel for the royal household and the various departments of government. This is why successive English kings from Edward II to Henry VIII found it politic to retain a direct supervision over the patronage of the college. Alone among English colleges, every fellow of the King's Hall, including the undergraduate fellows, was appointed individually by the king by writ of privy seal. In this matter English kings may have been influenced by arrangements at many of the Parisian colleges where founders assigned the patronage to an external body such as an archbishop, bishop, the head of a religious house or a group of university officers. Until the early-fifteenth century the King's Hall was supplied with a regular stream of youths or clerks from the chapel royal who were given the status of undergraduate fellows. After the first quarter of the fifteenth century, however, direct recruitment from the chapel

46. *Statutes*, I, ch. 5, pp. 4–7.
47. Lytle, "The social origins of Oxford students", p. 430 and Lytle, "Patronage and the election of Winchester scholars", p. 186.

royal appears to have dwindled, although links with the court and royal household continued until the dissolution of the college in 1546.[48]

Apart from recruitment from the chapel royal, the writs of privy seal for the appointment of undergraduate fellows reveal that, in the fourteenth century, the King's Hall provided an outlet for royal patronage in favour of superior and inferior household and court officials and high-ranking patrons who had government connections. For example, in 1349 Thomas of Wodeweston was nominated for a vacancy at the King's Hall at the request of the Earl of Lancaster along with Thomas, son of Walter the Smith, on the petition of Sir John Darcy, in recognition of Walter's services at the Tower of London. In the same year William, son of William Walkelate, king's sergeant at arms, was nominated on the supplication of Walkelate the elder, as was William of Walcote on the recommendation of Isabella, widow of the deposed Edward II. Nominations to vacancies at the college were also made in favour of Robert Nicole, cousin of Helmyng Leget, king's esquire and governor of Windsor Castle, Richard Lunteleye, cousin to the Bishop of Llandaff, confessor to Richard II, and John Cacheroo at the request of the confessor to the Duke of Ireland, in 1369, 1385 and 1387 respectively.[49]

Although the King's Hall recruited from all parts of England, the main intake was from the eastern counties north of the Thames, with Norfolk seemingly supplying more than any other county and closely followed by Yorkshire. The bias towards the eastern and northern counties at the King's Hall reflects what appears to be a similar recruitment pattern for Cambridge University as a whole.[50] In a purely geographical sense the English universities were regional rather than national in orientation. The southeast of England was apparently a low area for

---

48. For these features of the King's Hall see Cobban, *The King's Hall*, chs 1, 2, 5. The last known recruit from the chapel royal was John Fissher who was admitted on 3 December 1417 and vacated on 7 July 1432: *ibid.*, p. 188.

49. For Wodeweston, Thomas, son of Walter the Smith, Walkelate and Walcote see writs of privy seal of 11 March 1349, 30 November 1349, 1 February 1350 and 18 May 1350, Public Record Office, E101/348/4. For Nicole, Lunteleye and Cacheroo see writs of privy seal of 10 November 1369, 27 May 1385 and 8 February 1387, PRO E101/348/12/16/17.

50. For geographical recruitment patterns at the King's Hall see Cobban, *The King's Hall*, pp. 157–60. For geographical recruitment patterns to Cambridge University see Aston, Duncan & Evans, "The medieval alumni of the University of Cambridge", pp. 28–36, and A. B. Emden, *A biographical register of the University of Cambridge to 1500* (Cambridge, Cambridge University Press, 1963), pp. xxvi–vii (cited hereafter as *BRUC*).

recruitment for both Oxford and Cambridge, which is curious given the region's impressive resources of wealth and population. The significant intakes from the south of England by colleges such as New College, Oxford, and King's College, Cambridge, must have provided some corrective to the meagre level of admissions from the southeast to their respective universities. Even so, that the southeast provided only a limited supply of personnel for Oxford and Cambridge in the medieval period is a matter that is both surprising and hard to explain.

Illegitimacy does not seem to have been a major bar to university entry. One or two English colleges such as Balliol and All Souls College, Oxford, whose statutes of 1443 envisaged a few advanced undergraduates, did indeed exclude illegitimate entrants.[51] The general attitude, however, appears to have been one of tolerance. For example, Henry, son and heir of the Earl of Huntingdon, along with two bastard brothers, John and William, lived in the King's Hall as undergraduate commoners from 1439 to 1442.[52] In the fourteenth century John of Stirkeland referred to the death of a bastard son, Robert, who, 18 years previously, had been "killed by mischance" in the schools at Oxford.[53] William of Doune, who became a notary public in 1340, was of illegitimate birth and acquired degrees in arts and civil law at Oxford and, for a time, was in the employ of John of Grandisson, Bishop of Exeter, who granted William episcopal licence to continue study at Oxford between 1345 and 1349.[54] It has been reckoned that there were about 40 illegitimate sons at Oxford in the fourteenth century and just over 60 in the fifteenth century.[55] If these figures are in any way reliable, they suggest that student illegitimacy was of marginal concern at Oxford. The percentage of illegitimate students, although clearly small, cannot be determined because overall student numbers in the fourteenth and fifteenth centuries can only be a matter of broad estimate.[56] At some continental universities proof of legitimacy was at least a theoretical condition of entry. A declaration that one was legitimate would often

51. *Statutes*, I, ch. 1, p. 6; ch. 7, p. 20.
52. Cobban, *The King's Hall*, pp. 75–6.
53. *Calendar of inquisitions post mortem. Volume 8* (London, Fisher Unwin, 1913), p. 35.
54. Emden, *BRUO*, I, pp. 587–8. See also C. R. Cheney, *Notaries public in England in the thirteenth and fourteenth centuries* (Oxford, Clarendon Press, 1972), pp. 46–7.
55. Lytle, *Oxford students and English society*, p. 43.
56. See the discussion by T. A. R. Evans, "The number, origins and careers of scholars", in *HUO*, II, pp. 485–90.

suffice. Moreover, some universities required this affirmation of legitimacy only if the student wished to take a degree.[57]

The situation regarding the admission, number and subsequent treatment of English unfree students is wrapped in some obscurity. In general, unfree tenants were forbidden to send their sons to schools without the lord's permission and the purchase of an enabling licence.[58] This restriction on the education of villeins probably lessened in the course of the fifteenth century, and in some parts of the country it may have lapsed altogether. The attitude of the English universities towards unfree students was seemingly mixed. The statutes of All Souls College of 1443 enacted that all entrants had to be of free condition.[59] Many sets of college statutes do not raise the issue. In truth, very few English university students of unfree status can be positively identified. It is clear, however, that unfree status was considered to be a tainted condition and one that was not fully compatible with the academic life. This prevailing attitude prompted unfree scholars to seek manumission as soon as possible. For instance, Robert of He(i)ghington, a fellow of Merton and of villein status, acquired letters of manumission from the Bishop of Durham in 1312. Sometimes false accusations of servile origin were levied against a scholar who was obliged to obtain documentary proof of free status. A case in point is that of an Oxford scholar, Richard Stoketon, who acquired letters in 1343 from the Prior of Durham testifying that Richard's father was a freeman.[60] Apart from causing a measure of embarrassment and discrimination, the topic of servile origin does not appear to have loomed very large at medieval Oxford and Cambridge. The statutes of the faculty of arts of 1389 of Vienna University debarred from taking the master's degree not only unfree students but also those who had been manumitted.[61] This seems to be more discriminatory than anything to be found in the English universities.

---

57. Schwinges, "Admission", p. 171.
58. Orme, *English schools*, pp. 50–1.
59. *Statutes*, I, ch. 7, p. 20.
60. For Robert or Walter of He(i)ghington see Emden, *BRUO*, II, p. 903; A. F. Leach, *Educational charters and documents 598 to 1909* (Cambridge, Cambridge University Press, 1911), p. 270, and Lytle, *Oxford students and English society*, p. 144. For Robert Stoketon see Emden, *BRUO*, III, p. 1786 and Lytle, *Oxford students*, p. 144.
61. J. Paquet, "Recherches sur l'universitaire 'pauvre' au moyen âge", *Revue belge de philologie et d'histoire* **66**, 1978, p. 344.

As with illegitimacy and unfree status, there was no uniform perspective on physical handicap as a determinant for English university entry. There are occasional statutory rulings in English colleges whereby students are refused admittance on physical grounds. According to the earliest surviving statutes of New College of 1400 no scholar, including undergraduate members, was to be admitted who had either an incurable disease or grave bodily deformity, both conditions that would preclude holy orders.[62] On the other hand, there was obviously no objection to the admission to Oxford of students of exceptionally small stature. In the mid-fifteenth century two students who were about to determine as bachelors were allowed to do so in their own halls, instead of in the public schools, because of the embarrassment occasioned by their diminutive height.[63] An inspirational case from continental Europe is that of Nicasius Voerda, who had been blind since childhood and who entered the University of Louvain in 1459, qualified in arts and theology, and enrolled at the University of Cologne in 1489 and acquired a doctoral degree in canon law.[64]

There was no commonly prescribed age as a criterion of entry to the medieval English universities or indeed to universities across Europe. To a large extent this stemmed from the absence of formal entrance qualifications for universities in the medieval period. At the University of Bologna many law students, who had already experienced an advanced arts education, were aged between 20 and 25, and some were on the borders of 30 upon entry. It was not unusual for law students of this type, many of whom were wealthy and some were of noble birth, to have held ecclesiastical or secular office prior to their affiliation to the university.[65] By comparison with their university equivalents at Bologna and at universities in southern Europe generally, English undergraduates were usually less mature, less socially elevated and less experienced in worldly affairs. It is not possible, however, to state with any precision when most English students embarked upon their university studies. It is true that young boys were often present in the English universities

---

62. *Statutes*, I, ch. 7, p. 7.
63. J. M. Fletcher, "The teaching of arts at Oxford, 1400–1520", *Paedagogica Historica* **7**, 1967, p. 443.
64. Schwinges, "Admission", p. 172.
65. See, for example, A. B. Cobban, "Medieval student power", *Past & Present* **53**, 1971, pp. 38–9, and Cobban, *The medieval universities: their development and organization*, pp. 61–2.

and at Paris but not all of them were undergraduates. Some of them were attending grammar schools within the town with a view to raising their standards of Latin grammar to a point where they had the confidence to commence the university course in arts. At Paris several of the colleges catered for such advanced schoolboys as one of their resident categories. For example, the Ave Maria College received grammar students in their eighth or ninth year.[66] Oxford university statutes of the medieval period did not stipulate a minimum age of entry. The unofficial collection of early statutes and written customs for Cambridge, dating apparently from the mid-thirteenth century, is likewise silent on this matter. However, the late-fourteenth-century Cambridge statutes prescribe 14 years as the youngest age for admission. This, according to canon law, was the minimum age for taking an oath.[67] The statutes of 1215 of Robert of Courçon for Paris University also give a commencement age for the arts faculty of 14 years or even younger.[68]

English colleges occasionally stipulated entry ages and two that did so were the King's Hall and New College which, as previously mentioned, had large undergraduate intakes from their inception in the fourteenth century. The statutes of the King's Hall of 1380 set the minimum entry age at 14 years, and those of New College of 1400 insisted that new entrants had completed their fifteenth year.[69] The average age of entrants at New College seems to have been higher than the statutory minimum, and it has been reckoned that, in the fifteenth century, it may have been in the region of 17 years.[70] At least three members of the Paston family of Norfolk were quite young when studying at Cambridge in the fifteenth century. John Paston was at Trinity Hall from the age of 15 or 16 until 20 or 21 years of age. It is probable that two of John's brothers were at Cambridge when only

---

66. On youths at the English universities and at Paris who had not yet embarked upon the arts course see E. F. Jacob, *Essays in the conciliar epoch*, 2nd edn (Manchester, Manchester University Press, 1953), p. 210, and Jacob, "English university clerks in the later Middle Ages: the problem of maintenance", *BJRL* **29**, 1946, p. 308; A. L. Gabriel, *Garlandia: studies in the history of the medieval university* (Frankfurt, Knecht, 1969), pp. 97–124.
67. *Camb. Docs*, I, p. 337.
68. *Chartularium universitatis Parisiensis*, I, p. 78; Thorndike, *University records*, p. 28.
69. See the statutes of the King's Hall in W. W. Rouse Ball, *The King's Scholars and King's Hall* (Cambridge, privately printed, 1917), p. 67; also Cobban, *The King's Hall*, p. 59. For New College see *Statutes*, I, ch. 5, p. 7.
70. Lytle, *Oxford students*, pp. 189, 190.

13 and 15 respectively.[71] As a result of the expansion in the availability of pre-university education through the establishment of many new grammar schools in the fourteenth and fifteenth centuries, the ages of English students in the later-medieval period may well have become less diverse than in the thirteenth century. The average age may even have fallen in the first half of the sixteenth century. Another consideration is that the length of degree courses varied from university to university. This created divergencies in the age profiles of undergraduates pursuing similar courses in different universities. While no exactitude is possible, a suggested average entry age for English students of between 15 and 17 years is not perhaps too misleading.

In England, as in continental Europe, students arrived at university with very diverse educational attainments. There was no standardized educational system to prepare pupils for university entry. Exceptional schools, such as Winchester and Eton, were designed as feeder agencies for New College at Oxford and King's College at Cambridge. Most English schools, however, appear to have functioned independently of university criteria. The idea of a phased educational system where pupils progressed from elementary stages to the pinnacle of university entry is one wholly at odds with the unschematic nature of medieval English education. Indeed, it was possible to attend a medieval university without any prior formal tuition. Such instances were probably infrequent, but private tuition of good quality, lay or clerical, was a valuable supplement to school instruction for those pupils who belonged to families with the requisite resources.

The late-fourteenth-century statutes of the University of Perpignan, then in the Kingdom of Aragon, contain the disconcerting decree that all new entrants were to matriculate, including those who did not know how to write.[72] The Latin used makes it clear that, in this instance, the inability to write was not owing to physical handicap but to the lack of writing skill. This statutory provision may have resulted from the need to legislate for every eventuality, however remote, or it may have been formulated to draw attention to a real, if exceptional problem. This is not an isolated case. In 1455 the University of Vienna set up a commission to enquire into the state of a house of students, and it declared

---

71. Bennett, *The Pastons and their England*, p. 103.
72. Fournier, *Les statuts et privilèges*, II, p. 660.

that a large proportion of them did not know how to write.[73] It is apparent that these were students engaged upon degree courses, not children of tender years. The statutes of the University of Heidelberg of 1466 refer to students who did not know how to write and so could not take lecture notes. They were advised to listen in silence and without disturbing other students.[74] The Hungarian palaeographer and historian, I. Hajnal, assumed that students of this kind at Heidelberg would not be entirely illiterate but would be unable to write with any fluency, an interpretation that goes beyond the actual wording of the statutory provision. Even if a student could be admitted to a Spanish or German university with little or no writing ability, it is unlikely that this situation was paralleled in medieval England.

While a fair percentage of the English population possessed reading skills, it is true that far fewer of the laity had a mastery of writing.[75] Historians give widely differing estimates of lay literacy in England in the fourteenth, fifteenth and sixteenth centuries. There is general agreement, however, that literacy rates expanded throughout the entire social structure in these centuries.[76] Gentry and aristocratic families often employed professional scribes, secretaries or domestic chaplains to deal with correspondence. Writing was viewed as a professional activity and was doubtless so regarded by England's student population. Evidence for this is the fact that English students made extensive use of the formularies of model letters, compiled by professional writers or *dictatores*, that could be adapted quickly to a student's particular business. That English students preferred in the main to use model epistles that were in effect exercises in written rhetoric rather than devoting energy to composing original letters is by no means a sign that they were inexperienced in the art of writing. They simply wished to take advantage of the persuasive skills of the practitioners of rhetoric.

It is almost certain that potential English students, who were the product of either a school education or private tuition or both, would have acquired capable writing accomplishments. It is extremely unlikely that any English aspirant for university entry who was wholly

---

73. I. Hajnal, *L'enseignement de l'écriture aux universités médiévales*, 2nd edn (Budapest, Académie des Sciences de Hongrie, 1959), p. 65.
74. *ibid.*, p. 64.
75. See, for example, Moran, *The growth of English schooling*, p. 18.
76. *ibid.*, pp. 19–20.

deficient in the craft of writing would have been accepted. There is nowhere any suggestion of such a possibility in either English university or college statutes. In furtherance of this is the consideration that undergraduates could supplement their incomes through scribal activities. At Oxford it is probable that undergraduates engaged with stationers in the town to copy portions of the academic texts that were being studied in the university schools, payment being made as each piece or portion of text was copied.[77] The obsessive claims of the Hungarian scholar, I. Hajnal, that the elementary teaching of grammar and writing was a fundamental preoccupation of the English and all other medieval universities is a distortion that cannot be substantiated with reference to any body of convincing evidence.[78]

When undergraduates began to infiltrate English colleges, significantly from the late-fifteenth century, they became subject to close screening at the point of collegiate entry. Exceptionally, this had already been the case in the fourteenth century at the King's Hall, Cambridge, and at New College, Oxford, because of their substantial undergraduate cohorts.[79] Detailed assessments were certainly carried out for undergraduate entrants at King's College, Cambridge, and at Magdalen College, Oxford, in the second half of the fifteenth century.[80] Entry to Oxford halls and Cambridge hostels doubtless involved some form of academic assessment. Whether or not this was of a probing or perfunctory nature cannot be determined from available evidence. What is very clear is that when the undergraduate population transferred piecemeal from the unendowed halls and hostels to the colleges there was much improvement in the scrutiny of new entrants.

The lack of a centralized admissions policy at Oxford and Cambridge before the sixteenth century was patently one of the reasons for the high undergraduate wastage rate in England in the Middle Ages.

77. See G. Pollard, "The *pecia* system in the medieval universities", in *Medieval scribes, manuscripts and libraries: essays presented to N. R. Ker*, M. B. Parkes & A. G. Watson (eds) (London, Scolar Press, 1978), p. 156.
78. Hajnal's ideas are expounded at length in *L'enseignement de l'écriture aux universités médiévales*, ch. 3.
79. For screening at the King's Hall see the statutes of 1380 in Rouse Ball, *The King's Scholars and King's Hall*, p. 67, and for the emphasis placed on a training in grammar for new entrants to New College see *Statutes*, I, ch. 5, pp. 5–6.
80. For details of the selection of undergraduate scholars at King's College see *Camb. Docs*, II, pp. 484–92, and for the scrutiny of the qualifications of Magdalen's undergraduate demies see *Statutes*, II, ch. 8, pp. 15–16.

However, an important distinction has to be drawn between modern and medieval attitudes towards the attainment of degrees. The modern idea that a student who leaves university without obtaining a degree has contributed to the failure rate within that university is not one that easily transfers to a medieval context. Many students attended a medieval university without having the intention of acquiring a degree. They believed that a period of study at a university, as well as being an education in itself, would bring social and career advancement. A university education did not have to be crowned with the winning of an academic title for it to be perceived as having an intrinsic value. From the evidence of model testimonial letters it seems that such a spell of study at a university that did not entail a degree could be put forward with confidence in support of an application for employment.[81] University education in England was a deregulated activity, a form of private enterprise that owed little to state intervention beyond the provision of a framework of royal privileges that facilitated university development in a protected environment. University learning was encouraged through royal, aristocratic and ecclesiastical patronage, but it was not mandatory for any section of society. It was left to individuals and their families or guardians to decide if a university education was a valuable asset in terms of self-fulfilment or positive career advantage. If the answer was in the affirmative, a further decision had to be taken about the desirability or otherwise of aiming for a degree qualification. On impressionistic grounds it has been suggested that possibly more than half of medieval English undergraduates did not acquire a degree.[82] At the King's Hall there are instances of fellows who remained for periods of 20, 30, 40 and even 50 years without progressing beyond undergraduate status. The most extreme case is that of Robert (or Hugh) Lincoln who resided in the college from 1382 until death intervened in 1440 without obtaining any degree.[83]

Whether a degree was sought or not, some unfortunate students had to terminate their studies prematurely. In the absence of matriculation

---

81. Catto, "Citizens, scholars and masters", p. 190; H. E. Salter, W. A. Pantin & H. G. Richardson (eds), *Formularies which bear on the history of Oxford c.1204–1420* (2 vols), Oxford Historical Society, new ser. **4, 5** (Oxford, Clarendon Press, 1942), II, pp. 400–1, 465–6.

82. Aston, Duncan & Evans, "The medieval alumni of the University of Cambridge", p. 27; Evans, "The number, origins and careers of scholars", p. 497.

83. Cobban, *The King's Hall*, p. 56.

registers and accurate and complete degree lists, it is not possible to quantify student wastage at medieval Oxford and Cambridge. Nevertheless, detailed figures for wastage are available for New College, Oxford, and they give a graphic illustration of the scale of the problem. It has been reckoned that of 1,350 scholars recorded at New College between 1386 and 1547 about a third left prematurely, and many of these had not attained a degree. Moreover, of the 254 scholars who died in the college during this period 124 of them were undergraduates.[84] R. L. Storey has calculated that between 1386 and 1540 one in seven undergraduate scholars left before the expiry of the two probationary years required for election to a fellowship.[85]

New College was a magnificently appointed college, and all undergraduate entrants who transferred from the feeder school of Winchester had been rigorously examined on their competence in Latin grammar. If some undergraduate scholars of New College, who had benefited from a sound preparatory education at Winchester, found difficulties in coping with the early stages of the arts course, it is understandable that youths with fewer educational advantages would experience even greater problems in adapting to university study. Some would become disenchanted with academic life and decide to leave for fresh pastures. Others would soon realize that the stringencies of university study exceeded their abilities, and they would give up the unequal struggle. While individual masters may have given extra tuition to students in difficulties, Oxford and Cambridge, as corporate bodies, did not assume liability for the progress of their undergraduates after the manner of a modern university. They were not held accountable for the success or failure of their members. The guilds of masters provided the educational opportunity and the mechanisms for learning, and beyond this the responsibility for success or otherwise lay entirely with the student. However youthful some of the students may have been, they were treated as adults who were capable of making the important choices governing their sojourn at university.

Apart from loss of commitment, lack of ability, insufficient self-discipline, illness, death or the decision to make a career change, it is undeniable that some undergraduates had to terminate their studies

84. A. H. M. Jones, "New College", in *Victoria history of the county of Oxford. Volume 3*, p. 158.
85. Storey, "The foundation and the medieval college", pp. 17–18.

through financial exigency. If students had exhausted their monetary supplies and family members could not or would not send assistance, there were few alternatives but to withdraw from the university. In the thirteenth century undergraduates could take out loans from the Jewish moneylenders who were established in the towns of Oxford and Cambridge.[86] A security for a loan was required, and this sometimes took the form of a book. Not too many undergraduates of restricted means would have had such a pledge at their disposal. This borrowing option ceased with the expulsion of the Jews from England in 1290. In any case, those students who were disadvantaged financially would scarcely have been able to meet the high rate of interest charged on loans, although at Oxford some attempt was made to limit interest rates by royal edict. There is no known limitation on chargeable rates at Cambridge.

It may be thought that the many loan-chests that were established by benefactors at Oxford and Cambridge would have helped to alleviate students in the most straitened of circumstances.[87] By the early-sixteenth century Cambridge had about 15 university loan-chests and about a dozen collegiate chests as well as several administrative chests for the storage of valuables. Oxford had at least 21 university loan-chests and various administrative chests by 1511. These medieval loan-chests were in the nature of pawnshops that were endowed so that interest-free loans could be made to members of the academic community. The problem was that loan-chests were only of limited value for needy undergraduates. In order to secure a loan a pledge such as a manuscript, an item of plate, a candlestick, a piece of jewellery, a decorated belt, a vestment, a rosary, a cross and even an astrolabe had

---

86. On Jewish moneylenders at Oxford see C. Roth, *The Jews of medieval Oxford*, Oxford Historical Society, new ser. **9** (Oxford, Clarendon Press, 1951), pp. 126–50; also T. H. Aston & R. Faith, "The endowments of the university and colleges to *c*.1348", in *HUO*, I, pp. 274–5; M. B. Parkes, "The provision of books", in *ibid.*, II, p. 410.
87. For Oxford's loan-chests see Aston & Faith, "The endowments of the university and colleges", pp. 274–87 and G. Pollard, "The loan-chests", in *The register of congregation 1448–1463*, W. A. Pantin & W. T. Mitchell (eds), Oxford Historical Society, new ser. **22** (Oxford, Clarendon Press, 1972), pp. 418–20. For Cambridge loan-chests see Pollard, "Medieval loan-chests at Cambridge", *Bulletin of the Institute of Historical Research* **17**, 1939–40, pp. 113–29; M. Rubin, *Charity and community in medieval Cambridge* (Cambridge, Cambridge University Press, 1987), pp. 282–8; and R. Lovatt, "Two collegiate loan-chests in late-medieval Cambridge", in *Medieval Cambridge: essays on the pre-Reformation university*, pp. 129–65.

1. A Cambridge University chest of the fifteenth century. As a security device, several keyholders were required to be present to open the multiple locks. The chest is kept in the Old Schools, University of Cambridge.

to be deposited whose value usually had to exceed the size of the loan. For this reason, the borrowers tended to be the more advanced students who were not wholly devoid of means, university masters, college fellows and also colleges as corporate bodies. At Oxford, Balliol, Merton, Exeter and Queen's, and Peterhouse and the King's Hall at Cambridge, all borrowed extensively from either university or college chests to facilitate cashflow in the late-medieval period.[88]

Most loan-chests were governed by a sliding scale that allowed more senior academics to borrow more than those of lesser status. Moreover, the statutes of several chests confined loans to those who were of at least sophister rank, that is undergraduates of two-years' standing, so excluding many of the younger students from the potential benefits of the loan system. Students whose money had dwindled to virtually

88. Aston & Faith, "The endowments of the university and colleges", pp. 285–6, 301–2; also A. F. Butcher, "The economy of Exeter College, 1400–1500", *Oxoniensia* **44**, 1979, pp. 41–5. For the detailed workings of the Barnard Castle loan-chest of Peterhouse and the Billingford chest of Corpus Christi College, Cambridge, along with their pattern of loans, see Lovatt, "Two collegiate loan-chests in late-medieval Cambridge", pp. 129–65.

27

nothing had the option of interrupting their studies and returning to Oxford or Cambridge if and when their resources permitted. This option became more difficult to exercise when residence in a hall, hostel or college was made obligatory at Cambridge from the late-fourteenth century and at Oxford from the early-fifteenth century.[89] Clearly, the obligation of residence made it more complicated for a student to withdraw and return to the university according to fluctuating finances, although it was still possible to do so. Moreover, the growing apparatus of controls that permeated the student body in the later-medieval period institutionalized undergraduates to a greater degree than had been the situation in the thirteenth century, and this tended to place curbs on student mobility.

There were means by which a financially embarrassed student could earn a modest amount of money. For example, students could work in college or hall gardens. They could serve as casual labourers on building projects within the university precinct.[90] They might become servants to wealthier scholars or to masters, and they could perform menial duties by waiting at table or helping in the kitchen of the hall, hostel or college to which they belonged in return for a reduction in the cost of board and lodging. As previously mentioned, undergraduates could undertake paid work as copyists of manuscripts for stationers in the town. If particularly fortunate, a poor scholar might be the recipient of one of the charitable endowments that were established by a wide circle of benefactors, ranging from members of the royal family to former university bedels.[91] In extreme cases, a student could resort to begging in imitation of the mendicant friars. Begging licences were occasionally issued by the English university chancellors so that licensed students would be allowed to beg without incurring prosecution.[92]

89. For obligatory residence at Cambridge see *Camb. Docs*, I, p. 317, and for compulsory residence at Oxford see Gibson, *Statuta antiqua*, pp. 208, 226–7.
90. See, for example, payments to poor scholars for work in the garden of the King's Hall, Trinity College archives, King's Hall accounts, 0. 13. 1. – 26, III, fol. 96; XXVI, fol. 180. Poor scholars assisted in the building of the new library at Merton College between 1373 and 1378: see H. W. Garrod, "Merton College", in *Victoria history of the county of Oxford. Volume 3*, p. 101.
91. See below, Chapter 4.
92. See Salter, *Registrum cancellarii oxoniensis*, II, p. 40 for begging licences granted to two poor students of Aristotle Hall in 1461. On this topic of student begging see Rashdall, *Universities*, III, pp. 406–7 and J. Paquet, "Coût des études, pauvreté et labeur: fonctions et métiers d'étudiants au moyen âge", *History of universities* 2, 1982, pp. 15–52.

While licences were still being granted into the sixteenth century, they were given sparingly because of the social infamy and disorder associated with begging in the community at large. The English universities and Paris had problems with beggars who infiltrated the academic population and who tried to pass themselves off as genuine students. Official student begging in England was conducted on a small scale compared with the extent of the practice in many universities in continental Europe. For example, in Hungary the begging student was a well-established and popular tradition in the Middle Ages.[93] Doubtless, a certain amount of unlicensed begging was indulged in by English students which, because of its clandestine nature, has gone unrecorded.

These various options could only have had a marginal effect upon the situation of the most disadvantaged students. Some poor scholars would obviously have been helped by one or more of these measures, but for others there was no financial rescue and withdrawal from the university seemed the only course of action. The English universities had no systematic plan for dealing with impoverished students. This is probably because genuine student poverty was a more limited phenomenon at Oxford and Cambridge than in many continental universities. Arts faculties in several of the German universities, for example, dispensed poor scholars, either wholly or partially, from matriculation fees, from obligatory attendance at lectures and other academic occasions, from rules about prescribed dress and from compulsory residence in university premises.[94] Some relaxation in degree fees were made in favour of poor students at Bologna, Avignon and Aix-en-Provence in the fifteenth century. On the other hand, the statutes of the University of Toulouse made no concessions to poor scholars in respect of their debts.[95] Low-rate hostels for impoverished scholars were made available at the Universities of Freiburg, Erfurt and Vienna.[96] The definition of poverty varied within German universities, and in some centres students who pleaded poor status had to submit testimonial letters from their home municipalities in support of their claim.[97]

93. *ibid.*, p. 49, *n.* 146.
94. Fletcher, "Wealth and poverty in the medieval German Universities", pp. 423–35.
95. Paquet, "Coût des études", p. 20.
96. Fletcher, "Wealth and poverty", pp. 425–6.
97. *ibid.*, pp. 424–5. For the different forms of proof required by medieval universities to establish the threshold for student poverty see Paquet, "Recherches sur l'universitaire 'pauvre'", pp. 328–35.

The English universities appear not to have found it necessary to define undergraduate poverty, and there was probably only meagre official relief for the genuinely poor scholar. There are clear statutory statements that the fines of student malefactors could not be excused on the grounds of penury. At Oxford, statutes of 1410 and 1432 emphasized that all scholars of whatever condition who transgressed statutory regulations, including those who claimed poverty, were equally bound to pay their fines. However, the late-fourteenth-century statutes of Cambridge University decreed that regent masters were not to obstruct the admission of scholars who could swear to their poverty.[98] This may imply that such entrants were dispensed from some categories of fees, although the matter is ambiguous. In general, the attitude of the English universities towards the problems of student hardship was one of pragmatism. There were few sophisticated arrangements for alleviating undergraduate poverty. Indeed, the issue seems not to have led to anything that could be described as a co-ordinated university policy.

Whereas the English universities, as corporate bodies, did not give significant aid to poor undergraduates, several of the secular colleges made statutory provision for the charitable teaching of poor grammar youths. Strictly speaking, such youths were not undergraduates in a literal sense, but if they made good progress there was the possibility that they might be advanced to the position of scholar. For example, the earliest surviving statutes of Peterhouse, Cambridge, of 1344 envisaged charitable support for two or three grammar boys if the college finances would allow. If they proved to be promising, they might be promoted to scholarships, otherwise they were to be removed. A similar arrangement was made in the statutes of 1359 of Clare College, Cambridge, whereby ten poor boys were to be instructed in grammar, singing and logic until the age of 20, after which they were either to be made scholars or excluded from the college.[99] It has to be said, however, that most English colleges did not have the resources to sustain their statutory complements of fellows and so had little to spare for charitable teaching. The founder of Queen's College, Oxford, Robert of Eglesfield, had planned for the instruction of poor boys in grammar,

---

98. For Oxford see Gibson, *Statuta antiqua*, pp. 205, 241; for Cambridge *Camb. Docs*, I, p. 332.

99. For Peterhouse and Clare see *Camb. Docs*, II, pp. 24–6, 140–1.

singing, logic and philosophy up to the limit of 72. The founder's well-intentioned scheme, contained in the statutes of 1341, remained largely a dead letter because only a few charity boys had entered the college by 1500.[100]

Clearly, a top priority within English colleges was to preserve the level of financial support for their fellows. If the maintenance of charity boys diverted scarce resources from this central purpose, the statutory provisions for charitable teaching would almost certainly be severely curtailed. It is evident that the charitable teaching of grammar in English colleges was a very minor activity. It was far less developed than in some of the Parisian colleges, notably the College of the Sorbonne and the Ave Maria College.[101]

The genuinely poor undergraduate, however defined, was probably a minority figure in the medieval English universities and, so equally, at the other end of the social spectrum, was the son of a noble family. The universities had a natural interest in trying to attract youths of elevated status in the expectation of increasing political patronage and monetary contributions. In return, noble students would anticipate some relaxation of academic requirements and the enjoyment of certain privileges. However, it needs to be stressed that, prior to the sixteenth century, the preferential treatment accorded to English noble students was decidedly modest in comparison with that conferred upon noble scholars in many continental universities. It seems that the medieval English universities were tempted to exaggerate the extent to which they were the academic nurseries of the nobility. For example, in 1480 Oxford University sent letters to the Bishop of Salisbury, Richard Beauchamp, and to Edward IV concerning Edward de la Pole, second son of the Duke of Suffolk and nephew of the king, who had been brought up in the bishop's household. In the course of the correspondence the

---

100. *Statutes*, I, ch. 4, p. 30. On the actual and meagre provision made for poor boys see R. H. Hodgkin, "The Queen's College", in *Victoria history of the county of Oxford. Volume 3*, p. 132.
101. For the practice of charity at the College of the Sorbonne and the Ave Maria College see Cobban, *The medieval universities: their development and organization*, p. 150; see also A. L. Gabriel, *Student life in Ave Maria College, medieval Paris* (Notre Dame, Ind., University of Notre Dame Press, 1955), ch. 6, and Gabriel, "The practice of charity at the University of Paris during the Middle Ages: Ave Maria College", *Traditio* **5**, 1947, pp. 335–9.

university boasted that it had maintained many sons of noble families, and it gave the impression that it had for long been a natural venue for the education of the nobility.[102] Furthermore, in 1357 Richard FitzRalph, Archbishop of Armagh, chancellor of Oxford University between 1332 and 1334 and vituperative opponent of the friars, made a speech at the papal court at Avignon in which the friars were accused of bribery and enticing young undergraduates into their ranks without reference to their parents. The archbishop drew the conclusion that parents were now deterred from sending their sons to university out of fear of the mendicants.[103] In modern parlance, the friars were here viewed as a brainwashing cult. In 1358 an Oxford statute was passed that encapsulated FitzRalph's arguments. The statute stated specifically that noble families were among those who had ceased to send their sons to the university because of the reputation of the friars as virtual abductors of young undergraduates who had not yet reached the age of discretion.[104] These contemporary views are interesting, although they are not very illuminating about the extent of the noble contingents at Oxford in the medieval period.

Royal support for English noble students dates from the thirteenth century when Henry III maintained a half-brother, Aymer of Lusignan, and other distant relatives at Oxford, including Peter of Aubusson and Nicholas of Blaya. The king also maintained at Oxford Guy, brother of the Count of Auvergne.[105] Henry's support for Guy began in 1226 and arose from a military treaty made between the king and the count in 1225. Military alliances and kinship were the motivating factors behind Henry III's sponsorship of noble youths at Oxford. There is no evidence of direct monetary aid for noble university students on the part of Henry's successor, Edward I. Moreover, there are relatively few known instances of royal maintenance of noble scholars at either Oxford or Cambridge in the fourteenth and fifteenth centuries. The occasional royal support for individual non-noble students is found. In 1302 or 1303 Edward I maintained Thomas of Duns, a Scot, and Richard of

102. H. Anstey (ed.), *Epistolae academicae oxoniensis* (2 vols), Oxford Historical Society **35**, **36** (Oxford, Clarendon Press, 1898), II, pp. 453–6, 461–2.
103. A. G. Little, *The grey friars in Oxford* (Oxford, Clarendon Press, 1892), p. 79.
104. *ibid.*, p. 80; Lytle, *Oxford students and English society*, p. 40.
105. F. Pegues, "Royal support of students in the thirteenth century", *Speculum* **31**, 1956, pp. 455–8.

Nottingham at Oxford. Their daily allowance of 6d and their robes were charged to the Prince of Wales.[106] Rather than supporting individual students, however, English kings and their queens were more attracted to founding or refounding entire colleges. Cases in point are the King's Hall, King's College and Queens' College at Cambridge, and at Oxford, Oriel College and Queen's College.

Although sons of noble families were present at Oxford and Cambridge from the thirteenth century, it was not until the hundred years between *c*.1450 and *c*.1550 that their presence became especially significant. The introduction of humanist studies goes some way towards explaining the increasing attraction of a university education for the English nobility. Of particular importance here was the humanist ideal, fuelled by the influence of Plato's *Republic*, that only those who were qualified for government, either in terms of specific skills or of a broadly based education, were entitled to participate in the exercise of power. This was a notion that held threatening overtones for England's nobility. Unless the nobility embraced higher education as a leading priority, there was a danger that it would be excluded from the business of government and be rendered an emasculated class. Humanism brought with it the idea that a meritocracy was a surer and more equitable basis for government and administration than one built upon the outmoded concept of an aristocracy of birth. These arguments that were derived from political theory were conjoined with the practical consideration that the growing complexities of government under the Yorkists and early Tudors created an even greater demand than hitherto for the highly educated lay or ecclesiastical civil servant who was a product of Oxford or Cambridge or of one of the Inns of Court in London. Professional attitudes were coming to prevail in governing circles, and the nobility had to adapt to the changing climate or risk a partial eclipse. In an act of self-preservation the English nobility responded to the challenge, and the large influx of noble students in the sixteenth and early-seventeenth centuries transformed Oxford and Cambridge into highly stratified and privileged communities. The working milieu of the English undergraduate was very different in the sixteenth and

---

106. Emden, *BRUO*, I, p. 610 (Duns); *ibid.*, II, p. 1379 (Nottingham); D. E. R. Watt, *A biographical dictionary of Scottish graduates to AD 1410* (Oxford, Clarendon Press, 1977), p. 168 (Duns).

33

seventeenth centuries from what it had been in the less divisive and more heterogeneous university scene of the pre–Tudor age.

It has been calculated that between 1307 and 1485 at least 88 members of 42 noble families were admitted to the English universities. Of these, 69 are found at Oxford and 19 at Cambridge, while some obtained degrees at both. The distribution of noble entrants over the period was uneven, there being 51 in the fourteenth century and 37 in the fifteenth century.[107] This disparity may not be significant given the lack of centralized matriculation records before the second half of the sixteenth century. Most of the noble university students were younger sons. While some pursued secular lives as courtiers or landowners, in the main they followed ecclesiastical careers, and 15 noble students became bishops in the fourteenth century and 16 in the fifteenth century.[108]

Some noble families sent sons to university over several generations. At least eight sons of the Neville family received a university education as did five sons of both the Charlton and Scrope families. The Courtenay family sent four sons to university and the de la Pole family sent three.[109] It is known that some noble undergraduates had private tutors at university. Richard of Aston was granted leave of absence from an ecclesiastical living in 1312 to serve as a private tutor at Cambridge to Thomas of Segrave, son of Sir John of Segrave.[110] It is almost certain that all noble students would have retained servants, and some of them lived in style with their tutors and servants in private accommodation. In the fourteenth century the grandiose lodgings at Oxford of Edmund Arundel, son of Richard, Earl of Arundel, and of William Courtenay, fourth son of Hugh, Earl of Devon, and later Chancellor of England and Archbishop of Canterbury, were even fitted out with private oratories.[111] Other noble undergraduates were attached to a college as fee-paying commoners or were resident in halls, hostels or inns. It would have been very difficult for a noble undergraduate to acquire a fellowship

---

107. For this analysis of noble entrants see J. T. Rosenthal, "The universities and the medieval English nobility", *History of Education Quarterly* **9**, 1969, pp. 415–18.
108. *ibid.*, pp. 418–19.
109. Lytle, *Oxford students*, p. 129.
110. For Richard of Aston see Emden, *BRUO*, I, p. 68.
111. *ibid.*, I, p. 48 (Arundel), pp. 502–4 (Courtenay).

in a college where undergraduates were admitted as fellows or probationary fellows because most colleges excluded wealthy students from enjoying maintenance from the resources of the foundation.

As formerly mentioned, medieval English undergraduates made plentiful use of model student letters that were crafted by professional writers or *dictatores* according to strict rules of rhetorical composition. Although many surviving student letters are not originals but stereotypes adapted to meet the student's personal concerns, it may be supposed that they would be representative of the main features of undergraduate life. These letters are, however, rhetorical devices. They almost certainly exaggerate student hardships in order to evoke a sympathetic response in the recipient, whether a father, mother, brother, sister, uncle, cousin, guardian or influential patron. A persistent theme of these letters was the plea for more money for items such as room rents and board, university fees, degree expenses, articles of clothing, the purchase of texts for specific courses of study, a journey home and a host of other necessities.[112] Although these letters give incidental information about various aspects of the student condition, they reveal little of the teaching regime, the oral examinations and academic exercises, or of the routine of university life in college, hall or hostel. As a result, the letters do not allow the construction of a student's typical day. This is all the more vexatious when it is remembered that nothing approximating to a diary of an English tutor or student has been unearthed for the medieval period. It is only from the seventeenth century that there have survived detailed guidelines devised by tutors for the behaviour and studies of their pupils. Two of the most illuminating of these seventeenth-century sets of tutorial instructions are those of Richard Holdsworth, fellow of St John's College, Cambridge, and later master of Emmanuel College, and James Duport, fellow of Trinity College, Cambridge, and subsequently master of Magdalene College.[113]

---

112. C. H. Haskins, *Studies in medieval culture* (Oxford, Clarendon Press, 1929), ch. 1; also Salter, Pantin & Richardson, *Formularies*, II, pp. 331–450.
113. For the guidelines of Holdsworth and Duport see the discussion by M. H. Curtis, *Oxford and Cambridge in transition 1558–1642* (Oxford, Clarendon Press, 1959), pp. 108–14. See also a copy of Duport's rules, Trinity College, Cambridge, MS O. 10A. 33.

While most student letters emphasize depleted resources, it need not be assumed from this that the senders of these pleas for money were poverty-stricken in any absolute sense. A student who sent such a letter may have been suffering from a temporary lack of coin arising from the periodic shortage of hard currency that affected English society in the fourteenth and fifteenth centuries.[114] Again, the price inflation caused in part by lean harvests might squeeze the student's finances to an alarming degree. An affluent family could quickly alleviate a sudden financial hardship. On the other hand, if the student was guilty of monetary extravagance or riotous behaviour, or had failed to make satisfactory progress, the situation might not be so easily resolved. News of the youth's misdeeds would sometimes be communicated to the family or guardian or patron by the master with whom the student had registered, and monetary aid would be withheld until such time as a marked improvement had been monitored.[115] It was probably quite common for a family or patron to entrust the principal of a hall or hostel with an allowance for the undergraduate that would be dispensed in instalments either directly to or on behalf of the youth according to need. By this means, the principal could exercise a measure of social control over the student and, if misconduct arose, money could be held back as a disciplinary restraint.

While not underestimating the plight of undeniably poor students, it seems that most English undergraduates had reserves at a distance from which they could draw to tide them over a temporary crisis. As such, they should not be classified as living on the margins of poverty. Evidence for undergraduate expenditure in medieval Oxford and Cambridge is very hard to discover. However, a source of primary importance has been located in the unexpected guise of a logic notebook that belonged to master John Arundel who, in 1424, was the principal of an unnamed Oxford hall that may have been either Mildred Hall in Turl Street or (Great) Black Hall in School Street. Arundel was a fellow of Exeter College in 1424, and was later to become Bishop of Chichester and a

---

114. Jacob, *Essays in the conciliar epoch*, pp. 208–9, and Jacob, "English university clerks", p. 306.
115. See Salter, Pantin & Richardson, *Formularies*, II, pp. 360–1 for a letter in which money is withheld until bad conduct has been remedied. See also *ibid.*, II, pp. 370–1 for a letter in which a father hears good news of a son's progress from the youth's master and companions.

chaplain and physician first to Henry Beauchamp, Earl of Warwick, and then to Henry VI.

Arundel's logic notebook contains informal accounts of tutorial expenses that take the form of rough jottings made in a series of blank or semi-blank pages.[116] These accounts are probably the only undergraduate expenses to have survived from a medieval Oxford hall, and it seems that none have survived from a Cambridge hostel. The accounts show that Arundel acted as tutor to several undergraduate commoners and was in control of their finances. This evidence adds considerably to our knowledge of the living costs of undergraduate commoners in the late-medieval period. Arundel's record of tutorial expenses tends to corroborate the view that the expenditure of English undergraduates in the fifteenth century was of a relatively inexpensive character.

The only fully itemized account for a whole term is that for the undergraduate commoner, W. Clavyle, for the Michaelmas term of 1424. Clavyle's account embraced expenses for commons or basic items of food and drink, service charges and tips for domestic staff, the shared rent of a room, expenditure on feast occasions, books, clogs, clothes, linen and gloves, lecture fees, a payment for the light of St Nicholas and the cost of a journey home. In the aularian (hall) statutes of Oxford of the late-fifteenth century there is a requirement for all scholars in halls to contribute to the light of St Nicholas on 6 December, along with other communal expenses, under penalty of expulsion and seizure of goods.[117] Apart from Clavyle's account, there are two incomplete accounts that give totals for termly expenditure, those of the undergraduate commoners Okeford and Robert Canon.

116. These accounts are contained in North Devon Record Office, Barnstaple, MS B1/3960. For the analysis of Arundel's accounts that is given in the next two paragraphs and for further information see A. B. Cobban, "John Arundel, the tutorial system, and the cost of undergraduate living in the medieval English universities", *BJRL* **77**, 1995, pp. 143–59. Other types of hall expenses have survived. The expenses of John Hychcok (Hichcock), who was apparently a bachelor of St Mary Hall, Oxford, have been preserved in Bodleian MS Lat. misc. d. 83 fol. 1. The expenses of Thomas Jolyffe, principal of Glasen Hall, Oxford, are recorded in Bodleian MS Digby 26 fol. 140v. Jolyffe's expenses are extremely difficult to decipher. Both lists were compiled in *c.*1460.

117. Gibson, *Statuta antiqua*, p. 585. See also payments of 2d for the light of St Nicholas made by members of founder's kin at Merton College in J. M. Fletcher & C. A. Upton, "The cost of undergraduate study at Oxford in the fifteenth century: the evidence of the Merton College 'founder's kin'", *History of Education* **14**, 1985, pp. 6–8, 12, 14–15.

2. A fully itemized account of the expenses of W. Clavyle, an undergraduate commoner resident in an Oxford hall, for the Michaelmas term of 1424. This account is taken from the logic notebook of John Arundel, the principal of the hall, who acted as Clavyle's tutor and who kept a record of the expenses incurred on behalf of the pupil.

Assuming that all three undergraduates were resident in hall for a minimum three-term period of 36 weeks, and making allowances for journeys to and from Oxford throughout the year, Clavyle's total costs would have been in the region of £2 13s, Okeford's costs came to about £1 12s, and Canon would have incurred expenditure in the order of £2 0s 3d. The variations in expenditure are to be explained by the differing amounts spent on personal items and on battels, the extra food and drink ordered over and above basic commons. These sums for total expenditure give weekly costs for Clavyle, Okeford and

Canon of 1s 6d, $10\frac{1}{2}$d and 1s $1\frac{1}{2}$d respectively, that is, about $2\frac{1}{2}$d, $1\frac{1}{2}$d and 2d a day. This is cheap living, a point underlined by the fact that, in the early-fifteenth century, a building craftsman earned about 5d or 6d a day, a building labourer about 3d or 4d a day, a thatcher about $4\frac{1}{2}$d a day and a thatcher's mate about 3d a day. Both Clavyle and Okeford were charged only 6d a year for the rent of their rooms. It has to be remembered here that this low sum would be charged for only a share of the rent because it was usual for undergraduate commoners in Oxford halls to be housed two, three or four to a chamber. The annual sums of expenditure for Clavyle and Canon, though not for Okeford, are similar to those for founder's kin at Merton College, Oxford, in the second half of the fifteenth century. Over a three-term period of 36 weeks it has been reckoned that £2 12s 6d would have covered the expenses of a scholar of the founder's kin.[118] It has to be pointed out, however, that founder's kin were maintained from college resources and are not directly comparable with undergraduate commoners who were obliged to pay for their own board and lodging.

Apart from estimates of total expenditure, it is also possible to work out the cost of weekly commons, the standard food and drink requirements that were purchased each week by members of Arundel's hall. The outlay on commons for four undergraduate residents, namely W. Clavyle, Okeford, John Wode and John Russell, in 1424 is the only evidence of its kind so far discovered for any Oxford hall. In each of these four cases expenditure on commons amounted to less than 1d a day. This rate was similar to that paid by the grammarian, Robert Whittinton, who, as a student at Oxford in the late-fifteenth century, stated in 1520 that a commons rate of 7d a week was sufficient for an adequate standard of living. The low rates for Arundel's undergraduate commoners were far below those for fellows of most Oxford and Cambridge colleges. As a rule, the commons allowance for a college fellow was of the order of 1s a week, although this might be increased to statutory limits varying between 1s 3d and 1s 8d according to fluctuations in grain prices. Over and above this allowance, fellows had to find the money for extra food and drink from their own resources. In 1424, the year of Arundel's accounts, the average sums charged to each undergraduate and graduate fellow of the King's Hall, Cambridge, was

118. *ibid.*, p. 16.

just over 3d a day.[119] Fellows of the King's Hall received a flat rate allow-ance of 1s 2d a week or 2d a day from the exchequer for their commons, and had to bear the cost of any surplus from private income.

The undergraduate fellows of the King's Hall must have enjoyed a standard of living well above the average level that obtained for graduate fellows in most English colleges. It is also noteworthy that the commons rate for undergraduate fellows of this royal college was approximately three times that of the undergraduate commoners who lived in Arundel's unendowed hall and who were wholly unsubsidized. Assuming that the charges in Arundel's hall are typical of those normally levied on arts undergraduates in halls and hostels of the period, it may be deduced that a commons rate of just under 1d a day was probably representative of the daily outlay on basic items of food and drink of the average under-graduate commoner in the fifteenth century. It is almost certain, how-ever, that those few undergraduates who were college fellows before the sixteenth century were considerably better off than undergraduate commoners in halls and hostels.

In addition to the evidence from Arundel's hall, several annual grants to medieval students have been recorded that indicate a wide vari-ation in costs. In 1323 Richard Bruche, the son of a Lancashire gentry family, received £1 13s 4d for maintenance for one year at Oxford, and this included 13s 4d for a robe. In 1374 a wealthy London mercer, Robert of Brynkeleye, gave an itemized account for the support of a ward, Thomas, at Oxford for what appears to be about 13 years. Although the circumstances of Thomas' accommodation are unknown, total expenditure for each year seems to have come to £9 or £10. This level of expenditure was four or five times that of Arundel's under-graduates. On the other hand, John Cely received the annual sum of £2 13s 4d in the 1480s as a paternal gift towards expenses at Oxford. This is similar to the estimated expenditure for an assumed 36 weeks of £2 13s for W. Clavyle, the undergraduate commoner whose finances have been discussed.[120] Further examples of maintenance grants could

119. Cobban, *The King's Hall*, table 5 (facing p. 126), columns 1 and 16. For a full analysis of the standard of living of the fellows of the King's Hall see *ibid.*, ch. 4. For Whittinton's statement see A. B. Emden, *An Oxford hall in medieval times* (Oxford, Clarendon Press, 1927), p. 195.
120. For Richard Bruche see Evans, "The number, origins and careers of scholars", p. 504; for Robert of Brynkeleye see H. T. Riley (ed.), *Memorials of London and*

be cited, but there is a problem of comparability in that it is not always known if the amounts given are for all or only part of the student's expenses.

Whereas most arts undergraduates in halls and hostels probably paid less than 1d a day for their commons, an Oxford statute of *a.*1380 mentions three rates of commons for both masters and scholars living in halls.[121] The first rate covers those who paid up to 8d a week, and Arundel's undergraduate commoners fall within this category. The second and third categories embraced those who paid from 8d to 1s and those who paid more than 1s a week. It is indicated that these higher rates would be paid by masters or by law students who would be expected to pay more than arts students. It is known that some scholars embarked upon a law degree without a prior degree in arts. For this reason, halls for legists would have accommodated at least some undergraduate members. As a result, it is likely that legist halls had differentiated rates for commons to meet the needs of both undergraduate and graduate inmates.

The above estimates for total annual expenditure by undergraduate commoners do not take into account the heavy fees that students had to pay if they proceeded to the BA degree. These fees would be very disabling if the student did not have the assurance of financial support from the family or from an alternative source of patronage. John Lane, a member of the founder's kin of Merton College, was charged £1 14s 6d in 1424–5 arising from the admission and determination ceremonies involved in taking the degree of bachelor of arts. This sum was virtually the same as the cost of Lane's annual commons, although, in this instance, the expenditure was probably borne by the college.[122] If this expenditure on degree fees is at all typical for English undergraduates, it is easy to understand why some students had to postpone or even abandon plans to acquire the lower arts degree. High degree expenses were equally a problem in continental universities. For example, the University of Bologna had particularly onerous degree fees and, to

London life in the 13th, 14th and 15th centuries (London, Longmans, 1888), p. 379 and Lytle, *Oxford students*, pp. 10–11; for John Cely see A. Hanham, *The Celys and their world* (Cambridge, Cambridge University Press, 1985), p. 256.

121. Gibson, *Statuta antiqua*, p. 183.

122. J. M. Fletcher & C. A. Upton, "Expenses at admission and determination in fifteenth-century Oxford: new evidence", *English Historical Review* **100**, 1985, p. 335.

escape this burden, some students would enrol for courses at Bologna and would migrate to other Italian universities such as Padua, Pavia, Perugia, Siena and Ferrara so that they could take their degrees at more economical rates. In the medieval Spanish universities there are recorded cases of newly elected lecturers who, in order to take an obligatory degree, were driven to take out loans or to seek advance instalments of their salaries in an effort to meet the heavy degree costs.[123]

Despite the real hardship caused by high degree expenses, the potential range of support for students was quite extensive. Apart from close members of the family, undergraduates might receive assistance from surrogate relatives including stepfathers, godfathers and guardians of wards, as well as a considerable array of lay or ecclesiastical patrons ranging from archdeacons to bishops and abbots.[124] Furthermore, students often benefited from their fathers' wills. In 1416 John Brokeman, esquire of Hertfordshire, left £10 as a contribution towards the education of a son at either Oxford or Cambridge. By the codicil to a will that was added in 1509, the wife of Robert Rydon, a law graduate of Oxford and a justice of the peace, was entrusted with the family estate until their son would inherit at the age of 21 years. This arrangement was on the understanding that revenues from the estate would be used to give their son an education at Oxford.[125] From the evidence of inventories of the possessions of Oxford scholars of the mid-fifteenth century there is reason to suppose that the level of material comfort may have been somewhat greater in the fifteenth than in the thirteenth century. These inventories show that it was fairly common for fifteenth-century students to own, in addition to their clothes, bedding, knives, spoons, candlesticks, books, pairs of bellows, lanterns, coffers, gimlets and musical instruments.[126] This reinforces the impression derived from Arundel's accounts that most fifteenth-century undergraduate commoners enjoyed living standards that transcended the bare necessities.

123. For degree fees at Bologna see R. C. Schwinges, "Student education, student life", in *A history of the university in Europe*, I, p. 239. For degree fees in the Spanish universities see Cobban, "Elective salaried lectureships", pp. 667–8; see also R. L. Kagan, *Students and society in early modern Spain* (Baltimore, Md., The Johns Hopkins University Press, 1974), p. 165, *n.* 23.
124. See, for example, Evans, "The number, origins and careers of scholars", pp. 506–7; also Lytle, *Oxford students*, pp. 53–5.
125. *ibid.*, p. 45.
126. Salter, *Registrum cancellarii oxoniensis*, I, pp. 83–4, 160–1, 321, 352.

The undergraduate's life proceeded within an evolving disciplinary framework. Initially, the English universities attempted to exercise discipline by means of the matriculation rolls. The registration of students helped to separate out the committed from the false undergraduates who had no intention of following an approved course of study and who gave themselves over to idleness and the libertine pleasures of the university town. Beyond this, however, the disciplinary benefits of the matriculation system were rather limited. This was so because masters and registered students met normally within the context of the lecture room, and outside of this arena the students went largely unsupervised. The disciplinary net was much widened when the principals of halls and hostels and the heads of colleges assumed responsibility for undergraduate regulation. The Oxford aularian statutes of 1483–90 provide our sole insight into the code of discipline in the halls, there being no comparable set of statutes for the Cambridge hostels. By order of the chancellor's court at both Oxford and Cambridge a choice of punishments could be inflicted on undergraduates including fining, expulsion, imprisonment, excommunication and the denial of a degree. The statutes for the Oxford halls show that fining was the main form of retribution.[127]

The Oxford aularian statutes reveal that students would incur fines for causing a nuisance to fellow students, for creating disorder within the hall and for making derogatory remarks about particular countries or classes in society. Scholars were also fined for bringing the honour of the hall into disrepute, for consorting with persons of dubious character, for taking part in prohibited games, for climbing in and out of hall during hours of closure, and for spending a night away from hall without permission or leaving Oxford without licence. The carrying of weapons was forbidden except when a student was undertaking a journey. Otherwise, students were fined if found in possession of weapons or if they had loaned them to associates or if they had given them to a townsperson to hold secretly on their behalf. There were fines for bringing an unsheathed knife to table, for injuring a student with a fist or stone or by any other means. If blood was shed, the fine would be doubled, and if the assault was repeated, the offending student was to be expelled.

127. For much of the content of the following two paragraphs see the Oxford aularian statutes in Gibson, *Statuta antiqua*, pp. 574–88; see also Emden, *An Oxford hall in medieval times*, ch. 9.

Arising from the perceived threat of Wyclifism and Lollardy, students in hall were to be fined if they repeatedly expressed heretical views. An army of financial penalties were prescribed to ensure that students observed the regulations concerning academic courses and that they maintained a proper commitment to their studies. In common with the situation in most medieval universities, the Oxford aularian statutes insisted that only Latin was to be spoken within the precincts of the hall, although exceptions in the form of the vernacular were allowed on feast occasions and principal festivals. The requirement to speak Latin is highlighted in the *Manuale scholarium*, a treatise that assumes the shape of a rather stagy dialogue between two students at Heidelberg University in the late-fifteenth century. In this guidebook for freshmen there was an obligation on students to report others who failed to speak Latin in the university lecture rooms or in their lodgings. At Heidelberg and other German universities an official called the "wolf" (*lupus*) was specifically appointed to spy on students and keep a register of those who spoke the vernacular and to exact fines from offenders.[128] The "wolf" does not appear to have surfaced as an official in the English universities but, in addition to the Oxford aularian statutes, the stipulation to speak Latin is found in many sets of college statutes, although at Peterhouse and the King's Hall, Cambridge, and at Oriel and Queen's, Oxford, French was tolerated as an alternative.[129]

Some halls did not provide meals, a point that is made clear in the aularian statutes. Students from such places were obliged to eat in other halls where meals and lectures were available, their own hall being used primarily for sleeping and study. At the time of the aularian statutes there were two principal meals in the halls and colleges, namely dinner at about 10 or 11 am and supper at about 5 pm. Breakfast was still optional. Breakfast was presumed in the statutes of the King's Hall of 1380, and at the College of Verdale at Toulouse in 1337 breakfast might be given to youths under 20 years of age.[130] Moreover, in halls and colleges a measure of ale was sometimes served between dinner

---

128. R. F. Seybolt (trans. & ed.), *The manuale scholarium* (Cambridge, Mass., Harvard University Press, 1921), pp. 66–7, 72–3.
129. *Camb. Docs*, II, p. 31 (Peterhouse); Rouse Ball, *The King's Scholars and King's Hall*, p. 65; *Statutes*, I, ch. 3, p. 8 (Oriel), ch. 4, p. 14 (Queen's).
130. Rouse Ball, *The King's Scholars and King's Hall*, p. 65; Fournier, *Les statuts et privilèges*, I, p. 547; Rashdall, *Universities*, III, p. 407, *n*. 2.

and supper and before retiring to bed.[131] It is of interest that the aularian statutes tried to enforce good table etiquette, and unpunctuality or over-lengthy sessions at hall meals were punished by fines and forfeiture of food. Students were encouraged to have respect for their immediate habitat. They were fined for disturbing floor coverings of rushes or straw, for defacing hall property and for spillages on table-cloths, and they were expected to make monetary reparations for all breakages. Within the surroundings of the hall students were to be restrained by means of fines from running across the grass or trampling down plants, and they were to help in maintaining the gardens when required. In the interests of hygiene, hall residents were forbidden to wash their hands in the well-bucket. On the recreational front, hall students were forbidden to take part in gambling or to keep sporting dogs, ferrets, hawks and other small birds.

In contrast with the halls, the system of fines was only occasionally deployed in the colleges. In the statutes of Brasenose College, Oxford, of 1521 fines were imposed for feuding and for late attendance or disorderly behaviour at lectures. At the King's Hall fines were initially used as a method of discipline, but the system had apparently been discarded by 1380. There are no references to fining in the statutes of that year, and the voluminous college accounts are silent on the matter.[132] Apart from the ultimate deterrent of expulsion, the main disciplinary device that was employed in the colleges was the deprivation of commons for periods that varied according to the nature of the misdeed. Deprivation of commons persisted as a penalty through to the sixteenth century, and was clearly regarded as a proven and successful method of discipline.

Corporal punishment, as a mode of correction, appears to have been introduced into the English universities in the fifteenth century, although charity grammar boys were subject to physical correction at Queen's College, Oxford, in accordance with the statutes of 1341.[133] Clement Paston had received corporal punishment when studying at Cambridge before 1458. In that year Clement's mother, Agnes, wrote to Greenfield, the youth's new tutor in London, urging the use of

---

131. Emden, *An Oxford hall*, p. 211; Rashdall, *Universities*, III, p. 403.
132. For Brasenose see *Statutes*, II, ch. 9, pp. 16, 25–6; for the King's Hall see Cobban, *The King's Hall*, pp. 176–7.
133. *Statutes*, I, ch. 4, p. 30.

flogging, if necessary, as had been practised by Clement's master at Cambridge.[134] The Oxford aularian statutes charge the principals of halls with the task of administering corporal punishment to younger students on Saturday evenings as an alternative to fines.[135] The first known instance of corporal punishment in an English college occurs in the statutes of King's College, Cambridge, of the early 1440s whereby scholars and junior fellows could be beaten on the authority of the provost and the dean. The statutes of Magdalen College, Oxford, of 1479/80 permitted corporal punishment for the demies, the young scholars on the foundation in receipt of half of the fellows' allowance for commons. Physical punishment was prescribed for young fellows at both Christ's College, Cambridge, and at Brasenose College, Oxford, by their statutes of 1505 and 1521 respectively. A difficulty was to determine an agreed maximum age beyond which corporal punishment was deemed to be inappropriate. At Christ's College beatings were reserved for scholars of pre-adult age, the age of adulthood being left undefined. In the statutes of c.1525–7 of Thomas Wolsey, the founder of Cardinal College, Oxford, a maximum age of 20 years is stipulated. Dr Caius, in the statutes of Gonville and Caius College, Cambridge, of 1572, decreed 18 years as the uppermost limit for corporal correction. That physical punishment became a main form of correction for younger students in the sixteenth-century colleges may well be the result of the lowering in the average age of collegiate entrants in the Tudor era as the undergraduate population transferred gradually from halls and hostels to the colleges. Whipping was still being prescribed as a punishment for undergraduates of less than 18 years at Pembroke College, Oxford, founded in 1624, but it appears to have been seldom practised in English colleges by the end of the seventeenth century.[136]

There are few references to corporal punishment in continental universities before the sixteenth century, although a statute of 1413 at Vienna University contemplates flogging for the poorer category of students. At the opening of the sixteenth century the University of

134. Davis, *Paston letters and papers*, I, p. 41; Bennett, *The Pastons and their England*, p. 105.
135. Gibson, *Statuta antiqua*, p. 587.
136. For corporal punishment at Gonville and Caius, King's College and Christ's see *Camb. Docs*, II, p. 271 (Gonville), p. 556 (King's); III, p. 191 (Christ's). For corporal punishment at Magdalen, Brasenose and Cardinal College see *Statutes*, II, ch. 8, pp. 76–7 (Magdalen), ch. 9, pp. 16, 19 (Brasenose), ch. 11, p. 70 (Cardinal); for whipping as a punishment at Pembroke College see *ibid.*, III, ch. 14, p. 12.

Tübingen prescribed corporal punishment as one means of restriction to quell serious internal disorder. The College of Montaigu at Paris was a very austere foundation, and the new statutes of 1503, drawn up by Jean Standonck, the head of the resuscitated college, authorized physical correction for violence or acts of rebellion.[137] Flogging is occasionally found in other Paris colleges of the sixteenth century, although the impression is gained that it was deployed less than in the English universities.

Despite the disciplinary controls that came into force between the thirteenth and sixteenth centuries and the attempts made to enforce residence in halls, hostels and colleges, a minority of undergraduates remained persistent offenders and indulged in anti-social and criminal activities. In particular, the university authorities were concerned about the unattached students or "chamberdeacons", as they were called. Students of this kind were immortalized by Chaucer in the character of the student, Nicholas, of the *Miller's Tale*, who lodged in the town in the house of a carpenter and who was a cunning, licentious and likeable rogue.[138] In an Oxford statute of *c.*1410 these unattached scholars are described as "sleeping by day and haunting taverns and brothels by night, intent on robbery and homicide". This statute was not entirely effective, and in 1512 a further legislative effort was made to compel "chamberdeacons" to become institutionalized in halls and colleges.[139] Although there were at least 89 students in unlicensed lodgings in Oxford in 1562, it is clear that by the end of the sixteenth century the problem of "chamberdeacons" had been marginalized.[140] After a lengthy war of attrition the English universities had, by the seventeenth century, firmly established that members of the academic community had to be resident in approved accommodation and subject to university

---

137. For corporal punishment at the Universities of Vienna and Tübingen and at the College of Montaigu, Paris, see Rashdall, *Universities*, I, p. 527, *n.* 1; III, pp. 363 and *n.* 4, 369.

138. See J. A. W. Bennett, *Chaucer at Oxford and at Cambridge* (Oxford, Clarendon Press, 1974), ch. 4.

139. For the statute of *c.*1410 see Gibson, *Statuta antiqua*, p. 208; for the legislation of 1512 see C. J. Hammer, Jr, "Oxford town and Oxford University", in *The collegiate university*, J. McConica (ed.), vol. 3 of *HUO* (Oxford, Clarendon Press, 1986), p. 112; E. Russell. "The influx of commoners into the University of Oxford before 1581: an optical illusion?", *EHR* **92**, 1977, p. 731.

140. Hammer, "Oxford town and Oxford University", pp. 112–13.

jurisdiction. In the nineteenth century exceptions to this rule necessitated at Oxford the written permission of the vice-chancellor.[141]

It is surprising that the medieval English universities did not much use academic dress as a means of controlling the undergraduate population.[142] Before the sixteenth century there were few detailed regulations regarding the dress of undergraduates who lived in halls or hostels or in private lodgings beyond the obligation to wear decent clerical garb. Since this was ill-defined, clerical dress admitted of diverse styles and colours, and undergraduate dress was a medley of different hues and shapes for about three hundred years. Indeed, judging from items discovered in inventories such as red tabards and black and blue cloaks, there was probably not much to differentiate undergraduate dress from that of the laity of the period.[143] It was not until the sixteenth century that sombre, black gowns were imposed in an effort to achieve a uniformity that was thought to be conducive to good behaviour.

Undergraduates were sometimes tempted to ape the more decorative robes of graduates. In the fifteenth century Oxford had to legislate to prevent undergraduates from wearing hoods trimmed with silk or fur that were allowed only to masters or licentiates, persons of noble or royal blood, sons of members of parliament and those with private means of 60 marks or more annually.[144] Both undergraduates and graduates had to be restrained from emulating the fashions of lay society. In 1342 the Archbishop of Canterbury condemned the extravagance in the fashions of university scholars and clergy alike. Among the alleged outrages were long hair that was curled and powdered, stockings chequered with red and green, cloaks trimmed with costly furs, fingers bedecked with rings and expensive girdles that sported long knives.[145] Prior to the sixteenth century the only undergraduates who wore a recognizable uniform were those who were scholars or fellows of colleges with distinctive liveries. Liveries were certainly worn at Queen's, New College, All Souls, Magdalen and Corpus Christi, Oxford, and at

141. Pantin, *Oxford life in Oxford archives*, p. 10.
142. For Oxford academic dress see W. N. Hargreaves-Mawdsley, *A history of academical dress in Europe until the end of the eighteenth century* (Oxford, Clarendon Press, 1963), pp. 60–106, and for Cambridge pp. 107–37.
143. Catto, "Citizens, scholars and masters", p. 155.
144. Gibson, *Statuta antiqua*, pp. 239–40, 297; see also Anstey, *Munimenta academica*, I, p. 303.
145. Cooper, *Annals of Cambridge*, I, pp. 94–5.

Gonville, Trinity Hall, the King's Hall, and King's College, Cambridge.[146] Of these, only New College, the King's Hall and King's College had significant quotas of undergraduates before 1500. The colour of the livery is rarely specified, but prohibitions of dress at New College and King's College encompassed chequered hose of red and green, pointed shoes, knotted hoods and beads. The royal livery was permitted at the King's Hall where members wore tunics and tabards of a blue or bluish-grey colour.[147] Uniform academic dress was established in several of the medieval Parisian colleges. At the College of Navarre the livery was black, at the College of Dormans-Beauvais it was blue, and grey capes were worn at the College of Montaigu.[148]

The recreational side of undergraduate life and the often turbulent relations with the townspeople of Oxford and Cambridge will be discussed in Chapter 6. Suffice it to say here that the exuberant aspect of English undergraduate life did not manifest itself in any form of student power. The phenomenon of student power that had originated at the University of Bologna in the early-thirteenth century had fanned out to embrace other universities in Italy and several of the universities of provincial France and Spain.[149] In the universities in Germany, Bohemia, the Low Countries, Scandinavia, England and Scotland student controls did not take root. Here, the northern concept of a university, one that was governed by the masters with students in the nature of academic apprentices, went largely unchallenged. By way of explanation, it may be said that the average northern undergraduate was less politically and less legally sophisticated than the typical southern student. Many of the law students of southern Europe, who were the architects of student-power movements, were recruited from wealthy backgrounds, some were of noble birth and some had held professional positions in

146. *Statutes*, I, ch. 4, pp. 14, 16 (Queen's), ch. 5, pp. 45–6 (New College), ch. 7, p. 42 (All Souls); II, ch. 8, pp. 92–3 (Magdalen), ch. 10, pp. 84–5 (Corpus Christi); *Camb. Docs*, II, pp. 229–30 (Gonville), p. 419 (Trinity Hall), pp. 538–9 (King's), and the King's Hall statutes in Rouse Ball, *The King's Scholars and King's Hall*, p. 68.
147. For New College and King's see *Statutes*, I, ch. 5, p. 46; *Camb. Docs*, II, p. 539. For royal livery at the King's Hall see Cobban, *The King's Hall*, pp. 199–200.
148. A. L. Gabriel, "The college system in the fourteenth-century universities", in *The forward movement of the fourteenth century*, F. L. Utley (ed.) (Columbus, Ohio State University Press, 1961), p. 103.
149. The phenomenon of student power in the medieval period is examined by Cobban, "Medieval student power", pp. 28–66, and by Cobban, "Elective salaried lectureships", pp. 662–87.

society before coming to university. Mature students of this kind had a highly developed contractual view of university life. In the milieu of southern Europe, where universities were closely integrated with the organized professions, the students tended to see their universities as agencies whose services and staff were open to hire like any other business and which were to be used in the best interest of their paying customers. From the student standpoint, this necessitated varying degrees of control over the teaching staff who were to be made accountable to the student body for every aspect of their professional lives. These were remote assumptions for northern students who did not claim to constitute a fully-fledged profession, with all its concomitant rights, and they were content to be the academic equivalent of craft apprentices.

Oxford and Cambridge undergraduates were, in the main, adolescents and ill-equipped to generate and direct movements of student militancy. Moreover, they had little motivation to do so. In the English universities the masters' guilds afforded adequate protection for the undergraduate body. This contrasted with the situation in several of the southern universities where students were often rendered vulnerable in the face of the local commune, and they feared that their teachers could not defend them properly because they had identified too closely with communal rather than with student interests. Furthermore, the English universities did not accommodate a large foreign element. It was commonly the presence of foreign students in the universities of southern Europe that led to the formation of defensive student guilds, some of which went on to acquire a controlling voice in university affairs, or at least varying degrees of participation in areas of academic government. Nothing of this kind happened in the English universities. The sustained support given to Oxford and Cambridge by the English monarchy from the thirteenth century onwards helped to create an environment of relative security that acted as a brake upon the growth of student militancy.[150] Student unrest in the English universities usually took the mundane form of negative student violence between rival gangs of scholars or between scholars and inhabitants of the town.

The educational experience of most undergraduates in the medieval English universities revolved around their lectures and lecture notes,

---

150. See Cobban, *Medieval English universities*, p. 110; also P. Kibre, *Scholarly privileges in the Middle Ages* (London, W. Clowes for the Medieval Academy of America, 1961), ch. 9.

their disputations and other academic exercises, and what individual tutorial instruction may have been available. It is notable that the direct usage of books was not a prominent feature at the undergraduate level. Undergraduates did not apparently benefit much from the *exemplar-pecia* system.[151] This system is known to have operated in at least 11 of the medieval universities. It was a cheap method of manuscript production that enabled multiple copies to be made of portions of texts, commentaries, lectures and disputations from approved versions or *exemplars*. These *exemplars* were handed over to stationers in the town, and were divided into separate quires or *peciae* of varying length. Copies were made from the *peciae* either by professional scribes, by scholars of the university or by undergraduates who could add to their income by this laborious work. The finished copies were then made available for hire or purchase. So far as is known, the *pecia* system at Oxford was only in official use in the superior faculties of civil and canon law and theology where students had to own or borrow the prescribed texts.[152] However, it has been recently suggested that the *pecia* system at Oxford was not confined to stationers licensed by the university. Other booksellers, who had no connection with the university, may well have engaged in this activity on an independent basis.[153] If this is correct, Oxford undergraduates could have obtained copies of material relevant to the arts course from these unofficial booksellers. Whatever the case, there is no definite evidence for the *pecia* system at Cambridge, although it is improbable that it did not function there in some form.

Institutional libraries were of only limited use to English undergraduates before 1500. At Oxford the library begun by Thomas Cobham in *c*.1320 was, in 1412, confined to graduate use.[154] Likewise at Cambridge the university library was restricted to graduates in *c*.1490, although others in the company of graduates might also gain entry.[155] Most college libraries were primarily for the use of graduates. In those few colleges that had undergraduate members, such as the King's Hall and New College and later King's College, access to the college library

151. Pollard, "The *pecia* system in the medieval universities", pp. 145–61; Parkes, "The provision of books", pp. 462–70; and L. Bataillon, B. Guyot & R. H. Rouse (eds), *La production du livre universitaire au moyen âge: exemplar et pecia* (Paris, CNRS, 1988).
152. Pollard, "The *pecia* system in the medieval universities", p. 150.
153. Parkes, "The provision of books", pp. 467, 470.
154. Gibson, *Statuta antiqua*, p. 218.
155. *Camb. Docs*, I, p. 403.

was probably only through graduate fellows. In the halls and hostels principals and their graduate assistants would have possessed a modest store of books, and some of them were possibly made accessible to undergraduates. Bequests of books were made to halls and hostels, and at least two Oxford halls, Greek Hall and Hart Hall, appear to have had areas set aside as designated libraries.[156]

Ownership of books among undergraduates was almost certainly low, and this, combined with their restricted access to libraries, means that they were reliant upon oral forms of instruction to an extent that must have been a heavy tax on the memory. The cultivation of a good memory is a theme that is highlighted from time to time in contemporary educational comment. For instance, there are references to this in an early-fourteenth-century treatise that takes the form of a letter from a physician of Valencia to two sons studying at Toulouse.[157] The physician lays down the general precept that healthy exercise makes for a sound intellect and memory. In more bizarre vein, the physician urges the youths not to wear slippers in bed in summer because vapours will be generated that are bad for the brain and memory. Moreover, if exercise is not taken after a meal, noxious vapours will likewise harm the memory.

Given the fact that undergraduates were disadvantaged by having only a limited access to books, to at least one contemporary critic this would not have been a cause for lamentation. Richard of Bury, Bishop of Durham, bibliophile and formerly a tutor to the future Edward III, lambasted the treatment of books by young students. According to the author of the *Philobiblon*, students were liable to despoil books with catarrh from a running nose, with fragments of fruit or cheese or with spittle ejected from a mouth that was engaged in too much idle chatter. Further physical damage resulted from students taking naps with their heads on the books, or leaving straws as markers in a book when closed, or doodling in the margins, or cutting away margins to use for another purpose.[158] It is to be hoped that Richard of Bury's observations

156. Aston, Duncan & Evans, "The medieval alumni of the University of Cambridge", p. 17 and *n*. 22; N. R. Ker, "Oxford college libraries before 1500", in *The universities in the Middle Ages*, p. 293, n. 2.
157. This letter or treatise is printed by Thorndike, *University records and life in the Middle Ages*, pp. 154–60.
158. See M. MacLagan (ed.), *Philobiblon of Richard de Bury* (Oxford, Basil Blackwell, 1960), pp. 156–61.

applied to only a few irresponsible students and that most had a proper respect for these valuable and scarce products.

Accommodation in halls, hostels and colleges was generally at a premium, and undergraduates often had to live in crowded conditions with between two and four to a chamber. In order to give some privacy for study, cubicles or "studies" were commonly made by partitioning off the ends or corners of rooms. If possible, each "study" would command a source of light, and would probably contain a seat, a desk, a book-cupboard or book-shelf, and sometimes a chest and a table.[159] The main part of the chamber would be given over to communal living and sleeping quarters. Most of the furnishings had to be introduced by the students, only bedsteads being normally provided. So it was that undergraduates had to equip themselves with mattresses, blankets and sheets, and any other item that would afford a modicum of comfort amid a rather spartan environment. The mounting pressures for the creation of "studies" is shown at the King's Hall where, in the fifteenth century, a proportion of the entrance dues of new entrants that would normally have gone towards a breakfast for members of the college was often diverted for the funding of chamber "studies".[160]

The medieval English universities provided a relatively peaceful context for undergraduate study. Their populations were less cosmopolitan than those in larger continental universities. It is true that the impact of Wyclifism and Lollardy at Oxford in the late-fourteenth and fifteenth centuries and the disruption at Cambridge caused by the Peasants' Revolt of 1381 were far from negligible events. Furthermore, the temporary academic migrations from Oxford to Northampton and Stamford and from Cambridge to Northampton clearly had an intermittently unsettling effect upon the tenor of university life. The recurrent menace of plague and other diseases of the fever variety caused considerable interruption to studies as well as suffering and death. Interhall feuding and

---

159. For "studies" at English colleges see R. Willis & J. W. Clarke, *The architectural history of the University of Cambridge and the colleges of Cambridge and Eton* (4 vols) (Cambridge, Cambridge University Press, 1886), III, pp. 304–27; W. A. Pantin, "The halls and schools of medieval Oxford: an attempt at reconstruction", in *Oxford studies presented to Daniel Callus*, Oxford Historical Society, new ser. **16** (Oxford, Clarendon Press, 1964), pp. 86–7, 89. For the erection of "studies" at St John's College, Cambridge, in the seventeenth century see E. Miller, *Portrait of a college* (Cambridge, Cambridge University Press, 1961), p. 26.

160. Cobban, *The King's Hall*, p. 220; King's Hall accounts, IX, fol. 93v; X, fol. 1v.

the many brawls with townspeople or between rival parties of scholars could only have been a maddening distraction for those students intent on serious study.

Despite these problems, English undergraduates could look forward to a fair measure of continuity in their academic life, at least in comparison with the often lengthy and severe dislocations that occurred in continental universities. The University of Bologna was closed down in 1286–9 and 1306–9, in 1338 and in 1336–7 as a result of the imposition of papal interdicts on the city.[161] In addition to these closures, there were at least nine further cessations of lectures and migrations of Bolognese doctors and law students in the thirteenth and fourteenth centuries, and plague stoppages also happened on six occasions between 1348 and 1401.[162] Medieval English students were shielded from such excessive intrusions into their academic life. To that extent they were more fortunately placed than many of their continental counterparts.

161. Kibre, *Scholarly privileges*, p. 34.
162. *ibid.*, ch. 2; Rashdall, *Universities*, I, p. 589.

CHAPTER TWO

The postgraduate experience

A contemporary observer of the medieval English universities would probably have remarked on the general youthfulness of the teaching staff both in arts and in the superior faculties of law, theology and medicine. There were two main reasons for this. First, the idea of an organized academic profession was long in the making. A teaching position at a university was not generally seen as an end in itself. Rather it was an avenue for social advancement, a preparation for a new career move.[1] English university teachers or regents were mostly recruited from the ranks of the graduate students and so were often of middling to lower social origins. Since university teachers were generally located at the less influential end of the social spectrum, it is understandable that they would have a strong incentive to use their academic career as a springboard for greater recognition and reward. Whatever exalted notions they may have had of themselves, university teaching masters occupied only a modest niche in the social hierarchy of the age. The second factor that worked against the longevity of university careers in England stemmed from the absence of tenured posts. For almost three hundred years English university teachers had to exercise their craft without the benefit of salaried lectureships. Endowed lectureships had been gradually established in the universities of southern Europe in the course of the thirteenth and fourteenth centuries. The salaried university lectureship was a much later phenomenon in the

---

1. See, for example, the comments of J. Verger, "Teachers", in Ridder-Symoens (ed.), *A history of the university in Europe*, I, p. 167.

northern universities, and Oxford and Cambridge were among the last to institutionalize the system.[2]

Endowed lectureships first appeared in several of the English colleges in the fifteenth century, notably at the Cambridge colleges of Godshouse, later refounded as Christ's College, at Queens' and at the King's Hall. At Oxford, the three lectureships established at Magdalen College by 1479/80 at the latest were influential models for sub-sequent collegiate foundations. The earliest salaried lectureships to be successfully implanted in the English university sector, as opposed to the colleges, were launched at Cambridge in 1488 when three lectureships were endowed for classical authors, logic and philosophy.[3] In the remainder of the fifteenth and first half of the sixteenth centuries university lectureships at both Oxford and Cambridge were founded in some profusion, although this could not prevent the progressive decentralization of teaching in the colleges, a movement that was completed largely by the mid-sixteenth century.[4]

The effect of this reorientation of teaching around college and university lectureships was to create a more effective and stable teaching force than had been the case before 1450. To this extent English university teachers became more professional in character and outlook. It was the concept of tenure, whether limited or medium term and realized through endowed college and university lectureships, that above all transformed the condition of English university teachers. The lengthening of tenure brought with it a more defined status and a consequential increase in respect for academic practitioners. Before salaried lectureships became the norm, English university teachers were recruited in a rather haphazard way, and this unsystematic form of selection guaranteed neither sustained academic commitment nor intellectual maturity. The essence of the system, known as the "necessary regency" system, was the contractual obligation for every new master of arts or doctor in a superior faculty to remain at university to teach for periods of one or two years, depending upon the exact requirements of the particular faculty.[5] Looked

---

2. See the discussion by A. B. Cobban, "Decentralized teaching in the medieval English universities", *History of Education* 5, 1976, p. 204.
3. Cobban, *Medieval English universities*, pp. 196–201, 204–5; D. R. Leader, "Teaching in Tudor Cambridge", *History of Education* 13, 1984, p. 106; Leader, *The university to 1546*, pp. 242–3.
4. Cobban, "Decentralized teaching", pp. 205–6; Curtis, *Oxford and Cambridge in transition*, p. 104.

at from this point of view, teaching for many was a degree requisite rather than a career prospect. Even if a lecturer continued to teach for longer than was necessary, the aim was often to fund further study or to await an opportunity for advancement to arise outside the university. In the heyday of the "necessary regency" system a typical lecturer at Cambridge was probably obliged to deliver about 140 official or ordinary lectures in the course of the academic year or about 100 lectures if a disputation was held every week.[6]

In the fifteenth century there was a general movement towards a contraction in the "necessary regency" system of lecturing in arts at Oxford, and this situation was paralleled at Paris. Moreover, individual masters could be dispensed from all or part of their enforced regency, although they were sometimes required to provide substitutes in their place.[7] The register of Merton College yields the example of Gold, a regent master, who was licensed for the MA in February 1512 and was dispensed from "necessary regency" in January 1513 to enable the master to teach for a year and a half in a grammar school to relieve an impoverished condition.[8] General dispensations freed groups of masters from their statutory lectures. For instance, at Oxford in October 1506 all doctors and masters who had begun their regency in July of that year were dispensed from lecturing, that is after only about three months or less. In February 1511 all Oxford masters who had been created the previous July were allowed to reduce their lectures to 15 minutes each.[9] In the early-sixteenth century the traditional "necessary regency" system at both Oxford and Cambridge had become a mere shadow of what it had been. The number of days assigned for lectures each term in early-sixteenth-century Oxford had fallen to well below

---

5. Cobban, *Medieval English universities*, pp. 171–2. An Oxford statute of 1438 employs the term "necessary regent" (*necessarius regens*): see Gibson, *Statuta antiqua*, p. 258. According to the Cambridge constitution of pre-1250 all new regent masters were required to teach for at least one year: see Hackett, *Original statutes of Cambridge University*, pp. 198–301.
6. *ibid.*, p. 133.
7. J. M. Fletcher, "The teaching of arts at Oxford, 1400–1520", *Paedagogica Historica* **7**, 1967, p. 425; Fletcher, "Developments in the faculty of arts 1370–1520", in *HUO*, II, p. 333; T. A. R. Evans, "The number, origins and careers of scholars", in *ibid.*, II, p. 495.
8. H. E. Salter (ed.), *Registrum annalium collegii Mertonensis 1483–1521*, Oxford Historical Society **76** (Oxford, Clarendon Press, 1923), p. 433.
9. Leader, *The university to 1546*, pp. 244–5.

20, and sometimes to as low as four, whereas in 1431 at least 30 days were set aside for lectures each term.[10] "Necessary regency" had clearly been rendered a victim of the combined assaults of the salaried lecture-ship and the wide dissemination of printed texts that lessened the need for such a heavy quota of routine lectures. The transition from one method of lecturer recruitment to another was not marked in any formal manner, and neither Oxford nor Cambridge took the decisive step of abolishing the "necessary regency" system by official statute in the sixteenth century.

Before the advent of salaried lectureships English university lecturers depended in part or chiefly for their livelihood on student fees. These were not particularly lucrative, especially in the arts faculties. However, regent masters at both Oxford and Cambridge could expect to receive gifts from candidates taking degrees, and at Oxford a sum was distrib-uted annually to help needy lecturers so that they would not be lost to the University through poverty.[11] It must be stressed here that the teaching of the regent masters was heavily complemented by the teaching of bachelors who, as part of their statutory training to become masters or doctors in each faculty, were obliged to deliver a quota of lectures. Bachelors might continue teaching for two or three years, although they often had to wait longer for promotion to the appropriate superior degree. In the thirteenth century lecture fees were collected by regent masters as a matter of custom, not of compulsion. This inevitably created divisions within the ranks of the teaching masters because richer lecturers, who dispensed with their right to exact fees, drew audiences away from their poorer colleagues. In 1333 lecture fees were made compulsory in the Oxford faculty of arts.[12] The next develop-ment was that from 1432 the fees of all students in the faculty of arts at Oxford were to be pooled and divided equally among the regent masters.[13] However, even when lecture fees were made obligatory at both Oxford and Cambridge, they did not provide much of an incentive

---

10. Fletcher, "Developments in the faculty of arts", pp. 322–3.
11. Gibson, *Statuta antiqua*, pp. 73–4.
12. For the legislation of 1333 see *ibid.*, pp. 131–2. On compulsory lecture fees for regent masters in canon law at Oxford in the early-fourteenth century see *ibid.*, p. 47. For lecture fees at Oxford see further C. E. Mallet, *A history of the University of Oxford* (3 vols) (London, Methuen, 1924–7), I, p. 199 and G. Post. "Masters' salaries and student-fees in the medieval universities", *Speculum* **7**, 1932, p. 195.
13. Anstey, *Munimenta academica*, I, p. 303.

for young regent masters to contemplate a long-term career in university teaching.

The significant exodus of teaching staff, especially of the abler members, made continuity of university instruction a near-impossible goal to achieve with any consistency. Apart from the loss of young lecturers in arts to extra-university careers, a further problem arose when masters in arts enrolled to study in one of the superior faculties. No barrier was placed in the way of a master who wished to lecture in arts while studying in a higher faculty. The difficulty was that, in practice, few masters were able to combine the dual functions of teaching and study in different faculties because of the pressures of time and intellectual demands involved. In these circumstances, it often transpired that lecturing in arts would be sacrificed in favour of the pursuit of an advanced degree.

The lure of careers outside the university and the attractions of study in another faculty meant that, at any one time, there were many young and inexperienced lecturers in the arts faculties of Oxford and Cambridge. Many lecturers in arts were only in their early to mid-twenties, and the average age of masters in the higher faculties probably lay in the late-thirties. A similar situation pertained at Paris University in the fourteenth century. The age range of masters in arts at Paris, where known, was between 21 and 28, and many were below the age of 25 years. Regent masters in theology at Paris in the fourteenth century were mainly in their late-thirties and forties, and only a few were in their fifties.[14] It is interesting to reflect that university teachers in arts at the English universities and at Paris were commonly of similar age to those law students at Bologna and other southern European universities who helped to forge the plethora of student controls that came under the umbrella heading of student power. Teaching masters in arts at Oxford, Cambridge and Paris played a major role in the government of their universities. From this, it follows that the average age of those in authority in these northern universities was not all that different from that of members of the committees of law students who were responsible for the conduct of student-controlled universities in Italy,

---

14. W. J. Courtenay, *Teaching careers at the University of Paris in the thirteenth and fourteenth centuries* (Notre Dame, Ind., University of Notre Dame Press, 1988), pp. 24, 30; Courtenay, *Schools and scholars in fourteenth-century England* (Princeton, NJ, Princeton University Press, 1987), p. 24.

provincial France and Spain.[15] When regent masters ceased to teach either because they had embarked upon full-time study in another faculty or had left to pursue an alternative career they became non-regents and retained certain statutory rights in university government.[16]

It is abundantly clear that early retirement schemes were hardly appropriate for English regent masters in a context where long-serving teachers were thin on the ground. By contrast, in the Spanish universities in the fifteenth and sixteenth centuries a form of early retirement scheme was available. A lecturer, who had lectured for 20 years after taking a master's or doctor's degree, was entitled to the privilege of the Jubilee. This gave the lecturer the option of retirement because, if desired, the master's lectures could now be delivered by means of substitutes, and the master would still retain a good proportion of the normal salary.[17] Although retirement schemes had little relevance for the English situation, there are occasional and intriguing references to masters who were excused lecturing duties on the grounds of old age. The statutes of the King's Hall of 1380 contain such a clause, and two university graces of the early-sixteenth century exempted Cambridge masters from their academic obligations on account of senility and burdensome old age.[18] Curiously, the statutes of Cambridge University do not cite senility or old age as a reason for exemption from academic duties. Clearly, however, amid the generally youthful teaching scene issues of senescence and incapacity manifested themselves from time to time. Problems of vision may have caused some regents to cut short their academic careers, especially in the thirteenth century. The situation was improved as a result of the pioneering work on lenses by scholars such as Robert Grosseteste and Roger Bacon. A range of eyeglasses became available in England in the fourteenth century and enjoyed some popular usage. In a sermon delivered in 1306 the Dominican, Giordano of Pisa, praised the invention of eyeglasses 20 years before, and pointed out how beneficial they had been for those with sight

---

15. For student power see Cobban, "Medieval student power", pp. 28–66 and Cobban, "Elective salaried lectureships in the universities of southern Europe in the pre-Reformation era", pp. 662–87.
16. See below, Chapter 7.
17. Cobban, "Elective salaried lectureships", p. 669 and Kagan, *Students and society in early modern Spain*, p. 168.
18. Cobban, *The King's Hall*, pp. 89–90 and the statutes of the King's Hall in Rouse Ball, *The King's Scholars and King's Hall*, p. 66.

difficulties.[19] These devices would have been of considerable help to older masters in the superior faculties, but there is not much evidence that the use of optical instruments made a significant difference to the average length of the teaching career.

The youthful character of the teaching body of Oxford and Cambridge meant that the demarcation line between teachers and taught was not so clearly drawn as is usually the case in a modern university. Young and energetic lecturers might well make an easy academic rapport with impressionable students that would to some degree compensate for the lack of teaching experience and intellectual maturity. On the other hand, lecturers who were not far removed in years from their students would not always command the highest respect. Some of the ablest students would doubtless sense the inexperience of their teachers, and the spectacle of masters joining with riotous students in affrays with citizens of the town can have done nothing for the dignity of the teaching office. The rapid turnover of university masters and the fact that much teaching was shouldered by even younger bachelors as part of their academic training meant that it was difficult to create long-term master–student relationships. Among secular theologians regencies of two years was usual, and they did not often exceed five years.[20] This limitation applied not only to secular teaching but also to the mendicant orders in Oxford and Cambridge where regency was commonly as brief as one or two years.[21] In these circumstances, there were relatively few English masters who could make a sustained contribution to their disciplines while engaged in university teaching, although scholars such as Robert Grosseteste, Roger Bacon, Thomas Bradwardine and Richard FitzRalph continued scholarly writing in their post-university years. By contrast, John Wyclif, who spent about 30 years at Oxford from the early 1350s until his enforced withdrawal in 1381, is a good example of the minority of English teaching masters who passed much of their adult careers at university and who completed significant work during that time. Most teaching masters, however, did not become life-long professional scholars in the modern sense.

19. J. Gimpel, *The medieval machine: the industrial revolution of the Middle Ages*, 2nd edn (Aldershot, Wildwood House, 1988), pp. 149, 185–6.
20. W. J. Courtenay, "Theology and theologians from Ockham to Wyclif", in *HUO*, II, p. 4.
21. *ibid.*, p. 4 and Courtenay, *Schools and scholars*, p. 190.

It is interesting that the celebrated group of youthful scholars at Merton College, Oxford, in the early-fourteenth century that included Thomas Bradwardine, Richard Swyneshed ("the calculator"), John Dumbleton and William Heytesbury achieved their prominence in those subjects such as logic, mathematics and physics where the most valuable contributions are often made in the earlier phase of an academic career.[22] There is perhaps a grain of truth in the idea that the absence of tenure was a factor in channelling the intellectual energies of English teaching staff into areas that were particularly attuned to the youthful mind. However, any benefits that may have accrued from the release of youthful intellectual power have to be counterbalanced by the fact that the constant disruption to continuity caused by the rapid turnover in staff made it difficult to build up coherent schools of thought spanning several academic generations. It is true that there were some identifiable schools of thought in the medieval English universities. For example, the Mertonian school of the early-fourteenth century has just been mentioned. To this may be added the attempted imposition of Thomism by the Dominican Order on its members in the late-thirteenth and early-fourteenth centuries, and the dependence of the Austin Friars and the Franciscans on the works of Giles of Rome and Duns Scotus respectively in the earlier part of the fourteenth century.[23] Although definite schools of thought were prevalent at various times, it would seem that the predominant intellectual pattern was characterized more by the contributions of individual scholars than by the collectivist offerings of adherents to rigid and competing ideologies.

In the absence of student controls in the English universities the regent masters were not specifically accountable to the undergraduate body. Their responsibility was to the university statutes that defined

22. On these Mertonian scholars see J. A. Weisheipl, "Ockham and the Mertonians", in *HUO*, I, pp. 607–58; G. Leff, *Paris and Oxford Universities in the thirteenth and fourteenth centuries*, pp. 302–5; B. Lawn, *The rise and decline of the scholastic "quaestio disputata"* (Leiden, New York & Cologne, Brill, 1993), pp. 45–65; M. L. Colish, *Medieval foundations of the western intellectual tradition 400–1400* (New Haven, Conn. & London, Yale University Press, 1997), p. 322.
23. On schools of thought in fourteenth-century Oxford see Courtenay, *Schools and scholars*, ch. 6 and Courtenay, "The role of English thought in the transformation of university education in the late Middle Ages", in *Rebirth, reform and resilience: universities in transition 1300–1700*, J. M. Kittelson & P. J. Transue (eds) (Columbus, Ohio State University Press, 1984), pp. 111–12.

their academic duties. Statutes laid down the procedures governing the lectures and disputations of the regent masters and the teaching time-table for the year. The obligations of the teaching staff, however, went beyond the purely pedagogic. Regent masters had to take part in prescribed religious ceremonies, they participated in the government of the university and some of them held major administrative offices. Eminent teaching masters might be called upon to serve on diplomatic missions on behalf of the king or pope, and they were liable to be nominated by their universities to attend international ecclesiastical councils such as those of Pisa, Constance and Basel in the fifteenth century.[24] The absenteeism that necessarily resulted from these activi-ties was doubtless a problem at Oxford and Cambridge as it was in all medieval universities. Substitute teachers were deployed with some frequency in the southern European universities to cover for the legit-imate or illegitimate absences of full-time lecturing staff. The wide-spread use of substitutes in many of the southern universities generated a good deal of student criticism of substandard teaching by ill-qualified and inexperienced replacements.[25] There is not much evidence of adverse criticism of substitute teachers in the English universities, presumably because bachelors in the various faculties provided substitute teaching at an acceptable level.

English teaching masters enjoyed only modest privileges in compar-ison with some of their continental counterparts. For example, in 1319 Henry II of Castile and Léon conferred upon university masters who had taught for 40 years within these territories the privileges exercised by dukes, marquises and counts. These privileges embraced the right to bear arms in public and private, and the right to maintain four armed laymen or slaves. In 1420 Alfonso V of Aragon gave to the doctors and licentiates of civil law at the University of Valencia all the privileges of knights. The Emperor Charles V conceded to the doctoral college at Bologna in the sixteenth century the right to confer the status of knighthood upon teaching doctors. At the University of Salamanca the doctors of law came to exercise some of the fiscal and ceremonial

---

24. See, for example, J. I. Catto, "Wyclif and Wycliffism at Oxford 1356–1430", in *HUO*, II, pp. 241, 245, 254; also R. B. Dobson, "The religious orders 1370–1540", in *ibid.*, II, p. 577.
25. Cobban, "Elective salaried lectureships", pp. 669–75, 686–7.

privileges of the nobility.[26] Nothing of this kind permeated the English university scene. In England external authorities were apparently not keen to elevate teachers beyond their academic environment, although the prevalence of short tenures scarcely set up the conditions for privileged treatment. In southern universities many of the teaching doctors were laymen and married with families. Marriage could bestow on academics other forms of privilege. At Bologna, for instance, the law doctors attempted, for a time with some success, to make their positions hereditary. The commune eventually quashed this development, but there is no doubt that in the second half of the thirteenth century sons often succeeded to the teaching posts vacated by their fathers.[27] Another example of family privilege derives from the University of Avignon where, in the late-fifteenth century, the sons of teaching doctors were exempted from degree fees.[28] Before the sixteenth century most English teaching masters were of clerical status, and marriage brought an end to the academic career. This consideration greatly limited the scope for direct forms of nepotism.

English university teachers functioned in a free-enterprise culture. As individual regent masters, they were accorded a considerable degree of independence. Curricular and other professional concerns were generally settled by the self-regulation of the masters' guild. The academic regime and the examination criteria were internal matters that were not subject to external validation. The masters' guild did not experience the humiliation of having to produce banal and disingenuous mission statements or of having thrust upon it the inappropriate verbiage of a mercantile society to name only two of the albatrosses that so depress modern British universities. Regent masters were free to pursue lines of intellectual enquiry that were independent of the siren call of crude market forces. The only restriction was that university teachers were not immune from accusations of heresy, although they were largely shielded from the more draconian punishments that were reserved for errant members of the laity who lacked the protective mantle of an

26. For the privileges in the Spanish universities see *ibid.*, pp. 681–2; for the Salamancan privileges see R. Kagan, "Universities in Castile 1500–1700", *Past & Present* 49, 1970, p. 58; for the privileges at Bologna see Rashdall, *Universities*, I, pp. 228–9.
27. Rashdall, *Universities*, I, p. 214.
28. J. Verger, "Le coût des grades droits et frais d'examen dans les universités du Midi au moyen âge", in *The economic and material frame of the medieval university*, A. L. Gabriel (ed.) (Notre Dame, Ind., University of Notre Dame Press, 1977), p. 28.

academic status. For the most part, the masters of theology themselves had the right to evaluate the opinions of one of their peers if heresy was suspected.[29] Although the diocesan bishops, Lincoln for Oxford and Ely for Cambridge, were sometimes associated with a contentious issue, in most cases the adjudication of the masters of theology was sufficient to determine whether or not heresy had been involved. Only if the issue raised was of major import was it likely that the case would be referred for judgment to an extra-university authority such as the papal curia.

Censures of academic errors were directed usually against the offending opinions and only rarely against the person of the master whose subsequent career would normally survive this troublesome episode.[30] It is true that if a teacher persisted in voicing condemned heretical opinions, more serious action would follow. For instance, John Wyclif was forced to withdraw from Oxford in 1381 because of the subversive nature of doctrines repeatedly and aggressively expounded. At Paris, Nicholas of Autrécourt, a master who taught in the faculty of arts and who acquired a doctoral degree in theology, was summoned, along with five other theologians, to the papal curia at Avignon to answer charges of alleged errors. The examination extended over six years, and in 1346 Autrécourt retracted some of the controversial opinions. The regent master was also forbidden to teach again at Paris or at any other university, and was stripped of the degree in theology. In 1347 Autrécourt returned to Paris where a similar retraction was made and where one of the scholar's treatises, *Exigit ordo*, was publicly consigned to the flames.[31]

The cases of Wyclif and Autrécourt were rather exceptional, and academic censures were usually far less traumatic, causing only temporary embarrassment. From the early-fourteenth century newly qualified bachelors and masters, both in England and at Paris, had to declare publicly that they would not teach anything that was contrary to faith.[32] This binding oath provided a focal point for those who were motivated

---

29. For the situation regarding academics and heresy, especially at Paris, see W. J. Courtenay, "Inquiry and inquisition: academic freedom in medieval universities", *Church History* **58**, 1989, pp. 168–81.
30. *ibid.*, pp. 178, 180.
31. For the career of Autrécourt see Z. Kaluza, "Nicolas d'Autrécourt: ami de la vérité", in *Histoire littéraire de la France*, 42 (Paris, A. Bontemps, 1995), pp. 1–232.
32. Courtenay, "Inquiry and inquisition", p. 178.

to bring charges of false teaching against a bachelor or regent master. Censures appear to have been more frequent at Paris than in England, which is perhaps reflective of the more turbulent character of intellectual life in the French cosmopolitan university.

Some regent masters, who remained in the university beyond the obligatory teaching period, supplemented their incomes by renting halls or hostels and establishing themselves as principals. Others, who were either studying in or were regent masters in a higher faculty, became college fellows. It was emphasized sufficiently in Chapter 1 that, with one or two exceptions, secular colleges before the sixteenth century were largely postgraduate institutions.[33] In an age bereft of state educational funding, it was often financially impossible for a graduate with the BA or MA degree to remain at university to acquire a qualification in one of the superior faculties. Because of the length and costs of the courses in the higher faculties, there was an urgent need to make available accommodation and financial assistance for talented scholars who had ambitions to further their studies. Combined with this motive is the consideration that many secular colleges embodied a chantry element. The founders of secular colleges, whether kings, queens, ecclesiastics or members of the laity, viewed the founding of a college as a pious act of charity that would perpetuate their memory and allow masses to be said for themselves and named relations. This union of educational and spiritual motivation underlay the foundation of English university colleges right through to the sixteenth century.[34]

In their mature form English secular colleges were solidly endowed, self-governing corporations with their own statutes and common seals. It was the act of endowment that differentiated the college decisively from the Oxford hall and Cambridge hostel and set up the conditions for permanency within the university community. Founders sometimes stipulated that their colleges were designed for "poor scholars" or for "poor and indigent scholars". Balliol, New College, All Souls and

33. For a discussion of continental and English colleges see Cobban, *The medieval universities: their development and organization*, ch. 6 and, for the English colleges specifically, see Cobban, *Medieval English universities*, ch. 4.
34. On colleges and chantries see, for example, Cobban, *Medieval English universities*, pp. 112–13. At St Catharine's College, Cambridge, about one-sixth of the statutes concern chantry provisions: see the original statutes, St Catharine's muniments, XL/ 10 and the printed version in H. Philpott (ed.), *Documents relating to St Catharine's College in the University of Cambridge* (Cambridge, Cambridge University Press, 1861).

Magdalen at Oxford and King's College at Cambridge were all said to be founded for this kind of impecunious scholar.[35] However, in college statutes the term "poor scholar" is often used as a stereotype and implied no more than that the scholar needed a measure of financial support to sustain a lengthy course of study.

It seems evident that most college fellows would be possessed of average means and would have had an income additional to what was provided by a college fellowship. On the other hand, fellows were not intended to be wealthy. In order to exclude scholars who could easily afford to pay their own way, most English colleges of the fourteenth and fifteenth centuries prescribed "income ceilings". These "ceilings" laid down the level of personal income that was deemed compatible with the tenure of a fellowship. The amount of annual allowable income for a fellow from all sources such as a benefice, with or without cure of souls, a pension, corrodies or rents ranged from £4 at Trinity Hall, Cambridge, to £6 13s 4d at Clare College, Cambridge, with £5 being the commonly prescribed limit.[36] Whereas English college founders set fairly uniform permissible levels of income, French college founders tended to grade income limits according to academic disciplines so that, for example, theologians, canonists and artists were given their own separate ceilings.[37] The imposition of "income ceilings" in English colleges helped to ensure that fellowships were not turned into sinecures for affluent scholars.

It is very difficult to generalize about the length of tenure of college fellowships in the medieval period. At Queens' College, Cambridge, for instance, tenures were relatively brief in the fifteenth century. An analysis of 55 fellows of Queens' in that century reveals that the average tenure of fellowships was just under seven years, the actual lengths of stay ranging from several weeks to 25 years.[38] At Merton College, Oxford, the pattern was more mixed. Of 90 fellows present between 1415 and 1450 20 were resident for 7 years or less, 19 for 8 to 10 years, 28 for 11 to 15 years, 8 for 16 to 20 years, 5 for more

35. H. E. Salter (ed.), *The Oxford deeds of Balliol College* (Oxford, H. Hart, 1913), p. 280 (Balliol); *Statutes*, I, ch. 5, p. 1 (New College), ch. 7, p. 11 (All Souls); II, ch. 8, p. 5 (Magdalen); *Camb. Docs*, II, p. 481 (King's).
36. For a survey of college "income ceilings" see Cobban, *The King's Hall*, p. 146, n. 1.
37. A. L. Gabriel, "The college system in the fourteenth-century universities", in *The forward movement of the fourteenth century*, p. 90.
38. Twigg, *A history of Queens' College, Cambridge*, p. 78.

than 21 years, and, in the case of 10 fellows, the period of residence is unknown.[39] The situation at the King's Hall is characterized by a general lengthening of tenures between the early-fourteenth and mid-sixteenth centuries. Of the 472 fellows admitted between 1317 and 1450 at least 53 held fellowships for periods of between 20 and more than 50 years. Most of these long-tenured fellowships occurred in the hundred years from 1350 to 1450, there being only eight known instances of fellowships held for 20 years or more in the first half of the fourteenth century. Of the 245 fellows admitted between 1451 and 1543, 36 retained their fellowships in excess of 20 years, 15 of them being for periods of between 30 and 39 years.[40] Occasionally, a college set a maximum limit to the tenure of a fellowship. At Exeter College, Oxford, fellowships had to be vacated after about 14 years.[41]

Fellowships in medieval English colleges may be regarded from at least two different perspectives. On the one hand, fellowships that were held for brief tenures were often viewed as the first step on the way to an extra-university career. In this sense, they served a similar purpose to lecturing posts that were exercised for only a very few years as a prelude to moving to alternative employment. On the other hand, the long-tenured fellowship was one factor that, along with the late appearance of endowed college and university lectureships, helped to promote the reality of a more stable university profession by enabling a core of advanced scholars to study and function within the academic community for a significant period. Seen in this light, the college fellowship of the long-tenured variety was an important building block for developing the potential of the academic profession as a mainstream career.

It is clear that the English fellowship was designed to accommodate basic needs and to provide a range of communal comforts that mitigated some of the hardships of medieval academic life. Fellowships were not intended to be unduly lucrative, and the standard of living that they supported was adequate rather than lavish. Fellows were allocated a room or rooms, and were normally assigned a weekly sum from college revenues for their commons and an actual livery or an equivalent allowance for clothes. At New College the annual set of clothes was

---

39. Lytle, *Oxford students and English society*, p. 192.
40. For this analysis see Cobban, *The King's Hall*, pp. 56–8.
41. R. W. Southern, "Exeter College", in *Victoria history of the county of Oxford. Volume 3*, p. 108.

not to be sold, pawned or otherwise disposed of by a fellow for at least five years, although a livery that was five years old could be given free of charge to new fellows or probationary scholars. Fellows of All Souls who were found guilty of selling, pawning or giving away their college clothes were to be deprived of the next distribution of livery.[42]

The commons allowance for basic items of food and drink was, in many colleges, geared to a sliding-scale, with minimum and maximum limits and governed by fluctuations in grain prices, especially wheat and malt barley.[43] In the fourteenth century a usual allowance for commons was 1s per fellow per week. At New College, Oxford, this rate could rise to a maximum of 1s 6d in times of scarcity. At Oriel College the maximum limit for commons of 1s 3d was to come into operation when a quarter of wheat was selling at 10s or more in Oxford or in the surrounding area. In the mid-fifteenth century the commons rate at King's College, Cambridge, ranged from 1s 4d a week to an ultimate ceiling of 1s 8d. The fellows of Peterhouse, Cambridge, were not so fortunate. John Alcock, Bishop of Ely, inserted an ordinance in the statutes of 1489 limiting the commons allowance to 1s 2d a week, although this could be increased slightly in years of lean harvest.[44]

At the King's Hall, Cambridge, there was no such sliding-scale. Uniquely, the fellows were allowed a flat rate of 1s 2d a week that was paid directly from the royal exchequer.[45] The implication of this is that in the King's Hall, where the cost of living was noticeably high, the fellows certainly had to contribute from private income to meet the costs of their commons. Between 1382–3 and 1443–4 the King's Hall fellows were charged average sums fluctuating from 1s $2\frac{1}{2}$d a week in 1387–8 to 2s $3\frac{1}{2}$d in 1438–9, giving an average sum of 1s $8\frac{1}{4}$d a week over this whole period.[46] This is a high average charge, and it supports the notion that the King's Hall was a kind of *collège de luxe*, a suitable home for crown appointees, some of whom had connections with the court and royal household. Since the fellows were credited with 1s 2d

42. *Statutes*, I, ch. 5, p. 45 (New College), ch. 7, p. 43 (All Souls).
43. Cobban, *The King's Hall*, pp. 139–41.
44. *Statutes*, I, ch. 5, pp. 38–9 (New College), ch. 3, p. 15 (Oriel); *Camb. Docs*, II, pp. 527–8 (King's), pp. 48–9 (Peterhouse).
45. Cobban, *The King's Hall*, p. 129.
46. *ibid.*, p. 139 and table 5, column 16 (between pp. 126 and 127).

a week for commons by means of the exchequer subsidy, they had to find from their own resources an average sum of $6\frac{1}{4}$d a week which gives an average annual sum of £1 7s 1d. To this must be added the average amount spent by fellows on their sizings, the extra items of food and drink ordered beyond their commons and often called battels at Oxford. The combined annual sums for commons and sizings within the stated period ranged from £1 14s to £3, indicating an average annual amount of about £2 7s.[47] Further expenditure was incurred by the King's Hall fellows on matters such as lecture and degree fees, the purchase of texts used in study, travelling costs, the outlay on guests in college, exceptional expenditure on feast days and the expense of retaining private servants. The retention of private servants was not common before 1460. It became a regular feature from the late-fifteenth century. In the first half of the sixteenth century about half, and in some years two-thirds, of the fellows kept servants, presumably a sign of the growing standards of comfort within this royal foundation.[48]

It is not possible to give accurate figures for the total annual expenditure of the average King's Hall fellow. The range of expenses indicated above, however, suggests that the fellows would probably have to spend most of their allowable income each year. By statute, this was fixed at £6 13s 4d a year if derived from an ecclesiastical benefice, and set at £5 if acquired from temporal possessions, pensions or other revenues.[49] In 1490–1 about two-thirds of the fellows were beneficed. Most of these benefices were compatible with the statutory maximum income, although in the fifteenth century some royal licences were issued to fellows allowing them to receive the fruits of benefices that were valued in excess of the prescribed limit.[50] For a handful of years in the mid-fourteenth century the income of fellows of the King's Hall was supplemented by annual dividends from college funds to the value of one mark (13s 4d), payable in two equal instalments.[51] This is an early instance of college dividends. They did not become a regular feature of

47. *ibid.*, pp. 135–6.
48. For detailed figures on private servants see *ibid.*, pp. 242–4.
49. *ibid.*, pp. 145–6, and for the statutory entry Rouse Ball, *The King's Scholars and King's Hall*, p. 68.
50. Cobban, *The King's Hall*, p. 143.
51. *ibid.*, pp. 142–3; see also King's Hall accounts, XIV, fols 66v, 142v; XV, fols 26v, 86; XVI, fols 43, 46v; XVII, fols 100v, 126v; XVIII, fols 40, 45v, 66v; XIX, fols 24, 25; XX, fols 84, 85; XXI, fols 61v, 62v.

English colleges until the sixteenth century when they were often derived from entry fines paid by college tenants on taking over or renewing a lease.[52] Since the King's Hall did not depend upon estate management, its dividends were not acquired from this source. Just as fellows of the King's Hall needed a private income to maintain their collegiate position, so it has been reckoned that, at least in the fifteenth century, the expenses incurred by fellows at New College probably exceeded the financial value of a fellowship.[53] It is likely that the situation was similar at most English secular colleges.

The very detailed calculations that can be made concerning the expenditure of the King's Hall fellows on commons and sizings and on a wide diversity of miscellaneous items is not easy to parallel among medieval university colleges. The 26 volumes of the King's Hall accounts that extend, with a few breaks, from 1337 to 1544 comprise the longest series of paper collegiate records in medieval England and perhaps also in continental Europe.[54] As the King's Hall derived its revenue in the main from the exchequer and from a number of appropriated churches, it did not, as recently said, have to rely upon estate management. The result of this is that the voluminous accounts concentrate primarily upon internal economic and social matters. These accounts yield a vivid insight into the life and economy of a medieval college week by week and year by year for more than two centuries. The records of most English colleges of the pre-Reformation era, however valuable they may be in certain respects, simply do not allow such a detailed and comprehensive analysis. This being so, it is exceedingly hard to obtain distilled averages concerning the expenditure patterns of fellows in other colleges that can be used for comparative purposes. While this circumstance throws into sharp relief the importance of the King's Hall data, it has always to be appreciated that the average sums derived for expenditure by or on behalf of fellows of this royal college were almost certainly higher than in the generality of secular colleges.

The levying of entrance dues on new fellows does not appear to have been very widespread among English secular colleges. Of the many sets of college statutes that were framed between the late-thirteenth

---

52. T. A. R. Evans & R. Faith, "College estates and university finances 1350–1500", in *HUO*, II, pp. 682, 699.
53. Lytle, *Oxford students and English society*, p. 84.
54. Cobban, *The King's Hall*, p. 6.

and the seventeenth centuries, in only two, those of the Cambridge colleges of Peterhouse and Michaelhouse, are admission charges specified.

At Peterhouse a fellow had to give a mazer cup and a silver spoon to the college and, within three months, had to be equipped with a surplice. Similarly, at Michaelhouse a new fellow was required to have a white surplice and had to present the college with a silver spoon, a mazer cup and a napkin and cloth for the fellows' table.[55] Although entrance dues are not specified in the statutes of the King's Hall, the accounts make it clear that heavy admission charges were imposed upon new entrants. New fellows had to provide a breakfast or feast, valued at 20s, for all the established fellows. They also had to contribute 20s towards the running costs of the college boat.[56] The substantial total of £2 0s 4d for entrance dues at the King's Hall was not far short of the sum of £2 7s that represented the annual average cost of commons and sizings for each fellow. No trace of admission charges is to be found in any code of Oxford college statutes before the seventeenth century. As the case of the King's Hall illustrates, however, this does not preclude the possibility that dues were levied in one or two Oxford colleges despite the statutory silence. Entrance requirements took a very practical form in several of the Parisian colleges of the fourteenth century. At the Ave Maria College (1339) and the colleges of Boncour (1337) and Dainville (1380) new entrants had to provide items such as linen, towels and bed furnishings.[57]

Because undergraduates lived mostly in Oxford halls and Cambridge hostels before the late-fifteenth and early-sixteenth centuries, the secular colleges for long housed only a small fraction of the academic population. In the fourteenth century Cambridge's academic population may have fluctuated between 400 and 700 and that of Oxford may have reached about 1,500.[58] The eight Cambridge colleges in the fourteenth century yielded a statutory total of 137 fellowships, excluding headships.[59] Statutory complements are not always a reliable guide to the

55. *Camb. Docs*, II, p. 6 (Peterhouse); A. E. Stamp, *Michaelhouse* (Cambridge, privately printed, 1924), p. 29.
56. Cobban, *The King's Hall*, p. 138.
57. Gabriel, *Student life in Ave Maria College*, p. 94 and *n.* 6.
58. T. H. Aston, G. D. Duncan & T. A. R. Evans, "The medieval alumni of the University of Cambridge", *Past & Present* **86**, 1980, pp. 26–7.
59. For the statutory numbers in each college see Cobban, *Medieval English universities*, p. 121 and *n.* 27.

actual numbers present. Accepting the statutory figures for those Cambridge colleges where they are known to be reasonably accurate and estimating the actual numbers in colleges where the statutory totals are optimistic, the revised figure of about 80 fellowships is reached.[60] Small as this is, it is higher than the number of fellowships supported by the Oxford colleges before 1379 when the six secular colleges supplied about 63 fellows.[61] This number was virtually doubled with the foundation of New College in that year. Since Oxford's population was two or three times the size of that of Cambridge, it follows that, before 1379, the proportion of college fellows in the university community was greater at Cambridge than at Oxford. By the mid-fifteenth century Cambridge's population had possibly increased to about 1,300 and that of Oxford to about 1,700.[62] The actual number of fellows in Oxford and Cambridge colleges in the mid-fifteenth century cannot be computed with accuracy at present. Taking the statutory figures only, and recognizing that they may be to a degree misleading, Cambridge would have mustered about 225 fellows compared with between 150 and 200 at Oxford.[63] If these figures are broadly reliable, they show that Cambridge fellows in the fifteenth century continued to occupy a larger proportion of the academic population than did their equivalents at Oxford.

Although English college fellows comprised only a small segment of the university community, they exercised an influence that was wholly disproportionate to their numbers. Some combined their fellowships with the position of regent master in the various faculties and derived an income from lecturing in the university schools. In at least some of the colleges there were opportunities from the fifteenth century for fellows to serve as college lecturers or to act as tutors to undergraduate commoners. The latter were progressively introduced into colleges in the late-medieval period and they generated a useful source of revenue. Other fellows held administrative office within the university ranging from the keepership of a university or college chest to the

60. *ibid.*, pp. 121–2.
61. H. E. Salter, *Medieval Oxford*, Oxford Historical Society **100** (Oxford, Clarendon Press, 1936), p. 97.
62. Aston, Duncan & Evans, "The medieval alumni of the University of Cambridge", pp. 13, 19, 26.
63. *ibid.*, p. 14.

elevated position of vice-chancellor or chancellor. For example, 13
fellows of Peterhouse held university proctorships between 1450 and
1500, and ten of the King's Hall fellows are known to have served as
proctors of Cambridge University.[64] No fewer than eight wardens of
the King's Hall served as chancellors of Cambridge, and one of them,
Robert Ayscogh, was elected chancellor in 1447 while still a fellow of
the college and just before being appointed its warden in 1448.[65] In the
first half of the sixteenth century four of the fellows of this college
became Cambridge vice-chancellors at a time when the vice-chancellor
was becoming the effective head of the university, the chancellorship
now being held increasingly by non-resident governmental figures.[66] It
is not surprising that the King's Hall made a signal contribution to the
administrative life of Cambridge University because, until the foundation of King's College in 1441, the King's Hall was the largest and
most important of the Cambridge colleges. To take another Cambridge
example, in the fifteenth century the fellows of Queens' College filled a
number of university positions. They functioned as university preachers,
as keepers of university chests, as proctors, as writers of letters for the
university and at least one was a vice-chancellor.[67] A quantitative analysis
of university officers at Oxford reveals that between 1380 and 1419 the
fellows of Merton provided more administrative officers than any other
college.[68] In this regard, Merton was followed at some distance by
Queen's, with modest contributions from University College, Exeter,
Oriel, Balliol and New College. Between 1420 and 1479 New College
and Merton were now first equal as providers of university officers,
with Exeter a fairly close second. They were followed by Lincoln, All
Souls and University College, and some way behind by Oriel, Balliol,
Queen's and Magdalen. Between 1480 and 1499, however, the fellows
of Magdalen were the leading suppliers of candidates for university
offices, followed by Merton, New College and Lincoln. It is noticeable
that towards the end of the fifteenth century there was a decrease in

---

64. Lovatt, "Two collegiate loan-chests in late-medieval Cambridge", p. 163, *n.* 135;
Cobban, *The King's Hall*, pp. 295–6 and p. 296, *n.* 1.
65. Cobban, *The King's Hall*, pp. 285, 295; Emden, *BRUC*, p. 27.
66. Cobban, *The King's Hall*, p. 295.
67. Twigg, *A history of Queens' College, Cambridge*, p. 77.
68. For this quantitative analysis see Cobban, "Colleges and halls 1380–1500", in *HUO*,
II, pp. 623–4.

the number of university administrators who were recruited from collegiate sources.

An attractive career move for English fellows was to acquire the principalship of an Oxford hall or Cambridge hostel. This was particularly appropriate when many halls and hostels were purchased or leased by colleges in the fifteenth and early-sixteenth centuries for the purpose of housing undergraduate commoners. John Arundel, whose tutorial notes were evaluated in Chapter 1, was a fellow of Exeter College when principal of an Oxford hall in 1424. In c.1460 it seems that almost half of the fellows of Oriel College, Oxford, were or had been principals of halls, most of them belonging to the college.[69] At Cambridge, when a hostel was absorbed by a college, it was common practice for the college to appoint a fellow in residence as an external principal who would then approve the appointment of an internal principal who had been elected by the members of the hostel.[70] At Oxford the procedure was different, and it was usual for fellows to serve as the sole principals of the halls that were under the dominion of their colleges. Fellows also provided a reservoir of talent from which appointments to headships of colleges were made. The point may be illustrated from the examples of two Cambridge colleges.

In the second half of the fifteenth century Pembroke College, Cambridge, supplied fellows for the headships of at least four colleges. Edward Storey, Thomas Langton, Richard Stubbs and William Chubbes, all fellows of Pembroke in the fifteenth century, succeeded to the headships of Michaelhouse, Cambridge, Queen's College, Oxford, Clare College and Jesus College, Cambridge, respectively. In the early-sixteenth century Richard Shorton, another fellow of Pembroke, became the first master of St John's College, Cambridge, in 1511, and in 1518 was subsequently elected as master of Pembroke.[71] In similar vein, the King's Hall furnished fellows for the headships of at least six other Cambridge colleges.[72] Moreover, two of the wardens of the King's Hall had been fellows of Oxford colleges. John Blakman had been a fellow

---

69. Cobban, *Medieval English universities*, p. 159.
70. H. P. Stokes, *The medieval hostels of the University of Cambridge*, Cambridge Antiquarian Society, Octavo Publications **49**, 1924, pp. 34–7.
71. A. B. Cobban, "Pembroke College: its educational significance in late-medieval Cambridge", *Transactions of the Cambridge Bibliographical Society* **10**, 1991, p. 8.
72. Cobban, *The King's Hall*, p. 296.

of Merton, and Henry Bost had been both a fellow and provost of Queen's. At least five wardens were ex-fellows of Cambridge colleges. Nicholas Close was an ex-fellow of King's, Richard Dereham was a former fellow of Gonville, John Redman had been a fellow of St John's and two wardens, Robert Ayscogh and John Blythe, had been fellows of the King's Hall itself.[73]

An account of the reasons for the vacation of fellowships is to some extent equivalent to a survey of the career opportunities for university personnel. Along with graduates who had never held fellowships, English fellows vacated their college positions to acquire employment at all levels within the church. At the upper end of the spectrum they served as bishops and deans of secular cathedrals, and at the lower end they augmented the ranks of the inferior clergy as rectors, vicars, chaplains, chantry priests and as members of collegiate churches. Other lucrative areas of advancement lay within royal, noble and papal employment, although papal service was less favoured than the other two arenas. An analysis of fellows of New College who vacated their fellowships between 1386 and 1547 reveals that at least 312 of them entered the ranks of the beneficed clergy, many of whom remained as rectors or vicars until their deaths. No fewer than 80 returned to teach at Winchester, the preparatory school for New College, and 40 became schoolmasters at other schools. Another 70 fellows left to enter royal, aristocratic and episcopal households. The career of common lawyer accounted for 22 fellows, 20 became lawyers in ecclesiastical courts, 13 entered religious orders, 9 left to be married, 5 were expelled, 3 inherited estates that were incompatible with a fellowship and 2 were burnt as heretics. During the period surveyed, 254 fellows died while still at university, about half of whom were undergraduate fellows.[74]

Although New College was an exceptional secular college, this analysis is likely to give a broad indication of the career profile of ex-fellows throughout the English collegiate scene, bearing in mind that each college had its own concentration of studies and patronage links with extra-university society, all of which helped to determine career patterns. One college whose fellows had a larger than usual involvement

---

73. *ibid.*, pp. 280–90.
74. For this analysis see Lytle, *Oxford students and English society*, p. 231 and Lytle, "The careers of Oxford students in the later Middle Ages", in *Rebirth, reform and resilience*, pp. 221–3.

in royal service was the King's Hall, Cambridge.[75] King's Hall fellows vacated their college places to take up positions in the exchequer, the chancery, the king's council and the diplomatic sphere. They were also employed in the queen's household, and served as royal bailiffs, keepers of the forest and as judicial commissioners. Three of the King's Hall fellows served as master of the rolls, one was a keeper of the privy seal, one was a king's secretary and another was keeper of the great seal of England. It is pertinent to add here that the King's Hall was a main focus within Cambridge University for both civil and canon law, and produced just over a fifth of all university civilians in the fourteenth and fifteenth centuries.[76] The legal strength of the King's Hall was nurtured and positively promoted by successive English kings so that there would always be available a large pool of fellows with the appropriate training for royal government and administration.

To the reasons already mentioned for the resignation of fellows may be added the joining of a religious order, the neglect or failure to make progress in studies, an incurable illness, grave moral turpitude and various categories of crimes and sexual offences. These reasons are specified in the statutes of several Oxford colleges including Merton, Oriel and Queen's.[77] At New College, All Souls and Magdalen fellows could also be deprived of their fellowships if they absented themselves from the college for a stated proportion of the year without reasonable cause.[78] Moreover, fellows of Magdalen could be forced to resign if they refused to accept a college office to which they had been assigned.[79]

The situation in Cambridge colleges was broadly similar. In the statutes of Michaelhouse, for instance, fellows who became too ill to live among healthy colleagues or who entered a religious order or who were absent for three months without permission or who neglected their studies or religious duties or who acquired an income of £5 a year or who were guilty of flagrant immorality were to forfeit their

---

75. For a discussion of the careers of King's Hall fellows see Cobban, *The King's Hall*, pp. 290–9 and notes.
76. Cobban, *Medieval English universities*, pp. 226–7 and Cobban, "The medieval Cambridge colleges: a quantitative study of higher degrees to *c*.1500", *History of Education* **9**, 1980, p. 4 where table 2 monitors the King's Hall's share in university civil lawyers in each generation of 20 years between 1320 and 1499.
77. *Statutes*, I, ch. 2, pp. 6, 11, 27 (Merton), ch. 3, p. 9 (Oriel), ch. 4, p. 20 (Queen's).
78. *ibid.*, I, ch. 5, p. 64 (New College), ch. 7, p. 67 (All Souls); II, ch. 8, p. 46 (Magdalen).
79. *ibid.*, II, ch. 8, p. 82.

college places.[80] At Peterhouse, what may be construed as either incest or debauchery is given among the reasons for the enforced resignation of a fellow. On the other hand, at Clare College a fellow who developed what appears to be a form of leprosy was not to be ruthlessly expelled but was to be supported humanely for life from revenues of the college in suitable accommodation away from the other fellows.[81] Occasionally, fellows had to resign for failure to acquire a stipulated degree. This applied at Trinity Hall, Cambridge, which specialized in legal studies, where fellows who were unable to obtain the degree of doctor of civil or canon law were to be removed.[82] Several Cambridge colleges, including Gonville and the King's Hall, gave up to three warnings for certain categories of offences before resorting to expulsion.[83] Moreover, in one or two instances the King's Hall used the penalty of suspension from the benefits of a fellowship as a half-way measure along the road to full deprivation.[84] As a penalty, suspension, as opposed to permanent expulsion, does not seem to have been widely used in the English colleges.

College statutes give an inkling into the more boisterous side of life led by the more adventurous and rebellious of the fellows. At University College, Oxford, the fellows were to be restrained from fighting and using abusive language. They were to refrain from singing amatory songs and from telling tales of love, and they were not to cause ill-feeling by laughing at each other.[85] The fellows of Peterhouse, Cambridge, were prohibited from roaming around the town at night and frequenting alleys, taverns and other places of entertainment, indulging in gluttony and drunkenness. They were also forbidden to carry arms which might lead to a disturbance of the peace.[86] Many codes of college statutes have similar prohibitions, and this points to an undercurrent of restlessness and lawlessness that accords ill with the sober purpose that underlay the concept of a fellowship.

It is interesting that Robert of Eglesfield, the founder of Queen's College, Oxford, was determined to polish the manners and demeanour

80. Stamp, *Michaelhouse*, pp. 43–4.
81. *Camb. Docs*, II, p. 37 (Peterhouse), p. 139 (Clare).
82. *ibid.*, II, pp. 425–6.
83. *ibid.*, II, p. 230 (Gonville); statutes of the King's Hall in Rouse Ball, *The King's Scholars and King's Hall*, pp. 66, 67.
84. Statutes in *ibid.*, pp. 66, 69–70.
85. Anstey, *Munimenta academica*, I, p. 58.
86. *Camb. Docs*, II, pp. 29, 31.

of the fellows who were recruited preferentially from Cumberland and Westmorland. Eglesfield had been chaplain to Queen Philippa, consort of Edward III, and an effort was made to impart to the college something of the flavour of the royal court. Fellows were to be summoned to meals by a trumpet, and were to be allowed to speak French instead of Latin at table in imitation of the language of the court.[87] They were to behave in a courtly manner both towards each other and towards those of inferior status. The rough manners of fellows from northern counties were to be refined, and they were expected to live like gentlemen, showing generosity of spirit and other chivalrous traits. Eglesfield was idealistic, and the founder's vision was not matched by the resources available. Nevertheless, this was an intriguing attempt to use a college environment to raise standards of behaviour within a university community.[88]

The concept of sabbatical leave for fellows can just be dimly glimpsed and probably operated on a limited scale. The statutes of Peterhouse, Cambridge, permitted one or two of the fellows to study at Oxford with the support of a weekly commons allowance from the college. Moreover, it was permissible for fellows to study at other approved universities so long as they were maintained from non-collegiate resources.[89] In 1497 Richard Whitford, a fellow of Queens' College, Cambridge, was granted leave of absence for five years to take a pupil, Lord Mountjoy, to Paris for study purposes and for what may have been akin to a continental grand tour. In Paris Whitford had meetings with Erasmus.[90]

It was mentioned above that two fellows of New College suffered death by burning for heresy.[91] This highlights the fact that heresy, derived mainly from Wyclifism and Lollardy, became a live issue in at least some of the colleges between the late-fourteenth and sixteenth centuries. Despite the stringent efforts made to cleanse Oxford of Wyclifite and Lollard doctrines, the stigma of heresy hung like a murky cloud over the university throughout the fifteenth century. The principal

---

87. *Statutes*, I, ch. 4, p. 14.
88. J. R. M. Magrath, *The Queen's College* (2 vols) (Oxford, Clarendon Press, 1921), I, p. 33 and R. H. Hodgkin, *Six centuries of an Oxford college: a history of the Queen's College 1340–1940* (Oxford, Basil Blackwell, 1949), p. 15.
89. *Camb. Docs*, II, pp. 23–4.
90. Twigg, *A history of Queens' College, Cambridge*, pp. 82–3; Emden, *BRUC*, pp. 635–6; Leader, *The university to 1546*, pp. 291–2.
91. See above, p. 76.

motivation for the foundation by Richard Fleming, Bishop of Lincoln, of Lincoln College, Oxford, in 1427 was to establish a seminary for graduates in theology that would make an intellectual contribution towards the suppression of heresies and ecclesiastical error.[92] Curiously, at this most orthodox of colleges the crime of heresy is not actually specified among the reasons for the forfeiture of fellowships. At All Souls and Magdalen, however, the two fifteenth-century colleges that were founded in Oxford next after Lincoln, heresy is prescribed as one of the crimes for which a fellow had to resign.[93] The fifteenth-century Cambridge colleges, King's and St Catharine's, were both much concerned with heretical issues and heresy was cited as the first of the reasons for which fellows were to be expelled.[94] There was a comparable emphasis upon defending the purity of the faith at Queens' and Jesus, the other two fifteenth-century foundations at Cambridge.[95] Indeed, at Queens' fellows had to swear an oath against heresy that specifically mentioned the doctrines of John Wyclif and Reginald Pecock, the Bishop of Chichester who, claiming to refute Lollard errors, was bizarrely tried for heresy in 1457.[96] In view of Oxford's heavy involvement in Wyclifite and Lollard beliefs and Cambridge's relative freedom from the taint of heresy, it is surprising that the Oxford colleges, Lincoln excepted, did not make a more concerted effort to extirpate those doctrines that proved to be so injurious to the university's reputation in the late-medieval period.

Fellows of medieval English colleges had other important obligations apart from their studies, administrative functions and teaching duties, whether university or collegiate. Some colleges had a close affinity with chantry foundations, and the fellows had to perform a round of services in memory of the souls of the founder and named relatives. Several colleges imposed onerous chantry duties upon their fellows. King's

92. Cobban, "Colleges and halls 1380–1500", in *HUO*, II, pp. 600–1.
93. *Statutes*, I, ch. 7, p. 66 (All Souls); II, ch. 8, p. 45 (Magdalen).
94. *Camb. Docs*, II, p. 560 (King's); St Catharine's muniments, XL/10 fols 12v, 13; Philpott (ed.), *Documents relating to St Catharine's College*, pp. 24–5; see also A. B. Cobban, "Origins: Robert Wodelarke and St Catharine's", in *St Catharine's College 1473–1973*, E. E. Rich (ed.) (Leeds, Maney, 1973), p. 12. For King's see further *Camb. Docs*, II, p. 471 for the letters patent of Henry VI of 10 July 1443 where the king made it explicit that the rooting out of heresy was one of the purposes behind the foundation of King's College.
95. Cobban, *Medieval English universities*, p. 133.
96. Twigg, *A history of Queens' College, Cambridge*, p. 82.

College and St Catharine's College, Cambridge, and Queen's, New College and All Souls, Oxford, are examples of colleges that were cast heavily in the chantry mould.[97] By contrast, the religious regime of the fellows of the King's Hall was kept to minimal proportions.[98]

It was shown in Chapter 1 that the charitable teaching of poor grammar youths did not amount to much in practice in English secular colleges. Among Parisian colleges, however, the support of poor scholars from the revenues of the college was fairly widespread.[99] In another charitable direction English fellows lagged well behind their Parisian counterparts. Some of the college founders in Paris were acutely aware of the need to inculcate in their members a raised consciousness concerning the disadvantaged in the urban community. Regular contact with the distressed in society was seen as a humbling and learning experience for privileged academics who lived off the bounty of a college founder. For example, the founder of the Ave Maria College at Paris, John of Hubant, maintained two houses from college resources, one for ten poor and aged women and the other for ten poor and aged workmen. In addition, the fellows of the college had to distribute soup and bread every day to the poor of Paris, and had to be prepared to give away clothes and shoes that were not absolutely necessary for their minimal requirements. They were also obliged to tour the Paris prisons every year to give gifts of money to the inmates.[100] It is probable that Robert of Eglesfield, the founder of Queen's College, Oxford, was influenced by French collegiate ideas of charity. At Queen's, meals were to be served daily to the poor at the college gate, and 13 persons who were deaf or blind or dumb or lame, or in other ways incapacitated, were to be given meals daily in the hall. On Maundy Thursday 13 poor men and women were to receive fur-lined russet gowns, stockings and footwear.[101] It is far from clear that these good intentions were

97. A. B. Cobban, "The role of colleges in the medieval universities of northern Europe, with special reference to England and France", *BJRL* **71**, 1989, pp. 50–1; Rubin, *Charity and community in medieval Cambridge*, pp. 278–80.

98. See the arrangements for weekly commemorative masses in the King's Hall statutes in Rouse Ball, *The King's Scholars and King's Hall*, p. 65.

99. See above, pp. 30–1.

100. Gabriel, "The practice of charity at the University of Paris during the Middle Ages: Ave Maria College", *Traditio* **5**, 1947, pp. 335–9 and Gabriel, *Student life in Ave Maria College*, pp. 113–16; Rubin, *Charity and community in medieval Cambridge*, p. 277.

101. *Statutes*, I, ch. 4, pp. 33–4; Magrath, *The Queen's College*, I, p. 58; Hodgkin, *Six centuries of an Oxford college*, pp. 15–16.

fully implemented because of the tenuous resources at the disposal of the college in the fourteenth century. Eglesfield's charitable motives are notable, but it is improbable that charity on the scale of the Ave Maria College was ever practised by the English colleges.

Many fellows had to devote time and energy to college administration, so reducing the amount of time available for study or teaching. Most English colleges comprised a self-governing community of fellows and were organized, to a greater or lesser extent, along democratic lines. Although, following the French practice, at least five of the English colleges initially vested control of the patronage in an external authority, this was soon discontinued. With the notable exception of the King's Hall, where the right of appointment to the wardenship and to fellowships remained with the crown throughout its entire history, the fellows of English colleges came to have the right to elect to the headship and to co-opt to fellowships.[102] In most English colleges government was conducted jointly by the head of the college and committees of fellows who were elected to administrative positions. Generally speaking, colleges arranged their affairs so that most fellows, who resided for any length of time, would play some part either in the internal running of the college or in matters relating to estate management or appropriated churches, or they would be engaged periodically in travelling on college business. Evidence from Merton College in the late-thirteenth and fourteenth centuries shows that fellows were often absent from college for many weeks at a time while pursuing estate affairs. For instance, Walter of Cuddington, a Mertonian fellow, was at Cuxham for at least $17\frac{1}{2}$ weeks in 1289–90 overseeing agricultural processes.[103] On visits to Merton's estates in the north of England fellows would be absent from college for up to four, six or eight weeks. They would be occupied in auditing estate accounts and collecting revenues both in cash and kind.[104] Frequent absences of this nature must have played havoc with study and teaching commitments.

On the internal administrative front, the statutes of Queen's College, Oxford, laid down that every fellow, the provost and doctors in theology

102. Cobban, *Medieval English universities*, pp. 124–7 and Cobban, *The King's Hall*, pp. 148–51.
103. T. H. Aston, "The external administration and resources of Merton College to *c*.1348", in *HUO*, I, pp. 333–4.
104. *ibid.*, pp. 340–1.

and canon law excepted, was to serve as the seneschal or steward of the hall by weekly rotation. There were similar arrangements in place at New College, Oxford, and King's College, Cambridge.[105] An analysis of the annually elected committees of seneschals of the King's Hall reveals that, although there was a bias towards the more senior and experienced members of this society, there was a regular turnover of personnel that helped to guard against the dangers of oligarchical government by a ruling clique.[106] Even if fellows in English colleges suspected that oligarchical tendencies were afoot, there was always the ultimate deterrent of the college meeting that expressed the sovereignty that resided in the fellows acting together as a body or corporation. The consent of the fellowship, registered through the college meeting, would usually be required for matters such as large expenditure, for items of peculiar difficulty, and for deciding the fate of fellows who were charged with serious transgressions that carried the possibility of expulsion. The extensive involvement of many college fellows in internal administration or in estate management was undoubtedly a diversion from their primary academic tasks. On the credit side, it could be argued that participation in college business gave a good grounding in practical affairs that was of potential use in a future extra-university career.

Although fellows of medieval English colleges comprised only a small segment of the total academic population before 1500, their contribution to higher faculty studies was disproportionate to their numbers. While arts was the largest faculty at both Oxford and Cambridge between 1200 and 1500, theology was the largest of the superior faculties, assuming, in the case of Oxford, that civil and canon law are reckoned as separate faculties.[107] At both universities the faculty of theology was markedly strengthened by members of the regular orders comprising monks, the four orders of friars and regular canons. Of these, the friars made the most influential contribution to the membership

---

105. *Statutes*, I, ch. 4, p. 25 (Queen's), ch. 5, p. 42 (New College); *Camb. Docs*, II, p. 533 (King's).
106. Cobban, *The King's Hall*, pp. 181–2.
107. For details of the quantitative analysis that supports the statements in this and the following two paragraphs see A. B. Cobban, "Theology and law in the medieval colleges of Oxford and Cambridge", *BJRL* **65**, 1982, pp. 57–77 and Cobban, "The medieval Cambridge colleges", pp. 1–12. See also Cobban, "Colleges and halls 1380–1500", in *HUO*, II, pp. 581–633 and Cobban, *Medieval English universities*, pp. 209–39.

of the faculties of theology. In late-fourteenth-century Cambridge the mendicants formed the largest constituent of the theological faculty, with secular theologians accounting for only about a quarter of the total membership. The Oxford secular colleges reflected solidly the position of theology as the leading higher faculty. In eight out of the ten Oxford colleges founded before 1500 theology was the principal area of study. The fellows of the other two colleges, New College and All Souls, apparently subverted the intentions of their founders that theology was to be the main discipline, and considerably more of them pursued law than did theology. With these two important exceptions, it seems that prior to 1500 only a small proportion of college fellows engaged in legal study. Indeed, before the sixteenth century the Oxford halls were apparently more important centres for legal studies than were the colleges. This collegiate picture was very much at odds with the general situation regarding the popularity of law in the university at large where civilians and canonists combined probably outstripped theologians by a narrow margin.

At Cambridge, as at Oxford, the secular colleges were broadly supportive of the position of theology as the largest of the superior faculties. Of the eight secular colleges founded before 1400 six of them had significant numbers of fellows who were specializing in theology, the exceptions being the King's Hall and Trinity Hall. While law fellows were only a marginal presence in Oxford colleges prior to the establishment of New College in 1379, the Cambridge secular colleges before 1400 were rather more important as legal centres. The three key colleges in this regard were the King's Hall, Peterhouse and Clare. In the fifteenth century, however, the collegiate scene in Cambridge was characterized by a reduction in the number of fellowships available for legal studies and a corresponding increase in fellowships for theology. This development took place against the backcloth of a pronounced decline in the size of the faculty of theology, and with it a lessening in the dominance of the mendicants within the university. Of the Cambridge colleges founded before 1400 Peterhouse, Clare, Pembroke, Gonville and Corpus Christi all exhibited, in the fifteenth century, a curtailment in the number of law fellows and an expansion in the availability of fellowships allocated to theology. The King's Hall, that came near the base of the theological ladder in the fourteenth century, actually increased its corps of theologians in the fifteenth century, although it also added to its central strength as a nursery for law fellows. Trinity Hall remained exclusively a centre for law, but Michaelhouse, which was overwhelmingly a college for theologians in the fourteenth century, surprisingly saw a small reduction in the number of fellows studying theology in the next century. This intensification of theology in the older Cambridge colleges in the fifteenth century was reinforced by the heavy theological emphasis to be found in the new colleges established in this century, Queens', Godshouse, St Catharine's, King's and Jesus.

What seems to be detectable in fifteenth-century Cambridge is an attempt to stem the engulfing tide of legal studies in the university at large by a reaffirmation of the value of theological study in most of the colleges. As a society of student-priests, with an exclusive study regime of philosophy and theology, St Catharine's College, founded in 1473, was the fullest institutional expression of a line of thought that urged the advancement of theology and spiritual values and the rejection of materialistic preoccupations that many scholars and non-university observers alike identified above all with legal studies.[108] The effort to raise the spiritual ethos within Cambridge University through the medium of the colleges was an interesting experiment. However, an elevated gesture could not, by itself, halt the inexorable rise in legal studies on a long-term basis. In the sixteenth century this attempted theological reversion folded before the attractions of humanist education and the expanding legal needs of Tudor government. At Oxford, the collegiate scene did not mirror Cambridge's effort to resist the accelerating growth of legal studies. This may perhaps be explained by the fact that the fourteenth-century Oxford colleges had not embraced legal studies to the same extent as had those of Cambridge. Even when New College and All Souls emerged as prominent legal centres, there was no discernible reaction in favour of theology, and educational utility remained firmly entrenched at Oxford in the fifteenth century.

Taken as a group, the secular colleges of the medieval English universities were rather conservative centres of study before 1500. Clearly, the innovative work in the sphere of mathematics and physics at Merton College in the early-fourteenth century would not fit this general

108. See the discussion by Cobban, "Origins: Robert Wodelarke and St Catharine's", pp. 1–32.

observation. Nevertheless, it is hard to avoid the conclusion that the entrenchment of theology in so many of the colleges may well have inhibited academic innovation. In particular, this theological conservatism may help to account for the slowness with which Oxford and Cambridge came to accommodate the central strands of continental humanism.

It was emphasized in Chapter 1 that undergraduates had only a limited access to university and college libraries in the pre-Reformation era.[109] Libraries were, however, of cardinal importance for graduates who were regent masters or college fellows or both and for members of the orders of friars and monks. Scholars studying in the superior faculties were usually required to possess copies of the key texts. This obligation was actually prescribed by statute for legal studies at Oxford, although not at Cambridge.[110] Book-ownership among secular scholars before 1500 seems to have been decidedly sparse. It is to be assumed that most college fellows would own books judging from the frequency with which fellows deposited books as pledges in loan-chests, although it has to be said that the pledged books sometimes belonged to the college rather than to the individual fellow. Despite what was probably a fair incidence of ownership among college fellows, only about 10 per cent of recorded secular scholars at Oxford are known to have owned books, and the corresponding figure for Cambridge was about 9 per cent.[111] It is interesting that the incidence of ownership was much higher among secular theologians at both universities than among the legists.[112] Among the orders of friars and monks the recorded rate of ownership by individuals was about 10 per cent at Oxford and only about 4 per cent at Cambridge. The disparity in the figures is possibly to be explained by the fact that the friars were a larger presence

109. See above, pp. 51–2.
110. Gibson, *Statuta antiqua*, pp. 43, 44, 46.
111. T. H. Aston, "Oxford's medieval alumni", *Past & Present* **74**, 1977, p. 34; Aston, Duncan & Evans, "The medieval alumni of the University of Cambridge", p. 65. For a detailed investigation of the use of books as pledges for loan-chests by fellows at Peterhouse and Corpus Christi College see Lovatt, "Two collegiate loan-chests in late-medieval Cambridge", pp. 146–61.
112. Among secular theologians the figures for book-ownership are 33 per cent at Oxford and 30 per cent at Cambridge. The corresponding figures for legists are 11 per cent at Oxford and 8 per cent at Cambridge. Doubtless, many cases of book-ownership have gone unrecorded: Aston, Duncan & Evans, "The medieval alumni of the University of Cambridge", p. 65.

at Cambridge than at Oxford, and relatively few of the Cambridge friars are known to have owned as opposed to have borrowed books.[113]

Books were used extensively as pledges for interest-free loans from university and college chests, and they were also deployed as pledges by principals of halls and hostels when renewing annual leases and by teaching masters as security when hiring lecture rooms. In this way, books became a form of currency for several types of transaction within the medieval English universities, although their value was diminished with the advent of printing. Apart from the purchase of books available for sale, individual scholars, colleges and the universities often commissioned copies of works from scribes resident in the town, some of whom were foreigners living and practising their craft in England.[114] For instance, Henry Mere, a foreign scribe who worked in Oxford in the late-1450s and 1460s, copied a volume of postils by Hugh of St Cher for the warden of Merton, Henry Sever. In the 1450s another foreign scribe, John Reinbold of Zierenberg, copied a work by Duns Scotus for Richard Scarborough, a fellow of Merton.[115] Scholars also made personal copies of texts. From many examples, William Persson, a fellow of New College, copied a collection of letters and minor works of Peter of Blois at some point before 1435, and John Malberthorpe, a fellow of Lincoln College from about 1436 to 1445, copied no fewer than six books.[116] Moreover, members of the orders of friars in Oxford apparently copied works with some frequency, and there are instances of foreign friars who, while residing in Oxford, took the opportunity to copy books for assistance in their studies.[117] Similarly, monk-students at Oxford both commissioned copies of books and copied works for themselves.[118]

Apart from copying activities, friars and monk-students who were studying in the English universities were quite well-favoured concerning access to books. Books were assigned to friars and monk-students for short- or long-term loans or even for life from the convents and monastic colleges within the university town or from houses of the

113. *ibid.*, pp. 65–6.
114. Parkes, "The provision of books", in *HUO*, II, pp. 414–17.
115. *ibid.*, pp. 415–16.
116. *ibid.*, 426–7.
117. *ibid.*, pp. 441–3.
118. *ibid.*, pp. 453–5.

orders elsewhere in the realm. Sometimes a monastic house would give a sum of money to a monk-student for the purchase of books while studying at university.[119] Books acquired by friars or monk-students during their years of study usually reverted to the ownership of the relevant mendicant convent or monastic house.

The library collections of the friars and monks and their sophisticated network of loan services incurred the envy of secular masters. University libraries were slow to develop at Oxford and Cambridge, and they were not fully operational until the fifteenth century.[120] In view of the inadequacies of university library provision, the colleges acted quickly to establish collections of books for the use of their fellows. Of the Oxford colleges before 1500, Magdalen, New College, Merton and All Souls probably possessed the most extensive book collections. The largest of these belonged to Magdalen with more than 800 items.[121] College libraries in Cambridge were not, it seems, of the same order of magnitude, although the evidence is far from satisfactory. It is known that 302 books were listed at Peterhouse in 1418. The catalogue for Queens' of 1472 listed 224 volumes, the earliest surviving catalogue for King's of *c*.1452 listed 175 items, and the libraries of the King's Hall, Corpus Christi, Clare, Pembroke and Gonville had collections of between 100 and 200 books. Gonville, however, had increased its stock to more than 300 volumes in the early-sixteenth century.[122]

Following the model of mendicant libraries, most college libraries at Oxford and Cambridge eventually organized their volumes into a chained or reference part and a circulating or lending division. College fellows were at liberty to borrow from the circulating branch, usually by means of an annual *electio* or selection. At Oxford, an early account of this practice of distributing books among the fellows from the college collection on an annual basis is described in the statutes of Oriel of 1329, although a more restricted arrangement is contained in the statutes of University College of 1292 whereby fellows could

119. For example, in 1294–5 Worcester cathedral priory gave 30s to John Aston for the purchase of books as an aid for study at Oxford: *ibid.*, p. 452.
120. Cobban, *Medieval English universities*, pp. 82–3, 381.
121. *ibid.*, p. 383 and notes 142, 143, 144.
122. *ibid.*, pp. 384–5 and notes. For further details of college and university libraries in England and in continental Europe see J. Verger, *Les gens de savoir en Europe à la fin du moyen âge* (Vendôme, Presses universitaires de France, 1997), pp. 92–3.

borrow books only under the terms of an indenture that recorded the transaction.[123] At Cambridge, the Peterhouse statutes of 1344 give sparse details for the deployment of books. The college's books were to be kept in a communal chest, along with the archives and, at the discretion of the master and dean, they could be loaned to appropriate fellows.[124] However, the statutes of the mid-fourteenth-century colleges, Gonville College and Trinity Hall, yield a more detailed insight into library organization. The library arrangements were similar at both colleges. There was to be an audit of all books twice a year, and at Gonville volumes on logic, philosophy and theology and basic texts on civil and canon law could be borrowed by fellows for their personal use at the discretion of the master and three senior fellows. The more advanced works on civil and canon law were to remain in the chained section. The arrangements were the same at Trinity Hall except that, in a college devoted exclusively to law, no other categories of books are mentioned.[125] The size of the chained as opposed to the circulating library varied considerably from college to college. At the King's Hall about one fifth of the 101 volumes were chained in 1391. In the library of the College of the Sorbonne at Paris a similar proportion of books was chained in 1338, that is 330 out of a total of 1,722. At Peterhouse, Cambridge, less than half of the 302 volumes in the possession of the college in 1418 were chained. Merton College, Oxford, made far more books available for the use of fellows than were kept in the chained section.[126] The pattern of division into chained and lending sections was generally maintained down to the early-sixteenth century, after which the circulating parts of college libraries were much reduced and were eventually phased out. This was largely because of an increasing emphasis upon college security, and also as a result of the wishes of most donors to have their books kept securely in the reference department.

A small amount of evidence exists for the borrowing habits of fellows. The accounts of the King's Hall contain parts of four library

---

123. *Statutes*, I, ch. 3, pp. 14–15 (Oriel); Anstey, *Munimenta academica*, I, p. 58 (University).
124. *Camb. Docs*, II, p. 38.
125. *ibid.*, II, p. 236 (Gonville), p. 432 (Trinity Hall).
126. Cobban, *The King's Hall*, p. 249; F. M. Powicke, *The medieval books of Merton College* (Oxford, Clarendon Press, 1931), p. 9 (Sorbonne) and pp. 7–8 (Merton); Willis & Clark, *The architectural history of the University of Cambridge*, III, p. 403 (Peterhouse) and B. H. Streeter, *The chained library* (London, Macmillan, 1931), p. 8 (Peterhouse and Merton).

lending lists of the late-fourteenth century. Analysis of these lists reveals that the books borrowed were mainly texts or commentaries on civil and canon law, supplemented by medical treatises and a few volumes on grammar, logic and theology. It is interesting that the selection of books was not wholly confined to a fellow's faculty of study. Two of the fellows, Simon Godrich and William Waltham, who were bachelors of civil law, borrowed medical treatises in addition to books on their own subject.[127] At Merton College 137 volumes were distributed among 22 fellows in 1372, and in 1375 a total of 134 books were apportioned among 15 fellows. On both of these occasions the books that were distributed pertained to philosophy so that each fellow received a generous allocation of Aristotelian texts and commentaries on the same.[128] If the borrowing patterns at the King's Hall and Merton are in any way representative, it appears that English college fellows could expect direct access to many of the basic texts and commentaries required for study. This being so, and given the expanding resources of the university libraries in the late-medieval period, there can be no doubt that postgraduate study at Oxford and Cambridge was certainly more book-oriented than was the experience of the mass of undergraduates.

The periodic visitations of plague and associated diseases proved to be a serious assault upon the continuity of study at medieval Oxford and Cambridge. The impact of the Black Death of 1348–9 and subsequent epidemic diseases on the scholars of the English universities cannot be assessed with any exactitude. It may be that the youth of the scholars and the generally good level of diet of all but the poorest of them afforded a greater protection than was enjoyed by the populace at large.[129] An investigation of a sample of 87 theologians who were resident in Oxford in the years 1340–7 has indicated that the effect on Oxford University may not have been as severe as is often supposed. From this limited analysis, it has been suggested that the mortality rate at Oxford University may have been more in the region of 25 per cent rather than the rate of 40 per cent that has been detected for the rural

127. Cobban, *The King's Hall*, pp. 248–51 and Cobban, *Medieval English universities*, pp. 387–8.
128. N. R. Ker, "The books of philosophy distributed at Merton College in 1372 and 1375", in *Books, collectors and libraries: studies in the medieval heritage*, A. G. Watson (ed.) (London & Ronceverte, West Virginia, Hambledon, 1985), pp. 333–4.
129. See the discussion by W. J. Courtenay, "The effect of the Black Death on English higher education", *Speculum* **55**, 1980, p. 703.

poor and urban clergy.[130] However, one cannot extrapolate too much from a small sample. The town of Cambridge seems to have been much affected by the Black Death in 1349 and by the later visitation in 1361–2.[131] At the King's Hall 16 of the fellows died from the Black Death in 1349, and in 1361–2 the warden, Thomas Powys, and eight of the fellows perished from the plague.[132] In 1441 Henry VI cancelled a visit to Cambridge because of the "pestilence that hath long reigned" in the university.[133] Not much is heard of the plague in the King's Hall records for most of the fifteenth century. However, between 1498–9 and 1525–6, and again in 1541–2, the King's Hall accounts give an informative insight into the depressing frequency with which Cambridge was attacked by visitations of plague or sweating sickness.[134]

In the course of the fifteenth century plague outbreaks came to be associated more with urban than with rural areas so that a country retreat became a desirable option for English colleges in plague years.[135] The fellows of Merton had retreats in the Oxfordshire villages of Cuxham and Islip, and the fellows of Magdalen had sanctuaries at Ewelme and Witney in Oxfordshire, at Wallingford in Berkshire and at Brackley in Northamptonshire. The fellows of Lincoln College, Oxford, relied upon various villages in Oxfordshire and Buckingham-shire.[136] It is not certain that the fellows of the King's Hall had fixed retreats to which fellows could migrate. It is possible that the fellows made their own arrangements. Since plague and illnesses of the fever variety were in evidence during the warmer months of the year, migra-tions by English fellows in plague years generally occurred in spring,

130. *ibid.*, p. 702 and Courtenay, "Theology and theologians from Ockham to Wyclif", in *HUO*, II, p. 31. See also Evans, "The number, origins and careers of scholars", in *ibid.*, II, pp. 490–1.
131. F. A. Gasquet, *The Black Death of 1348 and 1349*, 2nd edn (London, Bell, 1908), p. 157; P. Ziegler, *The Black Death* (New York, Harper & Row, 1969), p. 172.
132. Cobban, *The King's Hall*, p. 221.
133. Cooper, *Annals of Cambridge*, I, p. 199.
134. King's Hall accounts, XIX, fols 143v, 177, 207; XX, fols 59, 149, 212v; XXI, fol. 68v; XXII, fols 37v, 133v; XXIII, fol. 168v; XXVI, fols 39v, 172v. See also Cobban, *The King's Hall*, p. 221.
135. J. M. W. Bean, "Plague, population and economic decline in England in the later Middle Ages", *Economic History Review*, 2nd ser. **15**, 1962–3, pp. 430–1.
136. P. D. A. Harvey, *A medieval Oxfordshire village, Cuxham 1240 to 1400* (Oxford, Oxford University Press, 1965), p. 91; N. Denholm-Young, "Magdalen College", in *Victoria history of the county of Oxford. Volume 3*, p. 195; V. H. H. Green, *The commonwealth of Lincoln College 1427–1977* (Oxford, Oxford University Press, 1979), pp. 120–3.

summer and autumn. When in retreat, the fellows were expected to carry on study and teaching as best they could, and they would usually claim their allowances for commons. In 1513–14 the King's Hall fellow, John Barow, was allocated commons for an absence of five months because of plague. Similar arrangements were made for the receipt of commons at plague retreats for fellows of Lincoln in 1514 and 1538, and for fellows of Merton in 1493.[137] Members of the college domestic staff sometimes accompanied fellows to a plague retreat.[138]

As a means of dealing with the dislocation of studies caused by epidemic disease, dispensations or graces were granted to scholars to allow them to count time spent in exile at another university or at a country retreat because of plague as equivalent to a statutory period of study at the home university. For example, in 1453 William Brown, BA, was allowed to count one year's study in arts outside Oxford as a substitute for a year at Oxford University. In 1455 Thomas Horn, a scholar of the faculty of arts, was allowed to reckon two long vacations and a few small vacations as the equivalent of the terms spent outside Oxford on account of plague.[139] There were similar dispensations at Cambridge.[140] In 1503 Richard Wether, a priest, was granted permission to take the BA degree at Cambridge, although three entire terms had been spent in the countryside.[141] The frequency of such dispensations indicates that the interruption to studies caused by the menace of plague and allied diseases was a problem whose seriousness ought not to be minimized. It is not easy to determine whether or not the effects of plague on Oxford and Cambridge were less or more severe than in continental universities. At the University of Padua the Black Death left all of the medical chairs vacant in 1349. At Paris the membership of the medical faculty shrank from 46 in 1348 to 26 in 1362.[142] The reduction in personnel at Padua and Paris may have resulted entirely

---

137. King's Hall accounts, XXI, fol. 68v; Green, *The commonwealth of Lincoln College*, pp. 120, 121; Salter, *Registrum annalium collegii Mertonensis*, pp. 172–3.
138. See, for example, Green, *The commonwealth of Lincoln College*, pp. 121, 122.
139. Pantin & Mitchell, *The register of congregation 1448–1463*, pp. 159 (Brown), 221–2 (Horn).
140. See, for example, the graces given to John Caunt and Alan Reed in M. Bateson (ed.), *Grace Book B Part I*, Cambridge Antiquarian Society, Luard Memorial Series, II (Cambridge, Cambridge University Press, 1903), pp. 100–1, 161.
141. Leader, *The university to 1546*, p. 215.
142. Figures quoted by R. S. Gottfried, *The Black Death* (London, R. Hale, 1983), p. 117.

from mortality or from a mixture of death and flight. Although figures can be cited from several continental universities, the basis for direct comparison with the results of plague in the English universities is lacking.

It is probably true to say that college fellows had more immediate access to supportive patronage than non-collegiate members of the postgraduate community. The unendowed halls and hostels had no ecclesiastical livings at their disposal. By contrast, advowsons, the right to appoint to livings, were often made part of a college's endowment. From the studies that have been made, it seems that quite a high proportion of college members who were presented to first livings owed their presentations to their college or to its visitor or episcopal patron.[143] From this consideration networks were formed whereby graduates, who had owed their first ecclesiastical placement to the college and who went on to senior positions within the church, in turn acted as patrons for members of their former college. In this way, collegiate dynasties were created. Sources of college patronage were especially important following the virtual collapse of papal patronage for the English universities in the early-fifteenth century. While the extent of college patronage ought not to be exaggerated, it was certainly a useful addition to the array of ecclesiastical and lay patrons, both corporate and individual, to whom university personnel had potential resort. The role of the colleges as patrons that was made possible by their endowments helped to integrate the colleges, and through them the English universities, more closely with an extra-university society that functioned on the principles of hierarchy and patronage.

143. See the discussion by G. F. Lytle, "Patronage patterns and Oxford colleges c.1300–c.1530", in *The university in society*, L. Stone (ed.), I, pp. 111–49, especially tables 3, 4, pp. 141, 142.

CHAPTER THREE

Commoners: undergraduate and mature

Any account of England's medieval academic population that did not give an appropriate weighting to university commoners would be sadly askew. Although fee-paying commoners or pensioners appear to have been an ample presence at Oxford and Cambridge in the medieval period, many may well have gone undetected in university and college records. As stated in Chapter 1, centralized records of university personnel in the form of matriculation registers were instituted at Cambridge only from 1544 and at Oxford only from 1565, and for the next hundred years or so the registers bristle with uncertainties, omissions and problems of interpretation.[1] Similarly, only in a minority of colleges do the extant records give anything like a comprehensive view of the fellows and commoners present from generation to generation, and quite a few colleges have especially scant or even negligible recall of their medieval personnel. Moreover, methods of accounting varied from college to college. Matters that were entered annually in one set of accounts may be only spasmodically entered in another or omitted entirely. This being so, it is extremely unlikely that anything approaching the full quota of commoners in residence can be retrieved from the surviving college records before 1600. The situation is even worse regarding the Oxford halls and Cambridge hostels. Before the early-sixteenth century these were the natural venues for most of the undergraduate commoners, and probably for a goodly proportion of the mature commoners as well. The unendowed halls and hostels generated far

1. See above, p. 10.

fewer records than did the endowed colleges, and no formal set of accounts has survived for any of these establishments, although the informal tutorial accounts of John Arundel, principal of an Oxford hall in 1424, are of inestimable value.[2] As a result of the inadequacy of the collegiate and aularian records, our knowledge of the names and numbers of the fee-paying commoner population in the medieval period is distinctly restricted.

The commoner population in the medieval English universities comprised men of mature years, many of whom were of graduate status, and the undergraduate commoners, who lived mainly in halls and hostels and who began to transfer to the colleges from the second half of the fifteenth century. The ranks of the commoners were divided into commoners and semi-commoners according to whether the commoners paid the full commons rate for board or only half of the commons charge. These grades of commoner and semi-commoner were used extensively throughout the accounts of the King's Hall, Cambridge, and this evidence proves that the stratified commoner system was in operation as early as the first half of the fourteenth century in at least one English college.[3] In addition to commoners and semi-commoners who had never at any time been supported from the revenues of a college, some colleges permitted fellows who had vacated their fellowships to remain in residence so long as they paid for their board and lodging. Commoners of this type may be usefully described as ex-fellow pensioners.

The terminology for academic commoners was very fluid in the medieval period.[4] The common terms used are *communarii* (and *semi-communarii*), *commensales*, *commorantes*, *sojournants*, *batellarii*, and *per(h)endinantes*. Of these, *per(h)endinantes* is the term that appears most frequently in Cambridge college statutes of the fourteenth and fifteenth centuries, whereas it is absent from the Oxford college codes of the same period.[5] The term *pensionarius* is found in the accounts of Pembroke College,

2. See the analysis above, pp. 36–40.
3. For commoners and semi-commoners at the King's Hall see Cobban, *The King's Hall*, pp. 259–75.
4. See the discussion of the terminology for commoners by Cobban, *Medieval English universities*, pp. 326–8 and Cobban, "Commoners in medieval Cambridge colleges", pp. 48–9.
5. For example, the statutes of Peterhouse and Queens' College in *Camb. Docs*, II, p. 27 (Peterhouse), III, p. 37 (Queens').

Cambridge, in 1438 and in the accounts of Gonville College in the early-sixteenth century.[6] The earliest statutory use of *pensionarius* at Cambridge occurs in the statutes of Christ's College of 1505, and in subsequent Cambridge college codes of the sixteenth century *pensionarii* and *commensales* are the terms most usually found.[7] The prevalence of *pensionarius* or pensioner as a designation for Cambridge commoners in the sixteenth century led to its firm adoption in later centuries as the standard usage for undergraduate commoners.[8] By contrast, Oxford settled ultimately upon commoner as the equivalent term for the Cambridge pensioner.

While the dimensions of the commoner population in relation to the total academic population cannot be determined, it seems that Oxford commoners and Cambridge pensioners were very unevenly distributed among the colleges, halls and hostels. The two colleges that appear to have accommodated the largest number of commoners were the King's Hall, Cambridge, and University College, Oxford. Between 1337 and 1500 the King's Hall lodged approximately 120 commoners, some of whom were undergraduate commoners, and about 100 semi-commoners.[9] The bursars' rolls of University College yield the names of at least 187 commoners who resided in the college between 1385 and *c.*1495.[10] It has to be said that contingents of collegiate commoners were usually much smaller. At Oxford, for example, the treasurers' accounts of Oriel of 1409–15 and 1450–82 indicate about 30 commoners, and the bursars' rolls of Lincoln College suggest that there were only about a dozen commoners in the fifteenth century.[11] The medieval accounts of Queen's prove that commoners were regularly present from the mid-fourteenth to the mid-fifteenth centuries, and at Exeter College there was certainly a significant number of commoners in the fifteenth century. On the other hand, Merton seems to have

---

6. Pembroke College archives, Registrum A, p. d, column 1; computus book of Gonville Hall (*c.*1423–*c.*1523), Gonville & Caius MS 365, pp. 74, 83.
7. See the statutes of Christ's College in *Camb. Docs*, III, p. 208.
8. On Cambridge pensioners in the eighteenth century see D. A. Winstanley, *Unreformed Cambridge* (Cambridge, Cambridge University Press, 1935), pp. 200–1.
9. Cobban, *The King's Hall*, pp. 259–79 and Cobban, "Commoners in medieval Cambridge colleges", p. 49.
10. University College archives, bursars' rolls, EE1/5–GG2/6.
11. Oriel College archives, treasurers' accounts, I (1409–15) and II (1450–82) and Lincoln College archives, bursars' books, I, II.

had very few commoners in the fourteenth and fifteenth centuries.[12] While many of the Oxford colleges permitted varying numbers of commoners to participate in the advantages of collegiate life, it is surprising that the voluminous bursars' and receipt rolls of New College that extend from 1376 to 1500 and the three bursars' books of All Souls of the second half of the fifteenth century yield no evidence of resident commoners. They uncover only guests and visitors such as university bedels, bailiffs and tradesmen.[13]

At Cambridge, the computus rolls of Peterhouse imply that before 1500 the list of commoners never rose above six a year.[14] Corpus Christi College seems to have maintained a few commoners before the sixteenth century, although the Corpus accounts are not easy to interpret and the presence of commoners may be masked.[15] Throughout the fourteenth and fifteenth centuries Gonville College admitted a number of commoners and, according to the earliest account books, the college accommodated 13 pensioners in 1508–9 and 12 in c.1510.[16] In addition to the commoners maintained within the college, Gonville also housed commoners in Physwick Hostel that came into its possession in 1393. The treasurers' accounts for Pembroke College survive only from 1557, but the transcriptions of lost accounts that were made by Matthew Wren in the seventeenth century reveal that the college admitted both mature and undergraduate commoners in the fifteenth century. As in the case of Gonville, Pembroke's commoner population was augmented when, in 1451, the college acquired St Thomas' Hostel and used it to house a sizeable number of commoners. In 1457 there were 34 pensioners in St Thomas' Hostel, and there were 28 in 1477.[17]

12. Data extracted from Queen's College archives, long rolls (transcripts), Exeter College archives, rectors' accounts, and Merton College archives, bursars' rolls.
13. New College archives, bursars' and receipt rolls, 1376–1499, 7711(1)–7459(136) and All Souls College archives, bursars' books for 1450–1, c.1495 and 1497–8, Bodleian MSS D.D. 6. 29.
14. Peterhouse archives, computus rolls; also entries in T. A. Walker, *A biographical register of Peterhouse men, part 1. 1284–1574* (Cambridge, Cambridge University Press, 1927).
15. Corpus Christi College archives, college accounts, 1376–1485.
16. Gonville College archives, computus books, c.1423–5, 1523, pp. 74, 83; see also for pensioners at Gonville, C. N. L. Brooke, *A history of Gonville and Caius College* (Woodbridge, Suffolk, Boydell Press, 1985), pp. 21–2, 25–6, 28, 30–3.
17. Cobban, "Pembroke College", p. 6; A. Attwater, *Pembroke College, Cambridge: a short history* (Cambridge, Cambridge University Press, 1936), p. 22; Pembroke College archives, Registrum Aa, p. y, column 2.

The available evidence uncovers little about the presence of commoners at Michaelhouse, Clare and Trinity Hall.

It is curious that neither the first nine volumes of accounts of King's College that extend from 1447 to 1507 nor the first book of accounts of Queens' College that spans the period from 1484 to 1518 make any references to pensioners resident in college beyond visitors and guests.[18] It is known, however, that both King's and Queens' admitted commoners to hostels in their possession, and it is likely that separate records were kept for these pensioners that have not survived. From a laconic entry in the King's accounts for 1490 it seems that there were then 20 pensioners in St Augustine's Hostel, a property that had been secured for the college by the founder, Henry VI.[19] Queens' College appears to have lodged its commoners in St Bernard's Hostel, a substantial structure with an ornate gallery, hall and chapel, although there is no indication of the actual numbers involved.[20] Godshouse, the Cambridge college founded specifically in 1439 for the training of grammar masters, is known to have rented rooms to pensioners.[21] When Godshouse was reincarnated as Christ's College, the statutes of 1505 clearly envisaged the reception of pensioners.[22] It is true that Christ's admitted one or two privileged fellow commoners. However, the earliest surviving volume of college accounts for the period from 1530 to 1545 is wholly silent on the matter of resident commoners of the more ordinary type.[23]

When medieval English colleges made statutory provision for commoners this seldom meant that commoners were regarded as a fundamental part of the collegiate foundation. They were usually valued for the income that could be derived from the charges for room and board and, in the case of undergraduate commoners, from teaching fees as well. The statutes of Jesus College, Cambridge, of the early-sixteenth century authorized the admission of commoners subject to the availability

18. King's College archives, mundum books, I–IX; Queens' College archives, journale I (1484–1518).
19. Stokes, *Medieval hostels*, p. 62.
20. *ibid.*, pp. 39, 63–4.
21. For Godshouse see A. H. Lloyd, *The early history of Christ's College, Cambridge* (Cambridge, Cambridge University Press, 1934); Cobban, *Medieval English universities*, pp. 196–8; D. R. Leader, "Teaching in Tudor Cambridge", *History of Education* **13**, 1984, p. 113 and Leader, *The university to 1546*, pp. 226–7.
22. *Camb. Docs*, III, p. 120.
23. Christ's College archives, college accounts, B. 1. 1.(1530–45).

of rooms and only after the fellows had exercised their right of first refusal of surplus chambers.[24] This typifies the general sense of collegiate priorities as between fellows and commoners. However important commoners were to become as a constituent of college life in the late-fifteenth and early-sixteenth centuries, the core and essence of the college remained the fellowship, commoners being a secondary consideration. It is understandable that colleges were cautious about the entry of commoners since the presence of only one or two of ill-disciplined character could lead to serious disruption that might even result in an expensive lawsuit. Most codes of college statutes counselled a wary attitude towards commoners.[25] This uneasiness is reflected even in the statutes of the King's Hall, although this proved to be no obstacle to the admission of an impressive force of commoners and semi-commoners.[26] In 1458 Thomas Estlake, a commoner of Lincoln College, brought the college into disrepute when convicted of stabbing Edward Steynor and was fined 10s for the offence in the chancellor's court. In 1459 Estlake was again convicted of a stabbing offence involving John Westerdale, although here the guilt was shared between the two parties.[27] As late as 1566 when the number of Oxford halls had dwindled to about eight and when the colleges had been recognized for some time as the natural home for undergraduate commoners, the founder of St John's College, Oxford, Sir Thomas White, felt impelled to reduce the statutory contingent of commoners from 16 to 12 because "inconvenyence cometh by borders in my colledge".[28]

The expectation that the renting of rooms to commoners would augment the finances of the college may have been generally realized, although this was not always the case. For instance, there were several mature commoners, among them John Trevisa and Richard Courtenay, the future chancellor of Oxford University, who were in serious arrears

---

24. *Camb. Docs*, III, p. 120.
25. For Oxford see, for example, the statutes of Merton, Balliol, Oriel, Queen's and New College in *Statutes*, I, ch. 1, p. 20, ch. 3, p. 8, ch. 4, p. 18, ch. 5, p. 43; for Cambridge see, for example, the statutes of Michaelhouse in Stamp, *Michaelhouse*, p. 44; the statutes of Peterhouse, Clare and King's in *Camb. Docs*, II, pp. 27, 136–7, 534–6.
26. See the statutes of the King's Hall in Rouse Ball, *The King's Scholars and King's Hall*, p. 66.
27. Salter, *Registrum cancellarii oxoniensis*, I, p. 412; II, pp. 24, 27; Green, *The commonwealth of Lincoln College 1427–1977*, pp. 19–20.
28. See W. H. Stevenson & H. E. Salter, *The early history of St John's College, Oxford*, Oxford Historical Society, new ser. **1** (Oxford, Clarendon Press, 1939), p. 421.

year after year at Queen's College in the second half of the fourteenth and early-fifteenth centuries. It seems that eventually a proportion of these long-term debts had to be written off.[29] Similarly, at the King's Hall 11 mature commoners in 1454–5 owed a combined total of £63 3s 10$\frac{1}{4}$d in arrears for commons, sizings, room rents and servants.[30] The fact that the commoner intake to the King's Hall was curtailed in the second half of the fifteenth century and almost ended in the early-sixteenth century may not be entirely unrelated to the financial problems associated with commoners. Doubtless, the commoner system was more effectively managed in some colleges than in others. It may be that marginal profits could generally be made from the residence of mature commoners in colleges, but virtually nothing is known of the economics of housing and teaching those undergraduate commoners who lived in halls and hostels that had been absorbed by colleges. Broad equivalents of English commoners were to be found among Parisian colleges. Early leaders in this field were the College of the Sorbonne, the College of the Treasurer, the College of Harcourt, the College of Narbonne and the College of Cornouaille, and a profit motive is to be assumed here as in England.[31] Since the first three of these colleges were thirteenth-century foundations, a case can be made out that academic commoners made an earlier appearance in France than in England.

Not all college founders had a wholly mercenary view of commoners. William Waynflete, the founder of Magdalen College, Oxford, initiated a statutory policy in 1479/80 whereby up to 20 commoners, the sons of nobles or other powerful personages, were to be a regular feature of college life. They were to live at their own expense and were to be under the supervision of a tutor.[32] It is true that there was a utilitarian

29. For Trevisa's arrears see Queen's College archives, long rolls (transcripts), III, p. 291; IV, pp. 381, 437, 453. Courtenay owed £25 1s 1d in arrears for room rent in 1413–14: *ibid.*, V, p. 73. For the debts of other commoners see, for example, *ibid.*, V, pp. 43, 57, 105, 123; VI, pp. 198, 222.
30. King's Hall accounts, XII, fols 26–8; Cobban, *The King's Hall*, p. 273.
31. See A. L. Gabriel, *The Paris Studium: Robert of Sorbonne and his legacy* (Notre Dame, Ind. & Frankfurt, Knecht, 1992), p. 80 and Gabriel, "The college system in the fourteenth-century universities", p. 93. See also Rashdall, *Universities*, I, pp. 515–16 and 515, *n.* 2. For commoners at the College of the Treasurer see J. M. Reitzel, *The founding of the earliest secular colleges within the Universities of Paris and Oxford* (PhD thesis, Department of History, Brown University, Rhode Island, 1971), p. 158.
32. *Statutes*, II, p. 60; Davis, *William Waynflete*, pp. 84–5.

element in Waynflete's thinking because it was hoped that this provision would enable the college to command the interest of wealthy and influential patrons. More importantly, Waynflete was concerned that members of the nobility should embrace university education in a more expansive way than hitherto. The gradual infiltration of humanist learning into the English universities towards the close of the fifteenth century was attractive to the nobility, and this helped to make Waynflete's commoner scheme a practical success.

Just as undergraduate commoners were an important feature of Waynflete's collegiate plan, so mature commoners were a considered part of St Catharine's College, Cambridge, from its inception. The founder, Robert Wodelarke, in the statutes that were framed between 1475 and 1481, authorized the admission of an unspecified number of commoners. Their collegiate role was to be strictly academic, and they were to engage in the study of philosophy and theology, the only two disciplines permitted to the fellows. In other words, the commoners were to be the academic counterparts of the fellows who would benefit, both intellectually and socially, from associating with mature commoners of like-minded interests.[33] In this sense, Wodelarke's mature pensioners were to provide an ever-present and stimulating company for a fellowship that might otherwise become too introverted.

The maintenance costs of mature commoners living in colleges are only occasionally revealed in collegiate accounts, and then only partially so. There is, however, quite a lot of data concerning room rents charged to commoners. The accounts of Oriel College, Oxford, of the fifteenth century indicate that 13s 4d was the most usual rate, with some rents set at 10s and 20s.[34] At Queen's College, Oxford, room rents of 13s 4d, 16s 8d and 20s are recorded.[35] As a commoner in Queen's John Wyclif was charged 20s for a room in 1365–6, 1374–5 and 1380–1.[36] The bursars' books of Lincoln College of the second half of the fifteenth century give a series of rates extending from 6s 8d to 16s.[37]

---

33. See the statutes of St Catharine's, St Catharine's muniments, XL/10, fol. 9; Philpott, *Documents relating to St Catharine's*, p. 19; Cobban, "Origins: Robert Wodelarke and St Catharine's", pp. 18–20.
34. Data extracted from Oriel College archives, treasurers' accounts, I (1409–15) and II (1450–82).
35. Information derived from Queen's College archives, long rolls (transcripts), I–VI.
36. *ibid.*, II, pp. 139, 233; III, p. 249.
37. Lincoln College archives, bursars' books, I and II.

Charges for rooms for the army of commoners resident in University College, Oxford, ranged from 6s 8d to 20s.[38] Room rentals were similar at Cambridge. For example, at Peterhouse the rents were generally fixed at either 13s 4d or 20s, and at the King's Hall room rents varied between 6s 8d, 10s and 13s 4d.[39] The renting of a single chamber was the norm for English commoners. Occasionally a commoner managed to acquire more than one room. For example, Thomas Marke, Archdeacon of Norfolk, rented two rooms in 1460–1 when a pensioner in Peterhouse at a charge of £1 6s 8d.[40]

Few sets of college accounts enable us to make estimates of commoner expenditure that go beyond room rentals. Fortunately, the accounts of the King's Hall yield a fair amount of data on this elusive matter. It seems that a typical rate for full commoners at the King's Hall in the fifteenth century was 1s 11d a week, and 6d would represent an average weekly expenditure on sizings, the extra items of food and drink ordered above basic commons.[41] This would give an annual sum of about £6 6s. Assuming that a full commoner retained a servant at the rate of half commons of approximately 10d a week, the yearly expenditure on servant provision would be in the region of £2 3s 4d. If 13s 4d is taken as the charge for the room rent, although it might be only 6s 8d or 10s, the total of these average sums for commoner expenditure comes to £9 2s 8d or about 3s 6d a week. The fellows of the King's Hall lived rent free, and they were subsidized for commons to the extent of 1s 2d a week, the subsidy being paid by direct exchequer grant. The amounts that they had to pay for commons and sizings from personal income were clearly much smaller than the costs of board and lodging for full commoners who were not subsidized in any way. As the name implies, semi-commoners had roughly half the expenditure outlay of full commoners. Probably the only costs that were equal for fellows and commoners at the King's Hall were those for the retention of servants. About 63 per cent of past fellows of the college who remained as pensioners retained one or more servants, and about 31 per cent of full commoners who had never been fellows did

38. Information extracted from University College archives, bursars' rolls, EE1/5–GG2/6.
39. Peterhouse archives, computus rolls of the fourteenth and fifteenth centuries; Cobban, *The King's Hall*, pp. 268–9.
40. Peterhouse archives, computus roll for 1460–1.
41. Cobban, *The King's Hall*, p. 271.

so.[42] Taking everything into consideration, it is likely that the total maintenance costs for a full commoner, whether a former fellow or not, were approximately three or four times the amount that a fellow had to find from private sources. It is probable that college commoners everywhere would have paid substantially more than subsidized fellows in order to sustain an equivalent standard of living.

Many of the mature commoners in medieval English colleges were of graduate status. Of these, a notable grouping comprised the ex-fellow pensioners, the fellows who had vacated their fellowships and who resided in college for varying periods paying for their full board and lodging. Some 52 fellows of the King's Hall subsequently became pensioners of the college between 1337 and 1501.[43] At Oxford, at least 12 fellows of Oriel College have been identified as ex-fellow pensioners in the accounts of the fifteenth century, although there is a gap in the records from 1400 to 1408 and a more serious one from 1416 to 1449.[44] Between the late-fourteenth and early-sixteenth centuries a dozen ex-fellow pensioners have been detected at University College.[45] The bursars' books of Lincoln College of the second half of the fifteenth century yield only one definite ex-fellow pensioner, John Tristrope, later rector of the college, and probably one other, Nicholas Langton, who is last known as a fellow in 1476. In that year a master Langton is recorded as a commoner for one term and may well have been the ex-fellow of the same surname.[46]

Most medieval English colleges would have had a company of ex-fellows as commoners. Some stayed for only a few weeks, others for several years. Ex-fellows had commonly vacated their fellowships upon

---

42. *ibid.*, p. 279.

43. *ibid.*, pp. 262–71.

44. These were: Thomas Lentwardyn, Richard Snetisham, Clement Smyth, Walter Peytwyn, Thomas Hawkins, John Swan, John Weston, Andrew Mankswell (Maukyswell), Thomas Wyche, John Hyll, Roger Hanley and Robert Holcote: data extracted from Oriel College archives, treasurers' accounts, I (1409–15) and II (1450–82). See also entries in Emden, *BRUO*.

45. These were: John Taylor, Edmund Lacy, Thomas Nafferton, Thomas Hunter, John Marshall, Thomas Butler, Thomas Pray, Thomas Thurlby, Gilbert Haydok, Robert More, Richard Hyndmersh and Edward Carr: data extracted from University College archives, bursars' rolls, EE1/5–GG2/6. See also entries in Emden, *BRUO*.

46. For Tristrope as a commoner see Green, *The commonwealth of Lincoln College*, p. 32; Emden, *BRUO*, III, p. 1909. For Langton as a commoner see Lincoln College archives, bursars' books, II, p. 11; for Nicholas Langton see Emden, *BRUO*, II, p. 1100.

promotion to incompatible benefices and had subsequently acquired episcopal licence to study for a number of years, supported from the income of the benefice. In this sense, a pensionership was a form of ecclesiastical scholarship. Other ex-fellows had gained employment in diocesan administration, and some of them continued to reside in their former college for at least part of their administrative service. Four cases from the King's Hall will illustrate this situation.[47]

John Wittilsey, an ex-fellow of the King's Hall, was an official of the Archdeacon of Ely between 1411 and 1415 and was a commoner of the college in 1412–13 and 1426–7. John Metefeld (Metford), who became the chancellor of the Bishop of Ely in 1389 upon vacating a fellowship, remained as a pensioner of the King's Hall from that year until at least 1391. Robert Leek, an ex-fellow, was vicar-general of the Bishop of Lincoln in 1421 when a commoner of the college. Finally, John Hole, a former fellow, was a pensioner from 1496 to 1499, and during that time was variously a canon of York and prebendary of Riccall, Archdeacon of Cleveland and Archdeacon of the East Riding. Sometimes a pensionership in an English college provided a convenient base for an ex-fellow in the interval between the vacation of one ecclesiastical position and the entering upon another. Moreover, there were former fellows who belonged to the "visiting" category of commoners who, typically, held ecclesiastical livings and visited the college for brief and congenial respites from the cares of a busy career. In these various ways ex-fellows of English colleges could retain either spasmodic or long-term links with their colleges, and this helped to promote their image as family institutions that were receptive to the needs of both past and present members.

It was not unusual for ex-fellows of one college to become commoners of another. University College, Oxford, had an exceptionally large concourse of commoners and was host, between the late-fourteenth and late-fifteenth centuries, to 10 ex-fellows of Merton, 6 ex-fellows of New College, 1 ex-fellow of Oriel, 1 former fellow of the King's Hall Cambridge, and 1, possibly 2, ex-fellows of Exeter.[48] In the fifteenth century Oriel welcomed William Penbukyll, ex-fellow of Exeter, as a commoner between 1411 and 1413 and Robert Gilbert, ex-fellow of

47. For details of these cases see Cobban, *The King's Hall*, pp. 265–6.
48. Information derived from University College archives, bursars' rolls, EE1/5–GG2/6, and entries in Emden, *BRUO*.

Merton, as a commoner in 1411–12 subsequent to a spell as a commoner at Exeter. Thomas Hawkins presents an interesting case, having been both a fellow of Exeter and a fellow of Oriel before becoming an Oriel commoner in 1459–60.[49] Walter Hart, who had a reputation as an astronomer, became a commoner of Lincoln College immediately upon the vacation of a fellowship at Merton in 1455. During the time that Hart was a Lincoln commoner the rectorships of Marnhull, Dorset, and St Martin's Vintry, London, were retained.[50]

Examples from Cambridge demonstrate that the transition from the status of fellow of one college to that of mature commoner in another was just as widespread as in Oxford. John Combe, vice-provost of King's College, John Reynold, a fellow of King's, John Redburne, a fellow of St Catharine's, and Thomas Tuppyng, a fellow of Michaelhouse, were all received as pensioners at Corpus Christi College for various periods in the second half of the fifteenth century.[51] Richard Davy, a fellow of Queens' College, and John Rumpayne, a fellow of King's, were pensioners in Gonville in 1498–9 and from 1506 to 1509 respectively.[52] Although the King's Hall accommodated some 52 of its own ex-fellows as pensioners, at least two others are discovered as commoners in Peterhouse, Henry Somer(s) in 1438–9 and Richard Laverok between 1466 and 1470.[53]

Apart from fellows who became commoners in colleges different from their own but within the same university, there are a few instances of Oxford fellows who migrated to Cambridge colleges as commoners. These include John Brygge, an ex-fellow of Merton and commoner of University College, Oxford, who was a pensioner in Peterhouse in 1403–4. Paul Gayton, a former fellow of All Souls, moved to Cambridge and resided as a pensioner in Corpus Christi College in 1474–5 and between 1480 and 1484, and was later a pensioner in Gonville

49. Emden, *BRUO*, II, pp. 766 (Gilbert), 891 (Hawkins); III, p. 1455 (Penbukyll or Penbogyll).
50. *ibid.*, II, p. 881.
51. Emden, *BRUC*, pp. 153 (Combe), 478–9 (Reynold), 475 (Redburne), 599 (Tuppyng).
52. J. Venn, *Biographical history of Gonville and Caius College 1349–1897* (3 vols) (Cambridge, Cambridge University Press, 1897–1901), I, p. 15; Emden, *BRUC*, p. 179 (Davy) and Venn, I, p. 16; Emden, *BRUC*, p. 496 (Rumpayne).
53. Peterhouse archives, computus rolls of 1438–9, 1466–7, 1469–70, 1470–1; Emden, *BRUC*, pp. 539–40 (Somer(s)), 356 (Laverok); also Walker, *Biographical register of Peterhouse*, I, pp. 44, 63.

College in 1505. John Dobbes resided as a Gonville pensioner between 1500 and 1515, having previously held an Oxford fellowship at New College that was vacated in 1498.[54]

Many of the mature commoners, who had never been college fellows, held a kaleidoscopic array of ecclesiastical livings and positions ranging from the relatively modest to those of the highest importance. Some were beneficed clergy who, in common with a proportion of the ex-fellow pensioners, had chosen to study for a time at a university, having obtained a licence to do so. During their university sojourn commoners of this kind were supported from the revenues of the benefice. In some instances, the bishop may have advised this course of action so that deficiencies in educational standards might be remedied. More often, however, the central purpose was to obtain either an arts degree, the MA if the BA was already possessed, or a degree in one of the superior faculties of law or theology. In a highly competitive ecclesiastical world there was a strong motivation to improve personal qualifications in the hope of gaining promotion to a wealthier benefice or to a more elevated ecclesiastical office.[55]

Not all mature commoners were intent upon acquiring an advanced degree. In parallel with some of the ex-fellow pensioners, there were commoners who looked upon a college pensionership as a comfortable base for use in the conduct of their non-academic careers. From many Oxford examples two may be selected from Lincoln College and one from University College as illustrative of the point. All three cases concern archdeacons. John Middelton, a canon lawyer and a commoner in Lincoln in 1455–6, was at this time an official of the Archdeacon of Wells, a position that was retained until 1477. Richard Cordon(e), a canon lawyer and advocate of the court of Canterbury, was Archdeacon of Rochester from 1416 until 1452 when Cordon died as a commoner in Lincoln. Robert Bowet, an illegitimate son of noble parents, was a commoner of University College from 1422 until at least 1428, and throughout the whole of that period was Archdeacon of Nottingham.[56]

54. Emden, *BRUC*, p. 102; Walker, *Biographical register of Peterhouse*, I, p. 32 (Brygge); *BRUC*, p. 254; Venn, *Biographical history of Gonville and Caius*, I, p. 16 (Gayton); *BRUC*, p. 188 (Dobbes).
55. For examples, see Cobban, *Medieval English universities*, p. 329; Cobban, "Commoners in medieval Cambridge colleges", p. 53.
56. Emden, *BRUO*, I, pp. 235 (Bowet), 486–7 (Cordon); II, p. 1277 (Middelton). For Middelton and Cordon see also Green, *The commonwealth of Lincoln College*, p. 19.

Two examples from Cambridge also involve archdeacons. Before becoming a pensioner of Gonville, William Sponne had been a justice of the peace for Cambridge. Sponne was intermittently a pensioner between 1434 and 1447 when discharging the office of Archdeacon of Norfolk.[57] When admitted as a commoner of Peterhouse in 1460, Thomas Marke was already Archdeacon of Norfolk. During Marke's pensionership, that seems to have ended in 1462, the archdeaconry of Cornwall and the rectorship of Hardwick, Norfolk, were also acquired.[58] It appears that Marke had used the pensionership to provide a suitable base in the course of a busy ecclesiastical career.

It is of considerable interest that commoners of noble birth were attracted to English colleges in the fourteenth and fifteenth centuries. Some of these noble entrants, in common with non-noble pensioners, already held ecclesiastical livings or offices when admitted to the college. Thomas Bubwith, a scholar of noble birth, was a commoner in University College in 1413–14 and held two canonries and one prebend prior to, during and for some years after the tenure of the pensionership. In 1422 Nicholas Preston, of noble origins, was granted a papal indult to farm a benefice for five years while studying at a university. At Oxford, Preston was a commoner of University College between 1422 and 1428, and during this time retained the position of vicar of Kirkby Stephen, Westmorland. Another noble commoner, Oliver Elton, resided in University College from 1435 to at least 1438 and remained rector of Chelmsford, Essex, throughout these years. John Lowe is recorded as a noble commoner of Lincoln in 1455–6. As Archdeacon of Rochester from 1452, succeeding in this position Richard Cordon(e), another Lincoln commoner previously mentioned, Lowe was still exercising this office in 1467. When William Scrope, son of Stephen, second Lord Scrope of Masham, was a commoner in Oriel between 1409 and 1412, a canonry and a rectorship were held in conjunction with the pensionership. Scrope moved on to become a commoner at Queen's College from 1420 to 1426 and combined this with the position of rector

57. Venn, *Biographical history of Gonville and Caius*, I, p. 8; Brooke, *A history of Gonville and Caius*, p. 25; Cobban, "Commoners in medieval Cambridge colleges", pp. 53–4.
58. Peterhouse archives, computus rolls of 1460–1 and 1461–2; Emden, *BRUC*, p. 391; Walker, *Biographical register of Peterhouse*, I, pp. 54–5; Cobban, "Commoners in medieval Cambridge colleges", p. 54.

of the free chapel of West Witton, Yorkshire, and with the canonry and rectorship held when a pensioner at University College.[59]

Examples of noble pensioners at Cambridge who were discharging ecclesiastical offices upon entry to a college include Gilbert, rector of Hal(l)sall, Lancashire, a commoner of the King's Hall between 1440 and 1452, Richard Moresby, Archdeacon of London, who was a King's Hall commoner from 1435 to 1442, and John and William, the illegitimate sons of the Earl of Huntingdon, who were both rectors when they were charged as commoners of the same college between 1440 and 1442.[60] Another member of the nobility, Humphrey de la Pole, the son of John de la Pole, the second Duke of Suffolk, was rector of Barrowby, Lincolnshire, when admitted to Gonville as a pensioner in 1490.[61]

It is probable that most noble commoners before 1500 were of the mature type. There were, however, a few sons of noble families who were only young boys when they entered as college pensioners. Robert Hungerford, later Lord Hungerford and Moleyns, was aged nine or ten when living as a commoner in University College in 1437–8. John Tiptoft, the future Earl of Worcester and humanist patron, was also a commoner at University College, and was about 13 years of age upon entry in 1440–1.[62] At Cambridge, John of Ufford, the third son of Robert, Earl of Suffolk, was about nine years old when commencing as an undergraduate pensioner at Gonville in c.1350. John Radclyffe, twelfth baron FitzWalter, was only about two years older when installed as a pensioner at Peterhouse in 1463.[63] As mentioned in Chapter 1, noble undergraduates often had private tutors while at university, and this applied to sons of noble families who were fee-paying college

59. Emden, *BRUO*, I, pp. 296 (Bubwith), 636–7 (Elton); II, p. 1169 (Lowe); III, pp. 1519 (Preston), 1660 (Scrope).
60. Emden, *BRUC*, pp. 282 (Hal(l)sall), 410 (Moresby), p. 322 (Huntingdon brothers). See also King's Hall accounts, IX, fols 161v, 162; X, fol. 13v.
61. Venn, *Biographical history of Gonville and Caius*, I, p. 14; Emden, *BRUC*, pp. 180–1; Brooke, *A history of Gonville and Caius*, pp. 22, 28–33.
62. Emden, *BRUO*, II, p. 985 (Hungerford); III, p. 1877 (Tiptoft).
63. For John of Ufford see Venn, *Biographical history of Gonville and Caius*, I, p. 1; Emden, *BRUC*, p. 603; Brooke, *A history of Gonville and Caius*, pp. 22, 23; for John Radclyffe see Peterhouse archives, computus roll of 1463–4; *BRUC*, p. 468; Walker, *Biographical register of Peterhouse*, I, p. 60.

commoners.[64] Both Robert Hungerford and John Tiptoft had private tutors as commoners in University College. Henry, son and heir of the Earl of Huntingdon, seems to have enlisted Richard Caudray, the warden of the King's Hall, as a tutor when a college pensioner from 1439 to 1442.[65] The presence of several extremely young noble commoners in the medieval English universities is a notable fact that anticipates a general lowering of the entry age in the post-Reformation period. Nevertheless, a small contingent of young boys of noble birth does not modify to any appreciable extent the thesis that before 1500 the average age of undergraduate entry lay in the region of 15 to 17 years.

A fair proportion of the mature and undergraduate noble commoners who were domiciled in colleges are known to have had a serious academic purpose in attending a university. At Cambridge, William Bardolf, brother of Thomas, fifth Lord Bardolf, who was a pensioner in the King's Hall from 1387 to 1390, studied civil law during these years, and Gilbert, rector of Hal(l)sall, John Huntingdon and Richard Moresby, noble pensioners of this royal college, were all possessed of degrees some years prior to entry.[66] Humphrey de la Pole acquired degrees in both civil and canon law when a pensioner in Gonville at the close of the fifteenth century.[67] At Oxford, William Scrope, a noble commoner first of Oriel and then of Queen's and University College, had obtained the degrees of BCnL and BCL by 1431, that is five years after being last recorded as a commoner of Queen's. Similarly, Thomas Bubwith had gained the same two degrees by 1414 while a noble commoner of University College. Two other noble commoners, Nicholas Preston of University College and John Lowe of Lincoln College, had both attained the degree of BCnL by the time that they had become commoners in

---

64. See above, p. 34.
65. Hungerford's tutor was master John Chedworth, the future Bishop of Lincoln, who was then a mature commoner of University College: *BRUO*, I, pp. 401–2 (Chedworth). Tiptoft's tutor was master John Hurley (Hurlegh): *BRUO*, II, p. 988 (Hurley). For Caudray as probable tutor to Henry Huntingdon see Cobban, *The King's Hall*, pp. 75–6; also King's Hall accounts, IX, fol. 123v.
66. For Bardolf see Emden, *BRUC*, p. 36; King's Hall accounts, III, fols 19, 43, 74v; E. F. Jacob, "Petitions for benefices from English universities during the Great Schism", *Transactions of the Royal Historical Society*, 4th ser. **27**, 1949, p. 58. For Hal(l)sall, Huntingdon, and Moresby see *BRUC*, pp. 282, 322, 410.
67. Emden, *BRUC*, pp. 180–1; Venn, *Biographical history of Gonville and Caius*, I, p. 14.

1422 and 1455 respectively.[68] It may be assumed that the noble and other well-connected commoners whom William Waynflete made an integral element of Magdalen College, Oxford, and who were to be regulated by tutors, would have been engaged in systematic study.[69]

An analysis by J. Rosenthal of members of the nobility who attended Oxford and Cambridge between 1307 and 1485 indicates that many of them acquired degrees, mainly in arts or law, with a few taking degrees in theology.[70] Noble commoners were widely dispersed and lived in colleges, halls, hostels or private lodgings, and some have undoubtedly gone unrecorded. It is clear that at least those noble commoners who were accommodated in colleges tended to follow the general pattern for nobles in the English universities at large. That is to say, most of the college commoners of noble birth seem to have been committed to academic pursuits, and some of them attained degrees, with perhaps a bias towards law degrees. It is true that there were noble commoners who had never at any point aspired to degree status. Nevertheless, the salient consideration is that so many of them did seek to acquire degrees. This rather belies the popular belief that members of the nobility attended the medieval English universities either for a social purpose or to study random topics of personal interest that were not part of a structured course leading to a degree. Such a scenario certainly applied to many noble entrants in the late-sixteenth and seventeenth centuries when college tutors could be found who would offer to commoners from the nobility and upper gentry a range of studies that were not embraced by the official curriculum. Subjects with a contemporary application such as history, geography, cosmography, cartography and navigation had a voguish appeal for sons of noble and gentry families who wished to follow palatable areas of interest without regard for courses of prescribed study that would lead to a degree.[71] There is not much evidence that this kind of two-tiered system of education, official and unofficial, was in operation in the English universities before the second half of the sixteenth century. Prior to 1550

---

68. Emden, *BRUO*, I, p. 296 (Bubwith); II, p. 1169 (Lowe); III, pp. 1519 (Preston), 1660–1 (Scrope).
69. *Statutes*, II, ch. 8, p. 60.
70. See Rosenthal, "The universities and the medieval English nobility", *History of Education Quarterly* **9**, 1969, p. 419.
71. On this topic see Curtis, *Oxford and Cambridge in transition*, ch. 4.

noble commoners appear to have been absorbed into the prevailing pattern of studies that widened, from the late-fifteenth century, to include strands of humanist learning.

There are occasional instances of commoners who had apparently never held a fellowship and who later became fellows either of the same or of another college. Obviously, the lack of reference to the tenure of a fellowship at any point in a recorded career is not conclusive proof that one had not been held. It may, however, be taken as a working assumption. Thomas Hardy, a commoner of Oriel in 1414–15, was admitted as a fellow of that college in 1417. John Eland and Robert Holywell acquired fellowships at Merton in 1411 and c.1420 respectively, and both were former commoners of University College. Oriel admitted John Weston as a fellow in 1445 nine years after Weston was recorded as a commoner of Exeter College.[72] At least five fellows of the King's Hall in the fifteenth century had been commoners of the college, and four had been semi-commoners. The commoners were Richard Moresby, Boynton, Screne, John Derby and Thomas Pykering, and the semi-commoners were John of Grimesby, Geoffrey Asteley, William Soole and John Coo.[73] Further examples could doubtless be cited, although not in any quantity. The clear impression is gained that the transition from fellow to commoner was much more frequent than the move from commoner to fellow.

A few commoners actually became heads of colleges. In all known cases except one, the commoner had previously been a college fellow. Thomas Lentwardyn and Thomas Hawkins had first been fellows and then commoners of Oriel before election as provosts of Oriel, Lentwardyn in 1417 and Hawkins in 1475. Similarly, John Tristrope was a fellow and commoner of Lincoln prior to succeeding to the rectorship of the same college in 1461. Rather different are the cases of Robert Gilbert, John Chedworth and Christopher Urswick. Gilbert was a fellow of Merton who eventually captured the wardenship of Merton in 1417. Several years before Gilbert had been a commoner, not of Merton, but of both Exeter and Oriel. Chedworth had started as a fellow of Merton, became a commoner of University College, was

72. Emden, *BRUO*, I, p. 633 (Eland); II, pp. 872 (Hardy), 955 (Holywell); III, p. 2024 (Weston).
73. For details see Cobban, "Commoners in medieval Cambridge colleges", p. 55, notes 48 and 49, and Cobban, *The King's Hall*, pp. 263–4.

appointed a fellow of the recently founded King's College, Cambridge, in 1443, and subsequently was made its second provost in 1446. Urswick had a fellowship at the King's Hall in 1470–1, was a commoner of University College in 1475–6, and returned to Cambridge as warden of the King's Hall in 1485. Robert FitzHugh, son of the king's chamberlain, Sir Henry FitzHugh of Ravensworth Castle, Yorkshire, was another warden of the King's Hall, appointed in 1424, having been made chancellor of Cambridge University the year before. An interesting point is that there is no evidence that a fellowship had been held in any college before FitzHugh succeeded to the wardenship of this prestigious royal foundation. FitzHugh's only recorded collegiate positions prior to the wardenship were as commoners of two Oxford colleges, Exeter and University.[74]

Several mature commoners rose to fill influential offices within the English universities. Just mentioned is the fact that noble commoner, Robert FitzHugh, became both chancellor of Cambridge University and warden of the King's Hall in the early-fifteenth century. Similarly, Richard of Goldynton, a commoner of the King's Hall, was made Cambridge chancellor a few years later in c.1345.[75] At Oxford, Henry Beaufort, the second illegitimate son of John of Gaunt, Duke of Lancaster, and future cardinal, was elected chancellor of Oxford University in 1397, having been a commoner at both Peterhouse, Cambridge, and Queen's College, Oxford.[76] Moreover, the Augustinian canon, Philip Repingdon, who was chancellor of Oxford between 1400 and 1403, is almost certainly to be identified with the canon, master Philip, who was a commoner in Queen's College in 1386–7. Richard Courtenay, nephew of William Courtenay, Archbishop of Canterbury, had recently been, and may still have been, a commoner of Queen's when created chancellor of Oxford in 1406. Courtenay was made chancellor again in 1411 and probably vacated the office in 1413.[77] At Cambridge,

---

74. For Chedworth, Lentwardyn, Hawkins and Gilbert see Emden, *BRUO*, I, p. 401; II, pp. 1131, 891, 766; for Tristrope see *ibid.*, III, p. 1909 and Green, *The commonwealth of Lincoln College*, pp. 31–2; for FitzHugh see *BRUO*, II, p. 689 and *BRUC*, pp. 231–2 and Cobban, *The King's Hall*, pp. 284–5; for Urswick see *BRUC*, p. 605 and Cobban, *The King's Hall*, pp. 288–9.

75. For Goldynton see Emden, *BRUC*, p. 264; King's Hall accounts, I, fols 48, 60.

76. Emden, *BRUO*, I, pp. 139–40 and *BRUC*, p. 46; see also Peterhouse archives, computus roll of 1388–9; Walker, *Biographical register of Peterhouse*, I, pp. 23–4.

77. For Repingdon see *BRUO*, III, p. 1566; for Courtenay see *BRUO*, I, p. 500.

two commoners of Corpus Christi College, Edmund Conyngsburgh and Thomas Tuppyng, who had previously been a fellow of Michael-house, were made vice-chancellors of Cambridge in 1471 and 1485 respectively.[78]

It was clearly possible to be employed on university business while still a commoner. For instance, an ex-fellow of Oriel, Richard Snetisham, was a commoner of Oriel between 1409 and 1414, and in 1411 was appointed a member of the committee set up by Oxford University to examine the works of John Wyclif. Another example is provided by Robert Fleming, the nephew of Richard Fleming, Bishop of Lincoln. The younger Fleming was a commoner of University College from 1430 to 1444 and from 1462 to 1472, and in 1438–9 acted as junior proctor of the university. A third example stems from the career of William Dowson, an ex-fellow of Merton and a commoner in Univer-sity College from 1432 to 1451, who served as senior university proctor in 1433–4.[79]

Quite a few commoners, whether former fellows or not, had not-able extra-university careers. Sir Henry Huntingdon, a commoner of the King's Hall from 1439 to 1442 and who became Earl of Huntingdon and Duke of Exeter, had a turbulent political career and exercised, among other responsibilities, the office of Admiral of England, Ire-land and Aquitaine. Huntingdon was drowned in the English Channel in suspicious circumstances upon returning from Edward IV's expedi-tion to France in 1475. Two noble commoners of University College, Robert Hungerford, later Lord Hungerford and Moleyns, and John Tiptoft, the future Earl of Worcester, had their high-profile, stormy careers terminated by execution, Hungerford in 1464 and Tiptoft in 1471. One of Oriel's most prominent commoners was Thomas Arundel, third son of Richard FitzAlan, Earl of Arundel, and commoner at Oriel in 1372–3, who rose to be Archbishop of Canterbury and Chan-cellor of England in the late-fourteenth and early-fifteenth centuries. Another commoner who attained prestigious office was Henry Beau-fort, the illegitimate son of John of Gaunt and commoner at both Peterhouse, Cambridge, and Queen's College, Oxford, who was Chan-cellor of England at various times in the first quarter of the fifteenth

78. Emden, *BRUC*, pp. 156 (Conyngsburgh), 599 (Tuppyng).
79. Emden, *BRUO*, I, 591 (Dowson); II, p. 699 (Fleming); III, p. 1725 (Snetisham).

century.[80] The celebrated canonist, William Lyndwood, may possibly have been a fellow of Pembroke College, Cambridge, and was certainly a pensioner of Gonville, probably in the opening years of the fifteenth century. Lyndwood held the office of keeper of the privy seal from 1432 to 1443, was a royal councillor, and was engaged on frequent diplomatic missions.[81]

A number of mature commoners were eventually translated to the ranks of the episcopate. They were mostly from Oxford colleges, a circumstance that fits the general scenario that between 1216 and 1499 Oxford produced 57 per cent of English bishops compared with the 10 per cent produced by Cambridge. Four of the commoners, Henry Beaufort, Philip Repingdon, Richard Fleming, who was a commoner both of University College and Queen's College, and John Chedworth, became Bishops of Lincoln, Beaufort at the close of the fourteenth century and the other three in the fifteenth century.[82] Beaufort was also Bishop of Winchester from 1440 until 1447, and Thomas Arundel was made Bishop of Ely in 1374 before reaching the position of Archbishop of York and later of Canterbury. Richard Courtenay was a commoner of Queen's in the early years of the fifteenth century and succeeded to the see of Norwich in 1413.[83] Two of the commoners, Robert FitzHugh and Robert Gilbert, were successive Bishops of London, FitzHugh from 1431 to 1436 and Gilbert from 1436 to 1448, and Edmund Lacy, a former fellow and commoner of University College, became Bishop of Hereford in 1417 and Bishop of Exeter in 1420.[84] William Lyndwood, the canon lawyer and at one time a pensioner of Gonville, ended an influential and varied career as Bishop of St Davids, a rather unassuming bishopric that seems a disproportionate reward for such an eminent figure.[85]

80. For Sir Henry Huntingdon see Emden, *BRUC*, p. 321 and King's Hall accounts, IX, fols 106v, 162; X, fol. 13v; for Hungerford and Tiptoft see *BRUO*, II, p. 985; III, pp. 1877–9; for Arundel see *ibid.*, I, pp. 51–3 and M. Aston, *Thomas Arundel* (Oxford, Clarendon Press, 1967); for Beaufort see *BRUO*, I, pp. 139–42 and *BRUC*, p. 46.
81. Emden, *BRUC*, pp. 379–81; Brooke, *A history of Gonville and Caius*, pp. 21, 22, 26.
82. For Richard Fleming see Emden, *BRUO*, II, pp. 697–8; see also Queen's College archives, long rolls (transcripts), V, pp. 43, 58, 73, 90, 142.
83. Emden, *BRUO*, I, pp. 500–1; Queen's College archives, long rolls (transcripts), V, pp. 30, 57, 73.
84. For Fleming, Lacy, and Repingdon see Emden, *BRUO*, II, pp. 697–8, 1082; III, p. 1566.
85. Emden, *BRUC*, p. 380; Brooke, *A history of Gonville and Caius*, p. 26.

Outstanding scholars are occasionally to be found among the ranks of medieval commoners. John Wyclif and John Trevisa were both commoners at Queen's College, Oxford, in the late-fourteenth century.[86] William Lyndwood, the canonist author of the *Provinciale seu constitutiones Angliae*, one of the most important of the English works on canon law down to the Reformation, has already been highlighted as a pensioner of Gonville. While it is true that only a few of the mature commoners who followed an academic rather than a social path scaled the highest peaks of intellectual endeavour, most of them seem to have reached a respectable level of achievement that enabled them to progress further in their chosen extra-university careers. The power that the English universities had to attract mature commoners in significant numbers from most sections of the social hierarchy added appreciably to the diversity and enrichment of the academic community, making the universities more representative of the society that they served.

Apart from members of the laity and of the secular clergy, commoners were also drawn from the monastic orders. At Oxford, regular canons of the Augustinian Order were sent to university in some numbers from the late-fourteenth century.[87] Initially, they lived as dispersed commoners in colleges and halls. Augustinian canons from Repton and Taunton are found as commoners of University College in the early-fifteenth century. Philip Repingdon, the future Augustinian abbot and Bishop of Lincoln, was probably a commoner in Queen's College in 1386–7, and several canons of the order were housed in Dagville's Inn in 1416.[88] Even after the first steps had been taken in 1435 to set up St Mary's College for Augustinian canons, resort still had to be made to rented accommodation.[89]

In the early-fifteenth century the main concentration of Cistercian students was located in Trillock's Inn where, in effect, they lived as

---

86. Wyclif was charged as a commoner of Queen's in 1365–6, 1374–5, and 1380–1: Queen's College archives, long rolls (transcripts), II, pp. 139, 232; III, p. 249. See also Hodgkin, *Six centuries of an Oxford college*, pp. 32–3. Trevisa was a commoner in 1386–7, 1394–5, 1395–6, and 1398–9: long rolls (transcripts), III, p. 291; IV, pp. 381, 400, 437.

87. R. B. Dobson, "The religious orders 1370–1540" in *HUO*, II, p. 554; S. Forde, "The educational organization of the Augustinian Canons in England and Wales, and their university life at Oxford, 1325–1448", *History of Universities* **13**, 1994, p. 34.

88. Dobson, "The religious orders 1370–1540", p. 554, *n*. 48; Forde, "The educational organization of the Augustinian Canons", p. 35.

89. Forde, "The educational organization of the Augustinian Canons", p. 33.

university commoners.[90] The founding of the Cistercian St Bernard's College in 1438 improved the situation to some degree, although the college had a chequered history for the remainder of the century, and a fair number of monk-students continued to be housed in rented rooms outside the college, living after the manner of commoners.[91] Benedictine monk-students probably fared better than the Augustinians at Oxford. Three Benedictine colleges, Gloucester, Durham and Canterbury, were established well before the appearance of the first Augustinian and Cistercian colleges, and the capacity to accommodate members of the order seems to have been reasonably good. It is noteworthy that the monk-fellows of Canterbury College in the second half of the fifteenth century received groups of monk-students from several prominent Benedictine centres, including Battle, Peterborough, Reading, Winchester and Worcester. These monk-students were to live as sojourners, one of the many alternative terms for commoners.[92]

Commoners from the monastic orders were no less in evidence at Cambridge. Monk-students at Cambridge were recruited in the main from monastic houses in East Anglia, in particular from Norwich Cathedral Priory and from Ely diocese. A few were also drawn from houses in Yorkshire.[93] Accommodation was an even greater problem at Cambridge than at Oxford. Oxford saw the foundation of five monastic colleges between the 1280s and 1438 while Cambridge had only Buckingham College, dating in a rudimentary form from the 1470s, although temporary accommodation for Benedictine monk-students had been improvised earlier in the century.[94] Because of the paucity of monastic housing, agreements were sometimes made between individual secular colleges and religious houses in East Anglia for the reception of

90. Dobson, "The religious orders", p. 552. For Trillock's Inn or New Inn Hall see Pantin, "The halls and schools of medieval Oxford: an attempt at reconstruction", pp. 71–9.
91. For the fluctuating fortunes of St Bernard's College in the fifteenth century see Dobson, "The religious orders", pp. 552–3.
92. *ibid.*, pp. 549–50.
93. Cobban, "Commoners in medieval Cambridge colleges", p. 58; Aston, Duncan & Evans, "The medieval alumni of the University of Cambridge", p. 56. For further details see J. Greatrex, "Monk students from Norwich Cathedral Priory at Oxford and Cambridge, c.1300 to 1530", *EHR* **106**, 1991, pp. 555–83.
94. For Buckingham College see D. M. B. Ellis & L. F. Salzman, "Religious Houses", in *Victoria history of the county of Cambridge and the Isle of Ely. Volume 2*, L. F. Salzman (ed.) (London, Oxford University Press, 1948), p. 312.

monk-students as pensioners. The most prominent example is that of Gonville College. Gonville accommodated monk-students from Norwich Cathedral Priory, St Albans Abbey, the Augustinian Priories of Westacre, Norfolk, and Butley, Suffolk, and from the Cluniac Priory at Lewes, Sussex.[95] One or two of the monk-pensioners at Gonville went on to important positions. Robert Catton, from Norwich Priory, who was a pensioner at Gonville in 1502–3, became Abbot of St Albans, succeeding Thomas Wolsey in that post. William Repps, also from Norwich, was a Gonville pensioner between 1509 and 1513 and was appointed Bishop of Norwich in 1536.[96] John Attleborough, another monk from Norwich, became Prior of Yarmouth, a dependency of Norwich, in 1501, having been a pensioner at Gonville from 1487 until at least 1500. In similar fashion, Woodbridge, an Augustinian canon and pensioner of Gonville in 1497, is recorded as the Prior of Pentey Priory, Norfolk, in 1520. Several monk-pensioners had already held responsible positions before moving to Gonville. For instance, John Wolman and John Stowe had been almoners of St Albans and Norwich Cathedral Priory respectively previous to their residence as pensioners of Gonville.[97]

Most of the monk-pensioners at Cambridge were not perhaps of the highest intellectual calibre. The occasional monk-pensioner already had a degree when admitted, some acquired respectable degrees in theology at university and others are not known to have taken a degree at all. Even a brief spell at university was considered a useful educative preparation for monk-pensioners who hoped to become preachers of the order.[98] Some monk-pensioners clearly advanced within their order as a result of their university experience and qualifications. It must be remembered, however, that the aspirations of the individual monk-pensioner were always secondary to the needs of the order. There was

95. See J. Venn, *Early collegiate life* (Cambridge, Heffer, 1913), pp. 70–3 and "Monks in college", *Caian* **3**, 1893–4, pp. 29–31; Leader, *The university to 1546*, p. 50.
96. For Catton and Repps see Venn, *Biographical history of Gonville and Caius College*, I, pp. 15, 18 and Brooke, *A history of Gonville and Caius*, pp. 49, 56.
97. For Attleborough see Venn, *Biographical history*, I, p. 14; Emden, *BRUC*, p. 23; for Woodbridge see Venn, I, p. 14 and *BRUC*, p. 644; for Wolman see Venn, I, p. 14 and *BRUC*, p. 648; for Stowe see *BRUC*, p. 561.
98. See the comments of B. F. Harvey, "The monks of Westminster and the University of Oxford", in *The reign of Richard II*, F. R. H. Du Boulay & C. M. Barron (eds) (London, Athlone Press, 1971), pp. 118–20.

a perennial tension between the monastic vocation and the pull of the monastic life. One can imagine that for some monk-pensioners time spent at a university was a liberating experience, and adjustment on return to the full monastic routine would be a frustrating matter.[99]

The main movement of fee-paying commoners from halls and hostels to the colleges occurred in the first half of the sixteenth century and continued through to the end of Elizabeth's reign. In the fifteenth century they had already begun to infiltrate a few of the colleges in small numbers. The earliest known presence of undergraduate commoners, as opposed to undergraduate fellows, in an English secular college dates from the 1430s. The college in question was the King's Hall, Cambridge.[100] As already mentioned, towards the close of the fifteenth century Magdalen College, Oxford, admitted fee-paying undergraduate commoners who were to be the sons of nobility or of other influential persons.[101] This provision was repeated virtually verbatim in Thomas Wolsey's lengthy statutes of c.1525–7 for Cardinal College.[102] Generally speaking, however, until the sixteenth century most undergraduate commoners were denizens of the unendowed halls and hostels that were scattered throughout the towns of Oxford and Cambridge. Some of the halls and hostels were either bought or leased by colleges and used as annexes for commoners, a proportion of whom would be undergraduate commoners.[103] In this sense, several Oxford and Cambridge colleges in the fifteenth century maintained fee-paying undergraduate commoners external to the college. This probably means that before 1500 far more undergraduate commoners were accommodated as appendages to the colleges than were housed within collegiate walls. During the sixteenth century the Oxford halls and Cambridge hostels were subject to a protracted decline.[104] In 1552 only about eight Oxford halls remained. Nevertheless, in a census of that year that embraced 13

---

99. For instances of this see Greatrex, "Monk students from Norwich Cathedral Priory at Oxford and Cambridge", pp. 577–8.
100. On this topic see Cobban, *The King's Hall*, pp. 67–72; Cobban, "Commoners in medieval Cambridge colleges", pp. 59–60.
101. See above, pp. 101–2.
102. *Statutes*, II, ch. 11, pp. 103–4.
103. For examples at Oxford see Cobban, "Colleges and halls 1380–1500", p. 630; for Cambridge see Stokes, *Medieval hostels*, pp. 34–7.
104. For detailed figures see Cobban, *Medieval English universities*, p. 158; J. McConica, "The rise of the undergraduate college", in *HUO*, III, pp. 52–3.

Oxford colleges and eight halls and included an unknown number of college servants and excluded scholars still living in private lodgings, one quarter of the thousand or so recorded in the census were said to belong to the surviving halls.[105] At Cambridge, the testimony of John Caius, writing in 1573, suggests that only nine hostels were operational in that year.[106] The gradual demise of the halls and hostels led to the physical incorporation of most undergraduate commoners within the colleges, rendering them an integral part of collegiate life. In tandem with this, the undergraduate commoner emerged as the main type of commoner in the English universities, and the army of mature commoners who had so enriched the academic community was substantially reduced. The entrenchment of the undergraduate commoners in the colleges in the sixteenth century was clearly an important directional turning point for the English universities. Not all colleges shared equally in the reception of undergraduate commoners. For instance, at Brasenose College, Oxford, in 1552 undergraduate commoners constituted about 40 per cent of the membership, whereas Merton had only a small undergraduate element in the sixteenth century and All Souls had scarcely any.[107] The rise of the collegiate commoner to a dominant position within the colleges accelerated the growth of collegiate teaching and tutorial facilities that resulted in the sixteenth century in the decentralization of much of the university instruction in the colleges and the few remaining halls and hostels. Moreover, the age of the undergraduate fellow seen at colleges such as the King's Hall and New College had now been replaced forever by the ubiquitous commoner.

---

105. Cobban, "Colleges and halls", p. 631 and *n*. 206; McConica, "Studies and faculties: introduction", in *HUO*, III, p. 153.
106. J. Caius, *Historiae Cantabrigiensis academiae ab urbe condita, liber primus* (London, Day, 1574), pp. 52–3; also Willis and Clark, *The architectural history of the University of Cambridge*, I, pp. xxii–iii.
107. McConica, "The rise of the undergraduate college", in *HUO*, III, pp. 12, 65–6.

CHAPTER FOUR

The academic periphery

The academic core of the medieval English universities comprised teaching and non-teaching masters, postgraduate scholars and college fellows, and undergraduate and mature commoners. There were, however, groupings on the academic margins that were important to the functioning of the universities and added to the general pageantry of university life. University and college benefactors, college founders, teachers of university extension courses, tradespeople who served the diverse needs of the academic community, university, college and hall servants, women in their various supportive roles and building operatives all contributed to the successful workings of the English universities. Through these satellite groupings the universities touched a range of external concerns, stimulated their urban economies and became significant employers of local labour. Moreover, the willingness of benefactors and college founders to invest in medieval Oxford and Cambridge is a powerful indicator of the value that contemporaries from different social backgrounds placed upon England's principal centres of learning.

The bestowal of money for the support of scholars or the giving of money or property to a university or college were acts that were expected to bring spiritual benefits to the donors. In return for a charitable investment, benefactors could command masses and intercessory prayers for their own souls and for those of their relatives. The Universities of Oxford and Cambridge commemorated their benefactors annually as an ensemble, and many benefactors were also remembered individually in anniversary services.[1] It is of some remark that among the earliest statutes of Cambridge University, dated between 1236 and 1254, arrangements were made for services to commemorate two of its principal benefactors after their deaths, Henry III and the current Bishop of Ely, almost certainly Hugh of Northwold.[2]

Following the lead of the university authorities, all of the secular colleges commemorated their benefactors on a regular basis. For example, at Peterhouse, Cambridge, the names of the founder and other benefactors were entered on a roll for recitation at several masses throughout the year. In addition, the master and fellows were to attend weekly masses for the soul of the founder, Hugh of Balsham, Bishop of Ely, and for the soul of Bishop Montacute, who gave to the college the statutes of 1344, and for the souls of Montacute's father and mother and other benefactors.[3] It is made clear that these spiritual rewards were in recompense for the receipt of valued temporal gifts. The commemoration of benefactors was rather more elitist at the King's Hall. In the statutes of 1380, given to the college by Richard II, the king enjoined the warden and fellows to attend a weekly mass for the souls of Edward II, the founder of the Society of the King's Scholars, Edward III, who endowed that Society as the royal College of the King's Hall, and for the soul of Richard II's father, the Black Prince, who does not appear to have had any particular bond with the college.[4] To take an example from Oxford. A heavy regime of devotional exercises was prescribed for the rector and fellows of Lincoln College, founded by Richard Fleming, Bishop of Lincoln, in 1427. The statutes envisaged by Fleming were never implemented. The code of statutes given in 1480 by the second founder, Thomas Rotheram, Bishop of Lincoln and later Archbishop of York, have survived. These statutes stipulate annual commemorative masses for Fleming and Rotheram, and prayers for Rotheram were to be said at all college masses. Moreover, whenever the rector or any of the fellows preached a sermon, prayers were to be recited for the souls of the two founders. The founders were also to be remembered in prayers every day after dinner. Other

---

1. Gibson, *Statuta antiqua*, pp. 1–14, 15–16, 98, 118–19, 134, 159; *Camb. Docs*, I, pp. 404–7, 413–15.
2. Hackett, *Original statutes*, pp. 25, 38–9, 217.
3. *Camb. Docs*, II, pp. 40–2.
4. See the statutes of 1380 in Rouse Ball, *The King's Scholars and King's Hall*, p. 65.

benefactors were to receive due attention in prescribed masses and prayers.[5]

The importance that colleges attached to these commemorative masses is shown by the fact that the attendance of the master and fellows was usually made obligatory, except for good cause. It has to be stressed here that many English secular colleges could be regarded to a lesser or greater degree as chantry foundations in which the fellows were required to participate in the performance of commemorative religious services for the souls of their founder and associated benefactors. The preoccupation with death and the post-mortem judgment that was especially marked in the fourteenth and fifteenth centuries was embodied in a formidable array of chantry foundations, ranging from the humble endowment of a single chantry priest to an ostentatious collegiate church or an academic college. The secular colleges that were endowed for permanency within the English universities were ideal subjects for the staging of perpetual intercessory services for the souls of both living and departed benefactors. Among the examples of English colleges that had a close affinity with the chantry idea are King's College and St Catharine's at Cambridge, and Queen's, New College, Lincoln and All Souls at Oxford. Indeed, at St Catharine's the founder, Robert Wodelarke, devoted about one-sixth of the original statutes to the elaborate intercessory prayers that were to be offered for the souls of the founder, Wodelarke's parents, Henry VI and other benefactors.[6]

In all of these colleges the fellows or scholars had heavy devotional functions to carry out that must have impinged upon the time available for study and teaching. The marriage of the chantry element and academic charity in a collegiate form was by no means confined to England. Colleges that encapsulated this spiritual and educative union are also to be found in Paris and in some of the French provincial universities. A fairly typical example is furnished by the College of Verdale that was established in c.1337 by Arnaud of Verdale, later Bishop of Maguelone, in the University of Toulouse. Arnaud, who set up the

5. *Statutes*, I, ch. 6, pp. 27–9.
6. On colleges as chantries see Cobban, *Medieval English universities*, pp. 112–13 and C. N. L. Brooke, "The churches of medieval Cambridge", in *History, society and the churches*, D. Beales & G. Best (eds) (Cambridge, Cambridge University Press, 1985), pp. 61–3. See also Rubin, *Charity and community in medieval Cambridge*, pp. 276–82. For the original statutes of St Catharine's see St Catharine's muniments, XL/10 and the printed version in Philpott, *Documents relating to St Catharine's College*.

college in a house in Toulouse, designed it for the education of 12 students and for the repose of the soul of a cousin, Pierre of Verdale, and for the souls of diverse relatives.[7] While chantry arrangements were in evidence in continental colleges, it is undeniable that the English secular colleges, taken as a group, are especially impressive with regard to the often elaborate and detailed chantry provisions that were made for the spiritual health and glorification of benefactors.

As educational centres, as providers of intercessory services and as objects of charitable investment, the colleges had evidently split roles to perform and this has caused some debate as to their central purpose. The question arises as to whether, in the minds of some college founders, the chantry or the educational motive was the more important. There is a temptation to say that where the chantry element was very pronounced the founder's need for intensive and perpetual prayers for the progress of souls must have taken priority over the academic objective.[8] The implication here is that modern historians have tried to impose misleading educational values on what was essentially a spiritual enterprise. However enticing, such a thesis does not accord with the impressive amount of effort that went into defining the instructional diet of most colleges, including those with a high chantry component. Indeed, the educational preferences set out in collegiate statutes were often the product of sustained consultations with either current or former university personnel who could give advice as to priority needs.

The detailed planning that went into the shaping of King's College, Cambridge, in the 1440s, a college with an extremely prominent chantry element, is a good illustration of the attention that was frequently lavished on the educational content. It seems that John Langton, then master of Pembroke College and chancellor of the university, was the leading spirit behind the academic venture that became King's College and Henry VI's principal agent in executing the project. Moreover, the commission of 1441 that was entrusted with the drafting of statutes for King's comprised Langton, John Somerset, a former fellow of Pembroke and physician, tutor and chancellor of the exchequer to Henry VI, William Lyndwode, the celebrated canonist and probably a past fellow of

---

7. Fournier, *Les statuts et privilèges*, I, pp. 538, 539, 561; see also C. E. Smith, *The University of Toulouse in the Middle Ages* (Milwaukee, Wis., Marquette University Press, 1958), pp. 110–11.

8. See, for example, the remarks of Brooke, "The churches of medieval Cambridge", p. 62.

Pembroke, William Alnwick, Bishop of Lincoln, and William Ayscogh, Bishop of Salisbury, whose brother Robert was to become the warden of the King's Hall in 1448.[9] King's was planned on an exceptional scale, and the amount and quality of the consultation and advice available to the royal founder was doubtless untypical. However, few college founders acted in an academic vacuum, and they benefited from advice, either directly or indirectly obtained, from contacts who were familiar with the intellectual trends of the English university world. It is then more than likely that the spiritual and academic aims of college founders were conceived as complementary, and that the educational purpose was generally in the ascendant. Nevertheless, it is well to remind ourselves that in the pre-Reformation era many college fellows had to assume the functions of chantry priests. This not only affected their outlook on the world but also ensured that the founder and other benefactors loomed large in the psychological make-up of collegiate life.

English college founders may have been confined to the margins of the academic community but their benefactions were eventually to transform medieval Oxford and Cambridge from universities of a centripetal to a centrifugal character. That is to say, by the time of the Reformation the colleges had become the primary teaching units within the English universities. The centralized university instruction had fallen into such a state of desuetude that, in the wake of the demise of the halls and hostels, the colleges had emerged as the foremost components of their universities in the course of the sixteenth century. Long-term projections of this kind must have been remote from the minds of college founders, at least before the mid-fifteenth century. From the late-fifteenth century, however, the burgeoning position of the colleges within the university system would inevitably have made college founders more attuned than previously to the constitutional changes underway. That the future of the English universities lay in a collegiate landscape would have been transparent to all but the most obtuse of potential college founders in the early Tudor period.

English college founders before 1500 were supplied in the main from the upper stratum of society and included kings, queens, archbishops, bishops, members of the lay aristocracy, a minister of state, a

9. Cobban, "Pembroke College", p. 7 and J. Saltmarsh, "King's College", in *Victoria history of the county of Cambridge. Volume 3*, p. 377.

chancery clerk, less exalted ecclesiastics and a Cambridge guild. The kings in question were Edward II, Edward III and Henry VI. In 1317 Edward II established a detachment from the chapel royal in Cambridge as the Society of the King's Scholars, and this was endowed in 1337 by Edward III as the royal College of the King's Hall.[10] Two major consequences flowed from this monarchical initiative. First, an organic link was forged between the royal household and court and the English universities. Secondly, the attraction of royal patronage to Cambridge altered the shape of English collegiate expansion. After the settlement of the King's Scholars in Cambridge only two colleges, Oriel and Queen's, were founded at Oxford in the remainder of the first half of the fourteenth century, whereas seven colleges were established at Cambridge between 1317 and 1352. It is clear that the coming of the King's Scholars to Cambridge and their subsequent embodiment in the King's Hall 20 years later had caused some college founders and benefactors, who might otherwise have given of their wealth to Oxford, to follow the royal lead by investing in the smaller of the English universities.

This scenario was repeated in the fifteenth century when Henry VI chose Cambridge as the host for King's College in 1441. Because Oxford's reputation had been seriously damaged by its association with Wyclifism and Lollardy, the king decided that royal patronage ought to be conferred upon the university that was relatively untainted by the stigma of heresy. Following the foundation of King's College, only one college, Magdalen, was launched at Oxford in the second half of the fifteenth century. By contrast, Queens', St Catharine's and Jesus were founded in the same period at Cambridge, and all of these were committed to shoring up that university as a bastion of orthodoxy and a sound investment for collegiate development. None of the Oxford colleges that were established before 1500 were directly founded by kings, although Oriel, originated in 1324 by the chancery clerk, Adam of Brome, acquired Edward II as co-founder.[11] Indeed, Oriel was sometimes referred to as the King's Hall or King's College because of Edward II's role as second founder. Similarly, Henry Chichele, Archbishop of

---

10. For the origins of the King's Scholars and the King's Hall see Cobban, *The King's Hall*, ch. 1.
11. W. A. Pantin, "Oriel College", in *Victoria history of the county of Oxford. Volume 3*, p. 119.

Canterbury, who founded All Souls College in 1437, named Henry VI as nominal co-founder.[12]

As their titles indicate, queens of England were associated with the foundation and promotion of Queen's College, Oxford, and Queens' College, Cambridge. In the case of Queen's, Oxford, the real founder was Robert of Eglesfield, chaplain to Queen Philippa, consort to Edward III. In 1341 Eglesfield acquired a licence to establish a college that was initially called the Hall of the Queen's Scholars of Oxford. Eglesfield, who gave the patronage of the college to Philippa and to subsequent queens consort, was anxious to have Philippa recognized as the foundress. In a charter of Edward III of 1350, one year after Eglesfield's death, Philippa is named misleadingly as the sole founder of the college. It is, however, more accurate to see Eglesfield as the driving force behind the foundation, with the queen acting in a secondary and supportive role.[13] At Cambridge, the first queen to be associated with the foundation of a college was Margaret of Anjou, consort to Henry VI. Inspired by Henry's foundation of King's College in 1441, the egotistical Margaret petitioned the king for permission to refound the existing College of St Bernard that had been established in 1446 by Andrew Dockett, rector of St Botolph's, Cambridge. In 1448 Queen Margaret issued a charter renaming the college as "the Queen's College of St Margaret and St Bernard". With the change of dynasty from Lancastrian to Yorkist, Elizabeth Woodville, consort to Edward IV, assumed the title of true foundress (*vera fundatrix*) in 1475, and the future of Queens' College was firmly secured.[14] The reasons for the promotion of the college by Margaret of Anjou and Henry VI were similar to those that prompted the foundation of King's College. These included the augmentation of the faith and clergy, the extirpation of heresy, and the stability of the church.[15] However, one motive that was expressed in Margaret's petition to Henry VI for leave to refound the existing College

12. *Statutes*, I, ch. 7, p. 12.
13. See Hodgkin, "Queen's College", in *Victoria history of the county of Oxford. Volume 3*, p. 132; Hodgkin, *Six centuries of an Oxford college*, pp. 7–10; Magrath, *The Queen's College*, I, pp. 1–22; *Statutes*, I, ch. 4, pp. 5–6.
14. On the foundation and early promotion of Queens' see Twigg, *A history of Queens' College, Cambridge*, pp. 1–12; R. G. D. Laffan, "Queens' College", in *Victoria history of the county of Cambridge. Volume 3*, pp. 408–9. For Elizabeth Woodville's self-description as "true foundress" see the preface to the statutes of 1475 in *Camb. Docs*, III, p. 18.
15. See, for example, Twigg, *A history of Queens' College, Cambridge*, p. 3.

of St Bernard is of more than usual interest. In the petition Queen Margaret requested that the college be refounded and renamed "to laud and honneure of sexe femenine" because no college had hitherto been founded in Cambridge by a queen of England.[16] This unexpected expression of fifteenth-century feminism was perhaps an early indication of Margaret's redoubtable, feisty and ruthless character as displayed on the political stage. These traits were presumably not fully formed at the time of the refounding of the college when the queen was only 17 or 18 years of age.

Margaret of Anjou was the first queen of England to be associated with the foundation of a Cambridge college but was not the first foundress of a college in that university town. That distinction belongs to Elizabeth of Burgh, widow of John of Burgh and youngest daughter of Gilbert, Earl of Clare and Joan of Acre, daughter of Edward I. Lady Clare had no surviving children when widowed, and was free to invest inherited capital in pious enterprises without fear of family opposition. As was the case with Margaret of Anjou, Lady Clare refounded an existing collegiate society. During the chancellorship of Richard of Badew, the university obtained a licence in 1326 for the incorporation of University Hall. This new college was ill-endowed and by 1336 was in a parlous state, and an appeal for assistance was made to Lady Clare who responded with alacrity. By 1346 the college had been soundly endowed and began life afresh as Clare College.[17]

Elizabeth of Burgh's example was followed by another immensely wealthy widow and close friend, Marie of St Pol, Countess of Pembroke,

16. This petition is printed by J. B. Mullinger, *The University of Cambridge* (3 vols) (Cambridge, Cambridge University Press, 1873–1911), I, pp. 313–14 and by W. G. Searle, *History of the Queens' College of St Margaret and St Bernard in the University of Cambridge, 1446–1662* (2 vols) (Cambridge, Cambridge Antiquarian Society, 1867–71), I, pp. 15–16. This point of "sexe femenine" is not mentioned by J. J. Bagley, *Margaret of Anjou Queen of England* (London, Jenkins, 1948), p. 57 when referring to this petition. See also Laffan, "Queens' College", p. 408 and R. A. Griffiths, *The reign of King Henry VI* (London & Tonbridge, Kent, E. Benn, 1981), pp. 257–8.

17. For Elizabeth of Burgh see F. A. Underhill, "Elizabeth de Burgh: connoisseur and patron", in *The cultural patronage of medieval women*, J. H. McCash (ed.) (Athens, Ga., University of Georgia Press, 1996), pp. 266–87. See also W. J. Harrison, "Clare College", in *Victoria history of the county of Cambridge. Volume 3*, pp. 340–1; A. C. Chibnall, *Richard de Badew and the University of Cambridge 1315–1340* (Cambridge, Cambridge University Press, 1963), pp. 14–18, 36–44; J. C. Ward, *English noblewomen in the later Middle Ages* (Harlow, England, Longman, 1992), pp. 158–9.

also known as Mary of Valence. Marie, who had no dependent children, was a descendant of Henry III and connected to the French royal family. Unlike Margaret of Anjou and Lady Clare, Marie of St Pol did not refound an existing college. Instead, an entirely new college was established in Cambridge in 1347, initially called the Hall of Valence Marie or Pembroke Hall, later Pembroke College, the planning of which appears to have begun in 1342. Born into a French aristocratic family, Marie also attempted to found a college in Paris in 1356, although the disruptive effects of the Hundred Years War brought this venture to nought.[18]

Another instance of a noblewoman who completed the foundation of an English college dates from the earliest phase of collegiate history. Lady Dervorguilla of Galloway, the widow of John Balliol, the father of John Balliol, King of Scotland, permanently endowed a community of scholars that Balliol had settled in Oxford by 1266 in expiation of a penance imposed by the Bishop of Durham, or so the tradition goes. Dervorguilla gave a body of statutes in 1282, and Oliver Sutton, Bishop of Lincoln, confirmed this reconstituted college in 1284.[19] The contributions of Lady Clare, Marie of St Pol and Lady Dervorguilla to the English collegiate movement are thrown into even stronger relief when it is realized that no male member of the nobility, apart from Dervorguilla's husband, sought to found a college at either Oxford or Cambridge before 1500. It is true that university education did not prove to be generally attractive for the nobility before the advent of humanism, although small groups of noble commoners were present in the English universities from the thirteenth century. Even if Oxford and Cambridge were for long relatively insignificant centres for the nobility, it is surprising that the chantry motive did not encourage male nobles to view the founding of an academic college as an ideal method for enshrining

18. For Marie de St Pol see H. Jenkinson, "Mary de Sancto Paulo, foundress of Pembroke College, Cambridge", *Archaeologia* **66**, 1914–15, pp. 410–46; Attwater, *Pembroke College Cambridge*, pp. 1–12; Leader, *The university to 1546*, pp. 83–4; E. Minns, "Pembroke College", in *Victoria history of the county of Cambridge. Volume 3*, p. 346; J. T. Rosenthal, *The purchase of paradise* (London, Routledge & Kegan Paul, 1972), pp. 67–9, 79, 80.
19. For the foundation of Balliol see J. Jones, *Balliol College: a history, 1263–1939* (Oxford, Oxford University Press, 1988), pp. 1–10, 281–3 (translation of Dervorguilla's statutes); Reitzel, *The founding of the earliest secular colleges within the Universities of Paris and Oxford*, pp. 221–34; Salter (ed.), *The Oxford deeds of Balliol College*, pp. 1–14, 277–83 (Latin text of Dervorguilla's statutes).

their memory, promoting their salvation and enlarging the scope of educational provision. This, however, did not happen. Instead, with the sole exception of John Balliol, it was left to three widowed noble-women with driving personalities, wealth and time on their hands to represent the nobility as college foundresses. In this way, these pion-eering women and the three queens who promoted the founding and refounding of colleges gave women a high profile as substantial ben-efactresses to the medieval English universities. The founders of academic colleges in continental Europe were mainly male, as in England, although notable exceptions occur. For example, Joanna of Navarre, consort to Philip IV, founded the impressive College of Navarre at Paris in 1305, and Joanna of Burgundy established the College of Burgundy in the same city in 1331.

Most of the Oxford college founders were ecclesiastics. Of the ten secular colleges founded before 1500 no fewer than nine had ecclesias-tical founders. Exeter, New College, Lincoln and Magdalen all had epis-copal founders, and Merton, although founded by Walter of Merton when Lord Chancellor, also acquired an episcopal founder when Walter became Bishop of Rochester in 1274.[20] One archbishop and one archbishop-elect were involved in Oxford's collegiate development. Henry Chichele, Archbishop of Canterbury, was the founder of All Souls in 1437, and William of Durham, Archbishop-elect of Rouen for a few months in 1235–6, may be regarded as the founder of University College, albeit that the circumstances leading to the foundation are complex.[21] The two remaining colleges, Oriel and Queen's, were founded by lesser eccle-siastics. Adam of Brome, an Oxford rector and chancery clerk, estab-lished Oriel in 1324 and, as previously mentioned, associated Edward II as co-founder when the college was refounded in 1326. Queen's came into existence in 1341 as a result of the initiative of Robert of

20. Exeter was founded by Walter of Stapeldon, Bishop of Exeter, in c.1314; New College and Magdalen were founded by William of Wykeham and William Waynflete, both Bishops of Winchester, in 1379 and 1457/8 respectively; and Lincoln College was founded by Richard Fleming, Bishop of Lincoln, in 1427. For Walter of Merton's career see J. R. L. Highfield, *The early rolls of Merton College Oxford* (Oxford, Clarendon Press, 1964), pp. 5–34, 52–4, 66–78.
21. For the circumstances surrounding the foundation of University College and for its early development see Reitzel, *The founding of the earliest secular colleges*, pp. 187–207; see also A. Oswald, "University College", in *Victoria history of the county of Oxford. Volume 3*, pp. 61–2.

Eglesfield, chaplain to Queen Philippa, whom Eglesfield tried to render as foundress. The only Oxford college of pre-1500 vintage to have a secular founder was Balliol in the person of John Balliol, Lord of Barnard Castle, with Dervorguilla as second foundress.

The situation at Cambridge was very different. Of the 13 Cambridge colleges established before 1500 only Peterhouse, Trinity Hall and Jesus had episcopal founders, and three, Gonville, Godshouse and Queens', were founded by rectors, although Queens' later acquired Queen Margaret of Anjou and Queen Elizabeth Woodville as foundresses.[22] The remaining seven colleges had secular founders. Two kings, Edward II and Edward III, were responsible for the establishment of the King's Hall, and one of Henry VI's few positive and enduring acts was the foundation of King's College. A chancellor of the exchequer of Edward II, Hervey of Stanton, founded Michaelhouse in 1324, and Clare and Pembroke were brought into being by two wealthy noblewomen, as previously discussed.[23] St Catharine's College is a most intriguing case. It was originated by Robert Wodelarke when provost of King's. In so doing, Wodelarke achieved a noteworthy English academic record. Wodelarke's career provides the only instance in medieval England of the head of one college who was at the same time the founder of another.[24] Corpus Christi College, for long styled Benet College, was unique in that it was the only college in England to be founded by a guild, in this case the amalgamated guilds of Corpus Christi and the Blessed Virgin Mary. Guilds had often played a part in founding grammar schools, but the founding of a university college was a far more ambitious undertaking. The enterprise that led to the foundation of Corpus Christi College was aided by obtaining the patronage of Henry, Duke of Lancaster, who secured a royal licence for the new college in 1352.[25] A foundation of this kind, where the interests of citizens and the

22. Hugh of Balsham, Bishop of Ely, founded Peterhouse in 1284; William Bateman, Bishop of Norwich, papal judge and royal diplomat, established Trinity Hall in 1350; and John Alcock, Bishop of Ely, founded Jesus College in 1496. The three rectors were Edmund Gonville, William Bingham and Andrew Dockett, and they founded Gonville College, Godshouse and the College of St Bernard, later Queens', in 1348, 1439 and 1446/8 respectively.

23. For Hervey of Stanton see Stamp, *Michaelhouse*, especially pp. 2–15.

24. Cobban, "Origins: Robert Wodelarke and St Catharine's", pp. 6–7.

25. C. P. Hall, "The gild of Corpus Christi and the foundation of Corpus Christi College: an investigation of the documents", in *Medieval Cambridge: essays in the pre-Reformation University*, pp. 65–91; J. P. T. Bury, "Corpus Christi College", in *Victoria history of the*

university merged, was an interesting experiment that ought to have improved relations between town and gown. This may have happened for a time. In 1381, however, during the turmoil of the Peasants' Revolt, Corpus Christi was one of the victims of the civil insurrection in Cambridge that was directed against the university and its privileges.

In continental Europe many colleges were founded for the benefit of foreign students. For example, colleges were established at Paris by Swedish and Danish cathedral chapters for the accommodation of scholars from these Scandinavian countries. These included the College of Upsala, Skara House, the College of Linköping and the College of Dacia. Paris also hosted the Scottish College, the College of Lombards and the College of the Germans. At Bologna the College of Spain, founded by Cardinal Gil Albornoz in c.1367, was designed for 30 Spanish or Portuguese students. Prague had its college for students from Lithuanian and surrounding territories.[26] By contrast, the English universities had no need for specific colleges for foreign students. Oxford and Cambridge attracted relatively few scholars from abroad, and most of these were members of the mendicant orders. Moreover, Oxford recruited only about 6 per cent of scholars from Wales, Ireland and Scotland, and Cambridge's percentage was only about 1 per cent.[27] In these circumstances, the English collegiate system was almost wholly geared to the indigenous scene.

If a potential English benefactor had neither the inclination nor the resources to found an academic college, the foundation of a university or college loan-chest was probably regarded as the best type of substitute benefaction. The establishment of loan-chests for university or college

county of Cambridge. Volume 3, p. 371; Rubin, Charity and community in medieval Cambridge, pp. 120–3.

26. For colleges for ethnic groupings at Paris see A. L. Gabriel, Skara House at the medieval University of Paris (Notre Dame, Ind., University of Notre Dame Press, 1960), pp. 15–47. For the College of Spain see B. M. Marti, The Spanish College at Bologna in the fourteenth century (Philadephia, University of Pennsylvania Press, 1966) and C. H. Clough, "Cardinal Gil Albornoz, the Spanish College in Bologna, and the Italian Renaissance", Studia Albornotiana 12, 1972, pp. 227–38. For the college for Lithuanians at Prague see Rashdall, Universities, II, p. 221 and n. 1. See, more generally, for ethnic colleges J. M. Fletcher, "The history of academic colleges", in I collegi universitari in Europa tra il xiv e il xviii secolo, D. Maffei & H. de Ridder-Symoens (eds) (Milan, Giuffrè, 1991), p. 16.

27. Aston, Duncan & Evans, "The medieval alumni of the University of Cambridge", p. 35.

personnel seems to have been particularly associated with the English universities. They arose first at Oxford in the mid-thirteenth century and at Cambridge towards the close of that century. Whereas most of the Oxford college founders were ecclesiastics, the founders of university loan-chests were far more diverse. Of the Oxford loan-chests founded before 1500 five had bishops as benefactors, two of whom also held the office of Lord Chancellor. The Chichele chest was founded by Henry Chichele, Archbishop of Canterbury, and two canons are recorded as having established chests. The lay benefactors who inaugurated chests included Queen Eleanor of Castile, consort to Edward I, Henry of Lacy, Earl of Lincoln, and Thomas Beaufort, Duke of Exeter, Ela Longespee, Countess of Warwick, a member of a noble household, a knight, three judges, an alderman of London, and Joan, widow of William Danvers.[28] Among the founders of university chests at Cambridge were an archbishop, a bishop, four clerics in episcopal employment, two rectors, three who were engaged in royal administration, a duke and two masters of colleges.[29] One conspicuous feature about the benefactors of university chests is that merchants were scarcely represented. This is rather curious since sons of merchant families were sent with some frequency to Oxford and Cambridge and merchants figured among college benefactors.

College loan-chests were generally founded by masters or fellows of the college for which the foundation was made. At Michaelhouse, Cambridge, two of the masters, William of Gotham and Henry Granby, founded loan-chests in c.1380 and c.1420 respectively. John Deveros(e), a fellow of Corpus Christi, added to the value of the Gotham chest, and another chest was set up by a fellow of Michaelhouse, Richard Baston, in the closing years of the fourteenth century.[30]

The spiritual obligations towards founders of college chests were usually less exacting than was the case with benefactors of university chests. It follows that college chests were of a more intimate nature than university chests, and they were designed to give charitable aid to

---

28. This analysis is based on the data on Oxford university loan-chests provided by Aston & Faith, "The endowments of the university and colleges to c.1348", pp. 276–7.
29. Rubin, *Charity and community in medieval Cambridge*, p. 285.
30. Stamp, *Michaelhouse*, pp. 34–5; Pollard, "Medieval loan-chests at Cambridge", *BIHR* **17**, 1939–40, p. 127. For Richard Baston and John Deveros(e) see Emden, *BRUC*, pp. 43, 186. Baston is not mentioned here as a founder of a chest.

fellows of a society of which the founder of the chest had often been a member. There is no doubt that some of the wealthier and more influential benefactors could have founded a college rather than a university chest. On the other hand, the university authorities were very keen on chests and they probably encouraged benefactors to fulfil this need. In a letter of 1432 from the University of Oxford to the Archbishop of Canterbury it is alleged that the foundation of chests gives sustenance to scholars just as water prevents vines from withering in the vineyard of the Lord.[31] Moreover, chests were less troublesome to establish than colleges, and their administration was a university responsibility. They did not involve the heavy legal costs attendant upon setting up a college or the securing of an endowment in the form of land, manors and appropriated churches, and there were no crippling building expenses. The spiritual rewards of intercessory prayers and anniversary masses were adequately upheld by the English universities for all founders of chests. In this way, benefactors, who chose to establish chests rather than colleges, did not lose out in this intangible area. In addition, borrowers from chests were usually required, by their statutes, to say private prayers for the founder.[32]

The role of benefactress was the one that allowed women to exercise their greatest influence on the English universities. One of the most prominent of these wealthy women who left their mark on English university life in the thirteenth century was Ela Longespee, the dowager Countess of Warwick, the wife and later widow of Philip Basset, justiciar and royal clerk. During their marriage Ela and Philip gave their manor of Thorncroft in Leatherhead to Merton College in 1266. As a widow, Ela founded the Warwick chest at Oxford in 1293, gave several grants to Merton and contributed to the building of the chapel of Balliol College.[33] Another notable benefactress was Queen Eleanor of Castile, consort to Edward I, who founded the Queen's chest at Oxford in the same year that Ela Longespee established the Warwick chest. Eleanor was also a benefactress to Cambridge, and in 1290 left 100 marks for

31. Anstey, *Epistolae academicae oxoniensis*, I, pp. 70–1.
32. Aston & Faith, "The endowments of the university and colleges", p. 284; Lovatt, "Two collegiate loan-chests in late-medieval Cambridge", p. 134.
33. Highfield, *The early rolls of Merton College Oxford*, pp. 27, 41, 445–9; Aston & Faith, "The endowments of the university and colleges", pp. 275–9; Reitzel, *The foundation of the earliest secular colleges*, pp. 235–6.

poor scholars at that university.[34] Less elevated than the Countess of Warwick or an English queen was Joan Danvers, a widow and foundress of the Danvers chest at Oxford in 1457. Another influential benefactress was Lady Isabella Parvyng who, as the widow of Sir Robert Parvyng, a Chief Justice of the Common Pleas, King's Treasurer and Lord Chancellor, gave the advowson of Newbold Pacey in Warwickshire to Queen's College, Oxford, in the mid-thirteenth century.[35] At Queens' College, Cambridge, three aristocratic women, Lady Margaret Roos, Dame Alice Wyche and Lady Joan Burgh, were generous benefactresses between 1469 and 1474.[36]

Benefactors to the medieval English universities and to their secular colleges were a mixture of lay and ecclesiastical, academic and non-academic, and are far too numerous to list here in their totality. However, a few examples, in addition to those already discussed, may be given to indicate the social range inherent in England's university benefactors.

At the upper end of the social spectrum Robert Winchelsey, Archbishop of Canterbury, supported scholars at Oxford and Cambridge between 1294 and 1313. Another Archbishop of Canterbury, Cardinal Morton, a chancellor of both English universities, bequeathed in 1500 £128 3s 8d per annum for 20 years for the support of some 20 poor scholars at Oxford, and for half that number at Cambridge.[37] Further down the social scale are found benefactors who were university members in that they were deemed to be servants of the English universities and were accorded the status of "privileged persons". At Oxford, Roger the stationer gave a tenement to the university at some point between 1240 and 1250. Two Oxford bedels are recorded as benefactors. Nicholas of Kingham, who was a bedel in the mid-thirteenth century, donated

34. Aston & Faith, "The endowments of the university and colleges", pp. 276, 283; Cooper, *Annals*, I, p. 62; T. Fuller, *The history of the University of Cambridge*, M. Prickett & T. Wright (eds) (Cambridge, Cambridge University Press, 1840), p. 130.
35. Aston & Faith, "The endowments of the university and colleges", pp. 277, 283; Hodgkin, *Six centuries of an Oxford college*, p. 19.
36. Laffan, "Queens' College", in *Victoria history of the county of Cambridge. Volume 3*, p. 411.
37. For Winchelsey see J. H. Denton, *Robert Winchelsey and the crown 1294–1313* (Cambridge, Cambridge University Press, 1980), pp. 13, 25. For Morton's bequest and payments to scholars see W. A. Pantin (ed.), *Canterbury College Oxford* (3 vols), Oxford Historical Society, new ser. **6, 7, 8** (Oxford, Clarendon Press, 1946–50), III, pp. 227–45.

a tenement to the university named Cat Hall. Reginald de la Lee, a former university bedel, left a house in 1294 to "the community of poor scholars", and also made arrangements for the annual distribution of bread to 100 poor scholars.[38] Similarly, bedels are found among the early benefactors to Cambridge University. One such, in the first half of the thirteenth century, was Thomas of Tudenham, who came from an Essex family and who, through marriage to Matilda of Walda, acquired property in Cambridge and the surrounding neighbourhood. The exact nature of Tudenham's donation is unknown, but it is likely to have been a property bequest.[39] Scholars sometimes gave property to the English universities. For instance, in 1321 Nicholas of Tingewick, a physician to Edward I and principal of Corbet Hall, donated Beef Hall and Corbet Hall to the University of Oxford so that an annual sum of £2 13s 4d would generate salaries for two regent masters to superintend the grammar schools within Oxford.[40]

All of the secular colleges received gifts including money, land, church livings, books, items of plate, missals and vestments for the chapel and contributions to building costs. College heads, fellows and ex-fellows figure prominently among college benefactors. In addition, members of the nobility and gentry, clergymen, merchants, citizens of London, craftsmen and the occasional burgess of Oxford and Cambridge helped to swell the ranks of those who gave of their largesse to collegiate foundations.[41] Whatever the size of the donation, whether an impressive gift of land or a minor object for college use, all benefactors expected to be treated with suitable deference. For instance, when Thomas Duffield, an ex-fellow of Peterhouse, gave money for the purchase of a lamp for the chapel of Queens' College, Cambridge, this donor was to be accorded the same commemorative rights and inter-cessory prayers as were given to benefactors who had made substantial donations.[42]

38. For Roger the stationer and the two bedels see Aston & Faith, "The endowments of the university and colleges", pp. 271–2; Salter, *The medieval archives of the University of Oxford*, I, p. 302.
39. H. P. Stokes, "Early university property", *Proceedings of the Cambridge Antiquarian Society* **13**, 1908–9, new ser. **7**, p. 165.
40. Aston & Faith, "The endowments of the university and colleges", p. 272.
41. See, for example, the variety of benefactors who donated to Queens' College, Cambridge, in Twigg, *A history of Queens' College Cambridge*, pp. 117–19.
42. *ibid.*, p. 118.

Apart from the prestigious role of benefactress, women served the medieval English universities in a variety of ways. As members of the towns of Oxford and Cambridge, women were prominent as ale-sellers and were involved in other retail trades, and some took advantage of the opportunities to act as landladies, at least in the period before residence in a college, hall and hostel was made obligatory for scholars. In the thirteenth century Jewesses in Oxford occasionally functioned as moneylenders and received books as pledges. In a dispute of 1278 the Carmelite convent claimed that it had deposited volumes with Margarina, the Jewess, who denied having received the pledge.[43] Women also held the leases of college tenements and even large portions of college estates.[44] From time to time, women are recorded as suppliers of materials to the colleges. For example, Laetitia Lynch supplied oil and wine to Merton College chapel between 1487 and 1491, and in 1501–2 a widow from Holywell sold cartloads of straw to the same college.[45] Women were employed by Merton as casual cleaners, seamstresses and as labourers engaged upon such tasks as preparing rushes, sorting out thatch for roofing purposes, planting saffron and weeding the saffron garden.[46] How typical this was for the generality of English colleges is difficult to say. Throughout the voluminous accounts of the King's Hall there is not a single reference to the employment of female casual labour. It may be that each college had its own policy on the matter.

Whatever the case regarding casual female labour, many colleges including Merton, Oriel, New College, All Souls and Corpus Christi, Oxford, and King's College, Cambridge, ruled that domestic college servants were to be males.[47] The presence of women on the domestic staff was generally considered to be most undesirable as they were alleged to constitute a threat to sexual propriety. There was, however, one unavoidable exception. Since male launderers were difficult to

---

43. Roth, *The Jews of medieval Oxford*, pp. 132–3
44. See, for example, the cases cited by J. M. Fletcher & C. A. Upton, "'Monastic enclave' or 'open society'? A consideration of the role of women in the life of an Oxford college community in the early Tudor period", *History of Education* 16, 1987, pp. 4–5.
45. *ibid.*, pp. 5–6.
46. *ibid.*, pp. 6, 7–8.
47. *Statutes*, I, ch. 2, pp. 19–20, 36–7 (Merton), ch. 3, p. 15 (Oriel), ch. 5, p. 94 (New College), ch. 7, p. 58 (All Souls); II, ch. 10, pp. 39–40 (Corpus); *Camb. Docs*, II, p. 596 (King's).

obtain, laundresses were often employed by colleges under stringent conditions. For example, at New College, All Souls and Corpus Christi, Oxford, and at King's College, Cambridge, it was specified that the laundress was to reside in the town and was to be of such an age and appearance that no sexual misdemeanour was likely to arise.[48] Such was the obsessional desire to keep physical contact between fellows and women within the college to an absolute minimum that all garments were to be handed to the laundress at the college gate by means of an intermediary servant.[49] At Peterhouse, the fellows were to have their heads washed in their rooms by males, if at all possible, and not by laundresses, and certainly not by young ones.[50] Similarly, at Queen's, Oxford, the heads of the fellows were to be washed by the barber, the laundress being expressly forbidden to perform this function.[51]

The other area in which women had an impact upon the academic community was that of prostitution. This presented an enormous problem for the university authorities in Oxford and Cambridge, and the frequent legislative efforts that were made to suppress the trade had only a limited effect. Prostitutes were subject to heavy penalties at the hands of the courts of the university chancellors who had acquired powers as guardians of the moral standards of the citizens of their university towns. It was argued that immoral conduct often provoked disturbances of the peace, and the chancellors felt impelled to pay close attention to urban prostitutes and the keepers of brothels.

The penalties that were levied on prostitutes included expulsion from the town for a specified period or for life, imprisonment or a spell on the pillory.[52] Despite the regular attempts to eliminate prostitution in Oxford and Cambridge, the most that was ever achieved was

---

48. *Statutes*, I, ch. 5, p. 94 (New College), ch. 7, p. 58 (All Souls); II, ch. 10, pp. 39–40 (Corpus); *Camb. Docs*, II, p. 596 (King's).
49. See the statutes of Peterhouse, King's, New College, All Souls and Corpus Christi, *Camb. Docs*, II, p. 30 (Peterhouse), p. 596 (King's); *Statutes*, I, ch. 5, p. 94 (New College), ch. 7, p. 58 (All Souls); II, ch. 10, pp. 39–40 (Corpus).
50. *Camb. Docs*, II, p. 30.
51. *Statutes*, I, ch. 4, p. 33.
52. For the Cambridge chancellor's power to drive prostitutes out of the town see, for example, Cooper, *Annals*, I, pp. 76, 83, 209–10; for the authority given by Edward IV in 1461 to the Oxford chancellor to banish prostitutes to places over ten miles from Oxford see Salter, *Medieval archives of the University of Oxford*, I, pp. 251–2. On punishments for prostitutes at Oxford see Salter, *Registrum cancellarii*, I, pp. xvii–xix, 332–3.

the reduction of the problem to manageable proportions. For Oxford, there is graphic evidence of prostitution in operation. This derives from an inquiry into prostitution in the town in 1443–4 under the auspices of the chancellor, Thomas Gascoigne.[53] This investigation revealed that many of the prostitutes were married women and that the trade was highly organized. Some of the women who came before the chancellor's court were made to abjure their activities as prostitutes, others had to swear to cease acting as procurers of women and others had to abjure both prostitution and procurement. Oxford scholars not only used the services of prostitutes but were even involved in promoting prostitution after the manner of pimps, and they were forced to renounce these activities in the chancellor's court. For example, Lewis Ydern, Richard May and John Raney, scholars, swore not to promote prostitution and procurement, and Hugo Blakton, a rector from Ireland, was imprisoned for disturbing the peace and for engaging in prostitution and procurement.[54] Moreover, Hugh Sadler, a scholar in priest's orders, who had appeared in the chancellor's court on charges of breach of the peace, pimping and furthering prostitution, was also alleged to have had, with other scholars, improper meetings with the nuns of neighbouring Godstow nunnery.[55]

It was not always easy to persuade witnesses to testify in the chancellor's court against prostitutes and their pimps because of the fear of retribution in the form of death or mutilation.[56] The involvement of at least some of the scholars either as users of prostitutes or as pimps or both was scarcely in accordance with the idea that education ennobles, a theme that was much elaborated in educational treatises of the later-medieval period.[57] In mitigation, it may be argued that the stringent suppression of contacts between women and scholars within the university precinct made association with prostitutes and brothels more intelligible. The rumbustious nature of life in university towns and the availability of female company were ever-present temptations for the wilder and more adventurous spirits among the academic community

53. Salter, *Registrum cancellarii*, I, pp. 92–9.
54. *ibid.*, I, pp. 98, 99.
55. Catto, "Citizens, scholars and masters", in *HUO*, I, p. 185; Salter, *Registrum cancellarii*, I, p. 97.
56. Salter, *Registrum cancellarii*, I, p. 95.
57. See, for example, Cobban, *The medieval universities: their development and organization*, p. 232.

who could not find an adequate outlet for their energies within the narrow circle of recreations permitted by the university authorities.

The prostitutes were decidedly not classified as "privileged persons". This was the status accorded to a veritable army of university, college and scholars' servants and to tradespeople who serviced the academic community. The categories of personnel that were to be included as "privileged persons" were defined at intervals, and between the thirteenth and fifteenth centuries there was a progressive enlargement of the groups that were recognized as "privileged".[58] Typically, "privileged persons" encompassed bedels, parchment-dealers, bookbinders, illuminators, scribes, the university bellringer, apothecaries, physicians, surgeons, barbers, common carriers and messengers in the service of scholars. To these were added the domestic servants employed in the halls, hostels and colleges, embracing manciples, butlers, cooks and launderers. Moreover, the personal servants of scholars were in time brought within the orbit of "privileged persons". Not only were the above reckoned to be "privileged", in some instances the privilege was extended to relatives and households. At Cambridge in 1502 there were 70 "privileged persons" attached to the university.[59]

The status of "privileged person" was much in demand because such a person was subject to the chancellor's court and was in large measure exempt from the jurisdiction of the borough courts, so avoiding many of the obligations and impositions that burdened their fellow citizens. Moreover, the protection of the chancellor's court was a useful defence for "privileged persons" who had enemies within the town. Indeed, there was a temptation for a townsman, who was in conflict with other citizens, to become a servant to a scholar in order to gain an added legal protection. Another advantage for a "privileged person" was that debts owed by scholars were often easier to recover through the chancellor's court than through the borough courts. Just as the colleges of the English universities built up extended families in the shires and

---

58. For details see Cobban, *Medieval English universities*, pp. 269–71. For the list of 1458 of those entitled to enjoy the privileges of Oxford University see Anstey, *Epistolae academicae oxoniensis*, II, pp. 344–5. For the categories of "privileged persons" that were agreed between Cambridge University and the town in 1502 see Dyer, *The privileges of the University of Cambridge*, I, pp. 97–8.
59. Peek & Hall, *The archives of the University of Cambridge*, p. 58.

towns through patronage networks, so the concept of "privileged persons" helped to create the sense of an extended university family within Oxford and Cambridge. Although the multiplication in the categories of "privileged persons" made the system rather unwieldy and some aspects of it were resented by the municipal authorities, the advantages probably outweighed the disadvantages and greater integration between the universities and their urban communities was undoubtedly furthered.

Of the "privileged persons" the domestic servants in the halls, hostels and colleges were of the utmost importance for raising the level of comfort for academic personnel who had to live in fairly austere conditions despite the grandeur of some of the collegiate buildings. Quite a few of the Parisian colleges had only one or two servants for the entire academic complement.[60] In the English colleges all but the smallest had an impressive array of domestics. For example, the statutes of Queen's College, Oxford, envisaged the employment of a steward, a cook and larderer, a kitchen boy, a baker, a brewer, a boy to grind the wheat and malt barley, a barber and janitor, a gardener, a laundress and a night watchman.[61] At Lincoln College, Oxford, the chief servants in the fifteenth century were the manciple, the cook, the laundress and the barber.[62] Over the fourteenth and fifteenth centuries the accounts of the King's Hall, Cambridge, reveal that the college employed at various times a butler, a cook, an undercook, a laundress, a barber, a baker, an underbaker, a brewer, a janitor and a book-bearer (*portitor* or *lator librorum*), a servant who was hired to transport the fellows' books to and from the lecture halls.[63] This latter servant was especially useful in colleges that were important legal centres. This is so because law students were obliged to possess copies of the bulky set texts and a human transport facility for these books was a welcome luxury. In addition to the King's Hall, book-bearers are found at New College and All Souls, Oxford, and at King's College, Cambridge.[64]

---

60. Gabriel, "The college system in the fourteenth-century universities", p. 94.
61. *Statutes*, I, ch. 4, pp. 31–2.
62. Green, *The commonwealth of Lincoln College*, p. 231; *Statutes*, I, ch. 6, p. 23.
63. For a detailed account of the domestic staff of the King's Hall see Cobban, *The King's Hall*, pp. 231–42; see also Cobban, *Medieval English universities*, pp. 339–43.
64. New College archives, bursars' and receipt rolls, 7711(1), 7330(2), 7332(4), 7336(8); *Statutes*, I, ch. 7, pp. 58–9 (All Souls); *Camb. Docs*, II, p. 596 (King's).

Colleges generally hired staff for the established domestic positions on an annual basis and according to a formal written contract.[65] Just as some of the English colleges are known to have prescribed a uniform livery for their fellows, so several colleges allocated livery to at least a proportion of the domestic staff. At the King's Hall there were six liveried servants until the late-fifteenth century, that is the butler, cook, baker, book-bearer, undercook and underbaker. By 1474–5, however, the barber, who had previously been recorded as non-liveried (*sine liberatura*), had been converted to a liveried servant.[66] The laundress, who was not permitted to board in college, remained throughout a non-liveried employee.[67] In recognition of the dignity of the office, the King's Hall butler, alone of the domestic servants, was in receipt of a robe (*roba*), once described as a full robe (*integra roba*).[68] The other domestic servants were supplied with gowns and caps, the former known variously as *gouna*, *gipon* and *tunica* and the latter as *pilius*.[69] Supplies of footwear and hose were also given to servants at various times but it is not clear that these were a regular part of the livery each year. In some years, the liveries were made up from material that was partly striped or rayed and partly of a uniform colour, and in other years the liveries were made entirely from woollen cloth of a single hue, usually green, grey or tawny.[70] The allowances of material for domestic staff at the King's Hall were more liberal than those at New College, and it is probable that they were untypically high.[71] Not all colleges, however, provided liveries for their principal servants. For instance, there is no mention of liveried servants at Lincoln College, Oxford, until the second half of the sixteenth century.[72]

---

65. For contracts (*conventiones*) of this kind at the King's Hall see King's Hall accounts, VII, fols 10v, 81v; XII, fol. 137v; XIII, fol. 112v; XV, fol. 72v.
66. Cobban, *The King's Hall*, p. 233.
67. *ibid.*, p. 234.
68. King's Hall accounts, III, fols 10v, 38v, 90, 92v, 133.
69. *ibid.*, III, fols 90 (*tunica*), 92v (*gouna* and *gipon*); XVII, fol. 40 (*pilii*).
70. For example, in 1430–1 the King's Hall's domestic staff were issued with a mixture of striped and blue cloth, *ibid.*, VIII, fol. 8v. In 1458–9 grey woollen cloth provided the domestic livery, in 1486–7 green cloth was bought for the livery, and in 1496–7 tawny material was purchased for the outfits of the servants: *ibid.*, XII, fol. 96v; XVIII, fol. 12v; XIX, fol. 72v.
71. Cobban, *The King's Hall*, p. 234.
72. Green, *The commonwealth of Lincoln College*, p. 231.

Although laundresses were non-resident and non-liveried, they were generally among the highest paid of the communal servants in English colleges. Most of the principal servants, if unmarried, were given accommodation and board as part of their remunerative package, and the wages of laundresses were presumably augmented by a monetary equivalent for the board and lodging from which they were usually excluded. Taking wages only into consideration, the laundress, with a stipend of 16s a year, was the highest paid servant in the King's Hall when it opened as an endowed college in 1337–8. Between 1400 and c.1465 the rate came to be fixed at £1 a year. This figure was raised to £1 6s 8d in 1475–6, and the stipend remained at this level until the last college account of 1544.[73] Typical stipends for the laundress at Merton College in the fifteenth century were 15s, £1 and £1 1s 8d, although these could be supplemented with payments for casual work in the chapel and allowances on ecclesiastical festivals.[74] At New College the laundress was given £1 6s 8d a year between 1381 and 1385, and £2 a year in 1390–1.[75] The laundress at Lincoln College was paid 13s 4d a year in the late-fifteenth century, a sum which had been increased dramatically to £1 16s by 1574. In this college the laundress was responsible, among other functions, for washing the linen of the chapel, hall and buttery.[76] Leaving aside accommodation and board, it is clear that the wage levels of laundresses were equivalent to those of senior college servants and this reflects the emphasis that English colleges placed upon hygienic standards.[77]

Judging from the situation at the King's Hall, college staff had to be versatile and ready to stand in for each other as required. For instance, the office of book-bearer was occasionally fulfilled by other domestic servants, by the baker in 1443–4 and by the barber in 1449–50.[78] There

---

73. Cobban, *The King's Hall*, p. 235.
74. See Merton College archives, bursars' rolls, 3727, 3737, 3750; for payments to laundresses at Merton in the late-fifteenth century see Fletcher & Upton, "'Monastic enclave' or 'open society'?", pp. 6–7.
75. New College archives, bursars' and receipt rolls, 7330(2), 7332(4), 7336(8).
76. Lincoln College archives, bursars' books, I, p. 26; Green, *The commonwealth of Lincoln College*, p. 233 and *n.* 6.
77. For details of wage levels for domestic staff at, for example, the King's Hall see Cobban, *The King's Hall*, pp. 235–40.
78. King's Hall accounts, X, fol. 62; XI, fol. 71v.

were opportunities for junior servants to be promoted to the superior domestic positions. At the King's Hall two of the butlers had entered collegiate service as book-bearers.[79] Some members of the King's Hall staff were long-tenured, but in general the turnover of personnel was fairly rapid. College servants would sometimes assist in external business. The manciple of Lincoln College would inspect the college estates in the company of the bursar and collect rents from tenants.[80] The barber of the King's Hall was occasionally deployed on missions far removed from tonsorial activity. In 1468–9 the barber undertook a journey on behalf of the college, and in 1505–6 the barber was sent to buy wheat.[81] Not all of the domestic staff in English colleges lived on the premises. Married staff were automatically precluded from doing so and were required to live in the town. A college such as the King's Hall helped to ease problems of accommodation for married staff, and indeed for ex-servants, by installing them as rent-paying tenants in urban properties belonging to the college.[82]

The medieval English universities and their colleges did much to stimulate the local building industry in and around Oxford and Cambridge. In the thirteenth century the structural development of the universities had been rather haphazard. In the fourteenth and fifteenth centuries, however, both universities embarked upon building programmes that were planned to meet specific academic needs. New university structures and the multiplication of colleges led to works of high architectural distinction, many of them conceived within the Perpendicular style.[83] The large-scale building projects, whether university or collegiate, and the need to maintain and repair existing structures necessitated the presence in Oxford and Cambridge of many skilled and unskilled building workers. Some of these were drawn from the university towns and neighbouring areas, and others were imported from further afield. At the highest level master-masons, who had made their reputations in royal service or in the employ of wealthy and influential clients, were hired for the most important and taxing building enterprises. At New College the main responsibility for the design and building lay with

79. Cobban, *The King's Hall*, pp. 236–7 and notes.
80. Green, *The commonwealth of Lincoln College*, p. 231.
81. King's Hall accounts, XIV, fol. 6; XX, fol. 127.
82. Cobban, *The King's Hall*, pp. 241–2 and notes.
83. J. H. Harvey, "Architecture in Oxford 1350–1500", in *HUO*, II, pp. 747–68.

the master-mason, William Wynford, and master-carpenter, Hugh Herland, supported by the advice of Henry Yevele, all three of whom had been in royal service.[84] William Vertue, master-mason, and Humphrey Coke, master-carpenter, who played the major part in the construction of Corpus Christi College, Oxford, had likewise been in royal employment.[85] Richard Winchcombe, the original architect of the Oxford divinity school, had also began an architectural career in the king's service.[86] Little is known of the early career of Richard Chevynton, the master-mason who was primarily responsible for the design of All Souls College, but Robert Janyns, the second-in-command, had a good architectural reputation that was to be enhanced with the building of the bell-tower of Merton College in the 1440s. The chief sculptor during the building of All Souls was John Massyngham, an artist of national repute who was hired from London.[87]

Principal craftsmen, whether master-masons, master-carpenters or sculptors, would often dine as honoured guests of the fellows of the college to which they were contracted so that they were made to feel a temporary part of the college's extended family. Sometimes a special feast was held to celebrate the completion of a major building operation.[88] Below the ranks of the master-craftsmen who designed and supervised building projects, there was a bustling workforce of masons, carpenters, joiners, sawyers, glaziers, carriers, smiths and labourers. Some of the more specialized work, such as the making of stained glass, was generally subcontracted. Building materials for university and college work had to be transported either from local sources or from a distance, and carriers or carters were in constant demand. At the King's Hall in the fifteenth century loads of stones were bought from quarries in Hinton and Burwell, Cambridgeshire, and from Barrington near Oxford, and carters from Cambridge, Stapelford and Hinton were hired

84. G. Jackson-Stops, "The building of the medieval college", in *New College Oxford 1379–1979*, pp. 156–64.
85. J. Newman, "The physical setting: new building and adaptation", in *HUO*, III, pp. 609–11.
86. Evans & Faith, "College estates and university finances 1350–1500", in *HUO*, II, p. 663.
87. For Chevynton, Janyns and Massyngham see H. Colvin & J. S. G. Simmons, *All Souls: an Oxford college and its buildings* (Oxford, Oxford University Press, 1989), p. 5.
88. See, for example, the situation at New College, Jackson-Stops, "The building of the medieval college", p. 159.

for their transport.[89] Broken stones or rubble ("roghwall" or "ragstone") and clunch (white limestone used for filling walls) were transported mainly from Burwell, slates from Stamford in Lincolnshire, timber from Haverill and Worlington in Suffolk, tiles from Wiggenhall in Norfolk, lime from Reach in Cambridgeshire, and sand and daub were bought locally.[90] From time to time, every college at Oxford and Cambridge had to contract for building materials, and the need for transportation must have been of prime importance for those engaged in the carrying trade. It is clear that the many master-craftsmen who, with their skilled and unskilled workers, were hired for university or college building projects were a significant, if temporary, component of the academic periphery. Through their building requirements, the English universities and their colleges made a vital contribution to their urban economies.

An arresting instance of the symbiotic relationship that existed between the English universities and the wider community resides in what may be called the Oxford system of "university extension". This operated on the fringes of the university and formed a link between the official teaching regime and the concerns of the business world. The kind of study involved was designed, not to prepare students for an official degree, but to give a training in practical subjects that would assist in non-academic areas of employment.[91] The subjects involved were related, in a much adulterated form, to *dictamen* and its legal counterpart, the *ars notaria*. *Dictamen* (*ars dictaminis*, *ars dictandi*) was the science of letter-writing and the rigorous drafting of different types of official documents, and the *ars notaria* pertained to the profession of notary. *Dictamen* provided an important training for clerks in papal, imperial, royal and episcopal service, and the *ars notaria*, the notarial art, was especially relevant for those areas of Europe wherever Roman or civil law predominated.[92]

---

89. King's Hall accounts, VII, fols 108v, 127v.
90. Cobban, *The King's Hall*, p. 217 and notes.
91. For this system of "university extension" see Cobban, *Medieval English universities*, pp. 344–8; Cobban, "Medieval universities in contemporary society", in *Intellectual life in the Middle Ages: essays presented to Margaret Gibson*, L. Smith & B. Ward (eds) (London & Rio Grande, Ohio, Hambledon Press, 1992), pp. 238–40; Evans, "The number, origins and careers of scholars", in *HUO*, II, pp. 523–6.
92. For *dictamen* and *dictatores* see Haskins, *Studies in medieval culture*, chs 1, 6, 9; see also Cobban, *The medieval universities: their development and organization*, pp. 221–2.

The *ars notaria* was not taught formally in England, and neither this discipline nor the *ars dictandi* were accorded faculty status at Oxford or Cambridge as was certainly the case in several Italian universities. Nevertheless, from the early-thirteenth century extra-curricular subjects were on offer at Oxford that contained elements of *dictamen* and the *ars notaria* and which had a direct bearing on many areas of employment. The topics in question included the drafting of charters, wills and letters, conveyancing, the keeping of accounts, court procedure, the French language, heraldry and possibly a training in estate management and husbandry for future bailiffs and seigniorial stewards.[93] The teachers of these subjects, who established their schools in the town of Oxford, were not necessarily graduates. They were, however, placed under the jurisdiction of two regent masters of the university, thereby acquiring at least a semi-official recognition.[94]

Prominent among the teachers of the "useful subjects" were Thomas Sampson, who taught in Oxford from *c*.1350 to 1409, and, in the early-fifteenth century, Simon O. and William Kingsmill, a London scrivener who had moved to Oxford.[95] While many of the students who frequented these licensed utilitarian courses appear to have come to Oxford for this specific purpose, others may have been casualties from the faculty of arts who had settled for a more practical and less onerous form of study.[96] An added attraction of these vocational courses was their brevity. Instead of the three or four years necessary for the lower arts degree, an intensive training in business studies could perhaps be compressed into six months or so.[97]

93. Gibson, *Statuta antiqua*, p. 240; H. G. Richardson, "Business training in medieval Oxford", *American Historical Review* **46**, 1940–1, pp. 259–80 and "An Oxford teacher of the fifteenth century", *BJRL* **23**, 1939, pp. 436–57; M. T. Clanchy, "*Moderni* in education and government in England", *Speculum* **50**, 1975, p. 685; D. Oschinsky, *Walter of Henley and other treatises of estate management and accounting* (Oxford, Clarendon Press, 1971), pp. 148, 226, 234.
94. Gibson, *Statuta antiqua*, p. 240.
95. On Thomas Sampson see J. J. Murphy, "Rhetoric in fourteenth-century Oxford", *Medium Aevum* **34**, 1965, pp. 16–17.
96. One of the letters of Thomas Sampson refers to the case of a youth who transferred from the faculty of arts to learn more practical skills under Sampson with a view to entering the service of a lay lord: see Salter, Pantin & Richardson, *Formularies*, II, p. 407.
97. See the model letter no. 21, *ibid.*, II, p. 372.

In the second half of the fifteenth century these business schools appear to have been gradually phased out at Oxford. In part, their disappearance may be explained by the superior competition provided by the Inns of Court in London where a parallel range of vocational studies was taught. No evidence has so far come to light to prove that a system of "university extension" operated in Cambridge, although the likelihood is that something similar to Oxford's system of vocational studies would have found an echo in England's other university. The fact that between the early-thirteenth and mid-fifteenth centuries Oxford University permitted non-degree courses to flourish shows that it was prepared to cater to some extent for the rudimentary and technical skills that did not properly fit the normal university experience. However, the teaching at Oxford of business and administrative techniques and elements of legal procedure was conducted on a more fragmented and less systematic plane than was the case with the sophisticated presentation of these topics in the Italian universities.

It is abundantly clear that the groups on the margins of the academic community made a substantial contribution to the life of the English universities. Whether college founders, university and college benefactors, university and college servants and "privileged persons", the varied role of women within the university environment, master-craftsmen and their skilled and unskilled workforces, and those engaged in "university extension", all of these groupings added to the vibrancy of university life and gave a necessary support to the academic core, the guilds of masters and associated students.

CHAPTER FIVE

Teaching and learning

Despite the many differences between the medieval universities in northern Europe and those in Italy, the Iberian peninsula, and the south of France, the essence of the system of teaching and learning at Oxford and Cambridge would have been immediately recognizable in any European centre of study. It is true that there were marked variations in the intellectual diets on offer. In the Italian universities legal studies predominated, often followed in importance by medicine. Arts subjects in Italy occupied a rather subordinate position until raised to prominence in the era of the Renaissance. Similarly, in the French provincial universities law was generally the leading area of study, although Montpellier was extremely important for medicine. The Spanish universities were less specialized and usually provided a fuller spread of disciplines, including theology, that had a rather low profile in the Italian and French provincial universities. The northern universities, those of England, Scotland, Scandinavia, Germany, Austria, Hungary, Bohemia and Poland, often had large arts faculties as an accompaniment to their superior faculty studies, and catered for a younger student clientele than was common in southern Europe. But whatever the particular academic concentrations of individual or groups of universities, the methods of teaching and learning were relatively similar throughout Europe.

Students at the English universities, in common with their counterparts right across continental Europe, were the recipients of a conservative teaching process. The main function of university teaching was to inculcate in students the appropriate segments of an inherited corpus of learning that was an amalgam of Greek, Graeco-Roman, Arabic and the European Christian traditions of scholarship. Whatever the disciplines in question, whether the arts subjects of the *trivium* and *quadrivium* or one of the superior faculties of law (Roman or civil and canon law), theology or medicine, university teachers aimed to transmit a cumulative body of learning that had been digested, debated and commented upon over the centuries by a series of accepted authorities. Study was usually conducted within the limits set by the recognized authorities in each discipline. Undergraduates were encouraged to question more as a form of training than as a genuine attempt to challenge the authoritative sources.[1] In theory, the accepted authorities were supposed to be subject to the supreme governance of the Bible, although the polarized nature of some of the ingredients of classical and Christian thought made this an often insoluble dilemma.[2] Scholars, both in arts and in the higher faculties, were expected to absorb in a measured form a body of received wisdom relating to their subject of study. At the same time, their critical acumen was developed through their training in Aristotelian logic. From the twelfth century logical analysis had come to be applied to virtually all branches of learning and students, whether in arts, law, theology or medicine, had to equip themselves to be adequate practitioners of logic. In so doing, they gained a facility in the application of rational argument to intellectual propositions, the essence of the scholastic method as it had evolved from the twelfth century and even earlier.[3]

The crucial role assigned to logic in the learning process is exemplified by the fact that Aristotelian logic and philosophy came to have primacy of place in the arts course leading to the BA degree at Oxford, Cambridge and Paris in the thirteenth century. That is to say, from an early stage in the lives of these centres of learning logic and philosophy had reduced grammar and rhetoric, the other subjects of the *trivium*, to subordinate positions.

The twin arts of grammar and rhetoric had been fundamental pillars of the literary humanism of the eleventh and twelfth centuries. But the

1. Cobban, *Medieval English universities*, pp. 170–1.
2. On the overriding authority of the Bible see Leff, *Paris and Oxford Universities in the thirteenth and fourteenth centuries*, p. 5.
3. On the revival of logic or dialectic see, for example, D. Knowles, *The evolution of medieval thought*, 2nd edn, D. E. Luscombe & C. N. L. Brooke (eds) (Harlow, England, Longman, 1988), pp. 85–97 and on scholasticism, pp. xiv, 76–82. On logic see also Cobban, *Medieval English universities*, pp. 12–13.

dramatic revival of logic that dates from the late-tenth and eleventh centuries and reached its apogee in the twelfth and thirteenth centuries led to an eclipse of the literary aspects of the classical heritage. The reduction of classical literary studies in the curricula of Paris and the English universities to basic Latin grammar and to elementary forms of rhetoric was the climax of a movement that, a shade earlier, had brought John of Salisbury, the Christian humanist scholar, into the field as trenchant critic. John of Salisbury was not opposed to logic or dialectic as such. Logic had a useful role to play as part of a broad educational programme. Logic, by itself, was an instrument of enquiry and not an education. John of Salisbury and fellow Christian humanists were deeply convinced that the excessive place accorded to logic in the arts faculties of Europe's earliest universities would produce shallow logicians who had taken short cuts in education and were ill-prepared as teachers of the next generation of students. They were not properly educated because they were not versed in the liberal arts and the classical authors.[4] Here was thrown into direct conflict the utilitarian or vocational and the non-utilitarian concepts of education. However, the intellectual currents of the age ran counter to the arguments of the Christian humanists, and the engulfing tide of logic could not be stemmed. The recovery of the greater part of Aristotle's logic seemed to provide scholars with a method of analytical enquiry whereby they could arrive at a more profound understanding of the apparently chaotic world. Through the subtleties of logical analyses, it seemed possible to penetrate to the heart of every field of human study. For its supporters, logic or dialectic was the embodiment of all that was innovative and exciting in the intellectual life and was the key that would unlock universal truths.

While logic is now generally regarded by society at large as a purely academic and even esoteric subject, in the medieval period it was viewed as a discipline of direct community value. A thorough training in logic was considered to be an excellent preparation for a legion of professional employments. Expertise in logical analyses sharpened the mind, attuned it for fine distinctions and placed a premium on intellectual

4. See John of Salisbury's views in D. D. McGarry (trans.), *The Metalogicon of John of Salisbury* (Berkeley, Calif., University of California Press, 1955), pp. 13–16, 93–5, 100–1, 244–5; see also McGarry, "Educational theory in the *Metalogicon* of John of Salisbury", *Speculum* **23**, 1948, pp. 659–75.

precision. These were the qualities of mind that were prized for almost any type of professional activity in the Middle Ages. Dialectical training was equally relevant for service in government or in the church, in the law, in a teaching post in a school or university, for service in a lay or clerical household, or for royal or papal diplomatic business. It is therefore no surprise that logic, and indeed the whole training in arts, was valued as a vocational branch of education, no less utilitarian than the disciplines of law or medicine.

There is some truth in the criticism of humanist scholars of the late-medieval period that logical excesses were a block to constructive argument. In the hands of less able scholars logical analyses could be reduced to an arid formalism, and nonsensical discussion of absurd propositions undeniably damaged the reputation of the scholastic method. But to imply, as did some humanist scholars, that this was the intellectual norm in the three centuries preceding the Renaissance era is a historical distortion of some magnitude. For the most part, a sound training in logic was both an essential grounding for most areas of study and an appropriate mental asset for extra-university careers.

It is clear that the study of logic dominated the lives of English students throughout the whole of the arts course, and overwhelmingly so in the first two years. The principal texts used were those works relating to the "old logic" and to the "new logic" of Aristotle, along with their many commentaries.[5] Supplementary to Aristotelian logic were treatises that were compiled in the medieval period and known as the *logica moderna* or modern logic. A Cambridge statute of the late-fourteenth century specified three that were in current use in the university lecture rooms.[6] The Oxford statutes do not actually mention logical texts of medieval vintage, but manuscript sources reveal that medieval logic was used extensively to supplement Aristotelian texts at both of the English universities.[7] Indeed, the proliferation of logical tractates by English scholars in the thirteenth and fourteenth centuries made Oxford an eminent European centre for logic. Writers on logic such as Robert Grosseteste, William of Sherwood, Robert Kilwardby, William of Ockham, Walter Burley, John Dumbleton, William Heytesbury,

---

5. For the main logical texts used at Oxford and Cambridge see Leader, *The university to 1546*, pp. 123, 124; Courtenay, *Schools and scholars in fourteenth-century England*, p. 32.
6. *Camb. Docs*, I, p. 384.
7. Leader, *The university to 1546*, p. 124.

Thomas Bradwardine, Richard Swyneshed and Richard Billingham produced logical texts that were widely used in continental universities, some of them being adopted as official works. This is not to say that these Oxford writers were everywhere well received. In particular, the works of Ockham, Heytesbury and Swyneshed that belonged to the nominalist philosophical school were unpopular among many Italian scholars who regarded their type of logical scholarship as pernicious and corrupting.[8] Nevertheless, there can be no doubt that Oxford University was a fertile producer of material for the study and teaching of logic in Europe's universities. Cambridge fared less well. It produced fewer writers on logic and it was clearly not as creative a centre of logical writing as Oxford. It is probable that many of the Cambridge texts on logic, some of them anonymous, were derivative versions of Oxford treatises.[9]

Apart from Aristotelian texts and their commentaries, the *logica moderna*, and specialist treatises dealing with logical questions, there were general primers on logic that were an aid to the undergraduate population. These primers were made up of tracts concerning different aspects of logic, some of them by named authors and others of anonymous attribution. The Cambridge tradition of primers was called the *Logica Cantabrigiensis*, and the corresponding Oxford tradition the *Logica Oxoniensis*. These were designed mainly for arts students who were not complete beginners, and they may also have been used by bachelors of arts for teaching purposes.[10] The commanding role of logic in the arts course at both Oxford and Cambridge is further underlined when it is considered that the four years that were usually necessary for a student to acquire the BA degree, the lower arts degree, was longer than that required for the MA, the superior arts degree, at many continental universities.

While logic was the bedrock of a training in arts in the English universities, grammar and rhetoric had subordinate but recognizable parts to play in the course leading to the degree of BA. Before a youth could embark upon the faculty of arts, a proficiency in Latin was necessary. The expectation was that this would normally be acquired in a

---

8. See Fletcher, "The faculty of arts", pp. 393–4.
9. Leader, *The university to 1546*, pp. 126–35.
10. For these primers see *ibid.*, pp. 133–4; also P. O. Lewry, "Grammar, logic and rhetoric 1220–1320", in *HUO*, I, pp. 407–9.

grammar school or through private tuition before the youth came up to university. However, some youths had not made adequate progress in Latin when they arrived at university, and this could be remedied by attending the school or hostel of a grammar master in the university town. One such grammar hostel in Cambridge was run by a master of grammar, Thomas Chambre, and later by Thomas Ayera, in the closing years of the fifteenth century.[11] Once launched upon the arts course, students would receive instruction in modal grammar, a type of speculative grammar concerned with the logical analysis of language, and with signification. Signification was an exercise that arose from the perennial question of universals that had resolved itself throughout Europe and in the English universities into the opposed realist and nominalist philosophical schools of thought.[12] In grammatical terms, signification was the act of determining within a particular sentence whether the words represented universals or only individual entities. For a realist, a word such as "women" was a general concept with its own inherent reality. For the nominalist, the term was only a name for a group of individual women. It had no meaning beyond this, and no reality as a general concept. In this matter of signification it is clear that grammar within the arts course incorporated both logic and philosophy. Such exercises in signification were probably quite taxing for arts students in their first or second year at university.

For those students at Oxford and Cambridge who were fired by an interest in grammar and wished to specialize in the subject, there were opportunities to train as grammar masters in order to teach either in a school or university. Teachers of grammar at both universities operated under the aegis of the faculty of arts, although they were not accepted as full members of it. It seems that very few students in any given year opted to pursue the specialist course in grammar that could lead to the MGram degree. Of those that did follow the course, some seemed not to have aimed for the degree. Rather, they persevered until they had reached the stage where they were deemed sufficiently qualified to teach grammar even without the formal seal of degree approval.[13]

---

11. Stokes, *The medieval hostels of the University of Cambridge*, pp. 46–7; Stamp, *Michaelhouse*, p. 21; Emden, *BRUC*, p. 25.
12. On signification see Leader, *The university to 1546*, pp. 112–13.
13. For a discussion of the grammar texts in use at both English universities see *ibid.*, pp. 111–16.

The third component of the *trivium*, rhetoric, remained a very sub-ordinate part of the arts course in the pre-humanist age. More often than not it was regarded as a mere element of grammar. It is difficult to define the content of rhetoric within the arts course at any given time because there were several different facets to this subject. It could include classical rhetoric, poetry, *dictamen* or the *ars dictaminis*, drama and preaching. Apart from *dictamen* at Oxford in the fourteenth century, there is not much evidence of systematic teaching of rhetoric at either Oxford or Cambridge before the fifteenth century.[14] What desultory teaching of rhetoric there was appears to have relied upon an amalgam of classical and medieval texts. With the coming of the northern Renaissance, however, there was a renewed emphasis upon classical and recent humanist works.[15]

While logic, supplemented by elements of grammar and rhetoric, dominated the lives of students at Oxford and Cambridge during their first two years, the third and fourth years of the course leading to the BA degree followed different patterns at each university. At Cambridge, the third and fourth years seem to have been largely given over to the study of Aristotle's natural philosophy.[16] By contrast, Oxford students were required by statute to study a series of texts relating to the quad-rivial subjects, broadly defined as mathematical and scientific, and treatises on natural philosophy are not specified.[17] However, the evidence of dispensations from statutory requirements in fifteenth-century Oxford indicates that at least some of Aristotle's natural philosophy was indeed studied.[18]

It is not possible to determine with complete accuracy the pre-cise ingredients of the course leading to the BA degree, and the same applies to the curriculum to be followed by a bachelor of arts in preparation for the MA. What may be said with reasonable surety is that it consisted of further study of quadrivial subjects in conjunc-tion with the three philosophies, natural and moral philosophy and

14. *ibid.*, p. 118; also Murphy, "Rhetoric in fourteenth-century Oxford", *Medium Aevum* **34**, 1965, pp. 13–14.
15. On rhetorical texts used in the English universities see Leader, *The university to 1546*, pp. 117–21.
16. Hackett, *The original statutes of Cambridge University*, pp. 297–9; Leader, *The university to 1546*, p. 93.
17. Gibson, *Statuta antiqua*, p. 200.
18. Leader, *The university to 1546*, pp. 94–5, 159.

metaphysics.[19] The quadrivial disciplines comprised arithmetic, music, geometry and astronomy.[20] In the English universities the average scholar did not pursue these subjects to any sophisticated level.

Arithmetic was a necessary groundwork for all study in the *quadrivium*, and was a skill that was fundamental for music, then seen as a branch of mathematics. Music, as a theoretical discipline, was concerned with the study of harmonic proportion, and this was balanced by a training in musical practice. Some scholars sought to specialize in music, and from the late-fifteenth century music degrees were granted at both Oxford and Cambridge. The first known recipient of a music degree at Cambridge was Thomas St Just, who became warden of the King's Hall in 1467 and who acquired a doctoral degree in music in 1461–2.[21] By the early-sixteenth century candidates for a musical degree were sometimes required to compose a mass and antiphon. Occasionally, it is stipulated that these compositions are to be performed on the day of the admission to the degree.[22] Some degrees in music were awarded, not so much on the basis of university study, but as a recognition of a successful career as a practising musician, although matriculation was always necessary.[23] Musical instruments are found in the inventories of goods of deceased university personnel that are listed in the Oxford chancellor's register of the fifteenth century. Among the items specified are an old harp (*antiqua cithara*), a broken lute (*lute fracta*), a hornpipe, and another *lewt* and harp (*harpe*).[24]

Geometry was an umbrella title for a variety of topics including geometry itself, optics, statics and the mechanical arts. It had important applications for measuring and surveying, and was a vital preparation for the study of astronomy.[25] In connection with geometry there is the intriguing case of William Malleveray who was made a "bachelor in

19. *ibid.*, p. 95; *Camb. Docs*, I, pp. 360–1; Gibson, *Statuta antiqua*, pp. 234–5.
20. Much information on quadrivial subjects in the twelfth century and earlier is provided by G. Beaujouan, "The transformation of the quadrivium", in *Renaissance and renewal in the twelfth century*, R. L. Benson & G. Constable (eds) (Oxford, Clarendon Press, 1982), pp. 463–87.
21. Emden, *BRUC*, p. 503; Cobban, *The King's Hall*, pp. 286–7.
22. F. Ll. Harrison, "Music at Oxford before 1500", in *HUO*, II, pp. 367–8; Leader, *The university to 1546*, p. 144.
23. Harrison, "Music at Oxford before 1500", p. 367; Leader, *The university to 1545*, p. 143.
24. Salter, *Registrum cancellarii oxoniensis*, I, pp. 37, 160; II, pp. 101, 129, 327.
25. Leader, *The university to 1546*, pp. 144–5.

156

geometry" at Cambridge in 1492.[26] If this was an attempt to establish a precedent for such a degree it seems to have failed because there are no further references to this type of degree at either of the English universities. Linked with geometry was the science of perspective (*perspectiva*). This was concerned with the properties of light and the study of light rays. Among the pioneering texts used for this subject were thirteenth-century works by Robert Grosseteste, Roger Bacon and John Pecham, and treatises by Witelo, the Polish scholar whose scientific interests were closely aligned to those of Grosseteste.[27]

Of the quadrivial studies, English scholars on the arts course probably devoted most attention to astronomy, using a mixture of classical, Arabic and more contemporary sources.[28] In addition to astronomical theory, astronomy had several practical applications. For centuries, astronomy had been used to calculate movable dates of the feast occasions of the ecclesiastical year. Because the planets were believed to have an influence on human affairs and on human health, physicians often acquired a knowledge of astronomy so that they could take account of astronomical data in their medical treatments. Physicians commonly had recourse to circular diagrams of signs of the zodiac as an aid to cures.[29]

Astronomical tables were widely circulated in European universities. Although they were not prescribed by statute at Oxford and Cambridge, there is abundant evidence from manuscripts belonging to scholars that they were in common use.[30] Many of these tables were modified versions of the celebrated astronomical tables that were compiled for Alfonso X of Castile, and others were of wholly Arabic origin. These tables were deployed to monitor the movements of the planets and to predict eclipses and other celestial phenomena. The interest in astronomy brought with it the need to invest in a certain amount of hardware. Astrolabes that were designed to take altitude readings might be owned by more affluent scholars as is evidenced by

---

26. For this case see Bateson (ed.), *Grace Book B Part I*, p. 38.
27. For more details see Leader, *The university to 1546*, pp. 145–6.
28. For the standard texts used in astronomy see, for example, *ibid.*, pp. 146–7.
29. Such a diagram is reproduced by M. Hussey, *Chaucer's world: a pictorial companion* (Cambridge, Cambridge University Press, 1967), p. 103 (plate no. 71).
30. Bennett, *Chaucer at Oxford and at Cambridge*, pp. 73–9; Leader, *The university to 1546*, p. 148.

the fact that they were sometimes given as cautions.[31] It is true that the young Oxford scholar, Nicholas, in Chaucer's *The miller's tale* kept an astrolabe at the head of the bed. This, however, is unlikely to have been typical for the average scholar because of the expense involved. It has to be borne in mind that, as the author of a treatise on the astrolabe, Chaucer had a special interest in this instrument and was likely to give it fictional prominence. In addition to the astrolabe, scholars who had the means might invest in a quadrant, an instrument for taking angular measurements, or a planisphere or globes made of wood or metal. Astrolabes and other instruments for the astronomer's craft were purchased by individual colleges, and Merton College, Oxford, had an impressive range of such objects as was fitting for a college with an innovative scientific reputation.[32]

Astrology was ambiguously regarded in the English universities as it was in universities throughout Europe. Many ecclesiastics denounced the subject because of its pagan associates and affinity with magic and the black arts. Some scholars argued that it was a flawed subject that did not rest on scientific principles.[33] Nevertheless, astrology had an organic relationship with the important university discipline of astronomy. A basic knowledge of mathematics and of astronomy was essential for an astrologer in order to perform the complex computations relating to the workings of the planetary system.[34] Using the framework of astronomy to confer a degree of respectability, scholars versed in astrology and astrologers outside the university context followed their predictive art in relation to mainstream and domestic events and to personal fortunes of the horoscopic kind. Magdalen College, Oxford, provides an interesting case of a college that officially hired the services of astrologers. In 1502 the fellows of Magdalen made payments to

31. S. M. Leathes (ed.), *Grace Book A*, Cambridge Antiquarian Society, Luard Memorial Series I (Cambridge, Cambridge University Press, 1897), pp. 181–2; Bateson, *Grace Book B Part I*, pp. 127, 207; M. Bateson (ed.), *Grace Book B Part II*, Cambridge Antiquarian Society, Luard Memorial Series III (Cambridge, Cambridge University Press, 1905), p. 18.
32. Bennett, *Chaucer at Oxford and at Cambridge*, pp. 75–6, 78; Leader, *The university to 1546*, pp. 148–9.
33. See the discussion by J. North, "The quadrivium", in Ridder-Symoens (ed.), *A history of the university in Europe*, I, pp. 357–8.
34. See, for example, M. Feingold, *The mathematicians' apprenticeship: science, universities and society in England 1560–1640* (Cambridge, Cambridge University Press, 1984), p. 18.

3. A brass astrolabe of *c*.1350 in the possession of Merton College, Oxford. This instrument was probably commissioned by the college or by one of the fellows and it is indicative of Merton's reputation as one of the foremost scientific centres of Europe in the fourteenth century. This astrolabe is similar to the one described in Chaucer's *Treatise on the astrolabe* of *c*.1380. It is known that Chaucer had connections with Merton.

several astrologers, one of them from Westminster, in an attempt to discover who had stolen £112 from the bursary.[35] The importance of astronomical data for the diagnosis and treatment of patients has already been mentioned. In this regard, the specific study of astrology may well have been promoted in European medical faculties in the fourteenth and fifteenth centuries. There was, however, considerable variation in the emphasis placed upon medical astrology in Europe's

35. R. Chandler, *The life of William Waynflete, Bishop of Winchester* (London, White & Cochrane, 1811), pp. 277–8, *n*. k.

universities. At universities such as Bologna and Padua the teaching of astrology for the benefit of medical students was seemingly actively encouraged.[36] There was probably less official endorsement of astrology in the English universities, but it was certainly a recognized component in the arts course, albeit one that sheltered within the respectability of astronomy, the parent subject.

In conjunction with further study in the quadrivial subjects, bachelors of arts in pursuit of the MA made a prolonged study of philosophy. It has already been pointed out that the third and fourth years of the arts course leading to the BA at Cambridge were heavily committed to the study of Aristotle's natural philosophy. At Oxford, undergraduates in their third and fourth years were obliged to place more weight on quadrivial subjects, although it is known that a fair amount of natural philosophy was studied as well. In the three years or so between the lower and higher arts degrees the three philosophies, natural, moral and metaphysical, formed a vital part of the curriculum. This training in philosophy was considered to be valuable for intellectual growth and a necessary preparation for scholastic theology. These philosophical disciplines were based upon the fundamental texts of Aristotle and augmented by the works of a galaxy of commentators ranging from the outstanding Arabic scholars, Avicenna and Averroes, to a lengthy chain of Christian theologians and philosophers. Of particular note were Boethius, Robert Grosseteste, Thomas Aquinas, Bonaventure, Duns Scotus, Walter Burley, William of Ockham, the Catalonian followers of Scotus, Antonius Andreas and John Marbres (Johannes Canonicus), and the enigmatic John Dedecus.[37] The central texts for natural philosophy were the *Libri naturales* or scientific works of Aristotle. These embraced the *Physics*, *De anima* (on the soul), *De caelo* (on the heavens), *Metheora* (meteors), *De generatione* (on generation), *De animalibus* (on animals) and the *Parva naturalia*, the lesser works on psychology.[38]

The texts of Aristotle, in conjunction with their many commentaries, were studied by means of the scholastic method. The essence of this

36. N. Siraisi, "The faculty of medicine", in Ridder-Symoens (ed.), *A history of the university in Europe*, I, pp. 376, 383–4.
37. See, for example, Leader, *The university to 1546*, pp. 155–9; Fletcher, "Developments in the faculty of arts", in *HUO*, II, p. 344.
38. Leff, *Paris and Oxford Universities in the thirteenth and fourteenth centuries*, p. 132; Courtenay, *Schools and scholars in fourteenth-century England*, p. 32.

methodology was the examination of propositions or questions from a text by means of logical analyses. Considering the opinions of different commentators on the issue, arguments for and against were adduced and compared, and conclusions were reached that seemed to embody the best rational solution to the problem. Sometimes Aristotelian propositions appeared to be wholly irreconcilable with Christian assumptions, and this was the inevitable consequence of trying to fit the cumulative body of Christian learning and doctrine within a pagan philosophical frame. This dilemma raised the massive problem as to whether philosophy was to remain forever the handmaid to Christian theology or whether it was to become an independent discipline. Allied to this was the question of whether a truth arrived at by philosophical means could be true even if it ran counter to theological truth. Such issues were fought out with fierce intensity at Paris University in the late-thirteenth century. The *Summa theologiae* of Thomas Aquinas of *c*.1270 had attempted the most mature and comprehensive synthesis of Aristotelian philosophy and Christian theology. Arguing that too many concessions had been made to Aristotle's philosophy, some of Aquinas' propositions were condemned in 1277 by the Bishop of Paris, supported by the conservative theologians of Paris. Eleven days later, and in imitation of Paris, the Archbishop of Canterbury, Robert Kilwardby, condemned several propositions of Aquinas at Oxford.[39] Presumably, the divisive theological and philosophical debates of Paris that found a reflection at Oxford would also have reverberated among Cambridge scholars. There is, however, no dramatic evidence of condemnations of intellectual propositions in late-thirteenth century Cambridge. Nevertheless, the repercussions of these monumental intellectual contests must have percolated down to English students who were studying philosophy on the arts course. The inherently controversial nature of the material would have given it a vibrancy and relevance that heightened its appeal even for the most mediocre of students.

Moral philosophy, divided by Aristotle into ethics, economics and politics, occupied a far smaller part of a bachelor's study for the degree

---

39. For the complexities surrounding these condemnations see, conveniently, Knowles, *The evolution of medieval thought*, 2nd edn, Luscombe & Brooke (eds), pp. 265–73; J. I. Catto, "Theology and theologians 1220–1320", in *HUO*, I, pp. 498–9; M. Haren, *Medieval thought: the western intellectual tradition from antiquity to the thirteenth century* (London, Macmillan, 1985), pp. 194–211.

of MA. The key texts employed were Aristotle's *Ethics* and *Politics*, with commentaries on these works by Thomas Aquinas and Walter Burley. Many classical texts, including those of Seneca, Ovid and Cicero, were harnessed to the study of moral philosophy as also were the works of humanist writers such as Boccaccio and Petrarch.[40] The availability of Aristotle's *Politics*, through the Latin translation in 1260 of William of Moerbeke, the Flemish Dominican, brought with it a radical challenge to contemporary political thinking. From this stimulus there emerged the *De regimine principum* (on the rule of princes), written in 1277–9 by the Augustinian friar, Giles of Rome (Aegidius Romanus), and which became a much studied work for moral philosophy at both Oxford and Cambridge. In addition, Boethius' *De consolatione philosophiae* (on the consolation of philosophy) remained a popular standard source for ethical debate.[41]

The third branch of philosophy, metaphysics, was considered suitable for only the most advanced students in arts. The fundamental text was Aristotle's *Metaphysics*, augmented by commentaries by Averroes, Aquinas and Duns Scotus. Of greater import than any of these, however, was the *Quaestiones super metaphysicam* (questions on the *Metaphysics*) by Antonius Andreas, a close follower of the realist philosophy of Duns Scotus.[42]

The discussion so far has concerned the arts curriculum before the impact of humanism. The humanist infiltration from the second half of the fifteenth century was a gradual process. It began in a superficial and haphazard manner, put down deeper roots towards the close of the fifteenth century and became more institutionalized through endowed university and college lectureships in the course of the sixteenth century.[43] Moreover, St John's College, founded at Cambridge in 1511, and Corpus Christi College, established at Oxford in 1517, were in part designed as havens for humanist teaching. Despite these developments, there was no comprehensive humanist plan for the systematic reformation of teaching and learning in the English universities, only

---

40. Leader, *The university to 1546*, p. 163.
41. *ibid.*, pp. 163, 165, 166.
42. *ibid.*, p. 168.
43. See, for example, R. Weiss, *Humanism in England during the fifteenth century*, 2nd edn (Oxford, Basil Blackwell, 1957) and J. McConica, *English humanists and Reformation politics* (Oxford, Clarendon Press, 1965), pp. 76–105.

an incorporation of selected elements of the new learning done in a piecemeal manner. During the sixteenth century no more than modest adjustments were made to the arts course, and this also applied to the curricula in theology, civil law and medicine, canon law being suppressed in 1535.[44] For this reason, the English universities never became prominent centres of humanist activity comparable in scale with many universities in continental Europe. Humanist tracts were added to the arts course in the English universities, especially in relation to rhetoric and mathematics, and there was an emphasis on Greek, humanist Latin and Hebrew, the languages that were important for the comparative study of biblical texts.[45] At Cambridge there was a statutory reduction in 1488 in the amount of logic to be studied.[46] This apart, the Aristotelian system of logic remained largely intact. One beneficial effect of humanist influence on logic is that it may well have countered some of the more introspective technicalities of the discipline. By setting logic within a humanist framework, the subject was probably rendered a more suitable training for scholars who were to participate in public service in a world that had partially succumbed to Renaissance values.[47]

Taking stock of the arts course leading to both the lower degree of BA and the higher degree of MA, it can scarcely be said to measure up to a realization of the Graeco-Roman notion of the seven liberal arts, the theoretical underpinning of medieval education. While there was a laudable spread of disparate elements, the overriding grip of Aristotelian logic and philosophy prevented an equal emphasis on each of the trivial and quadrivial subjects. This was a clear departure from the concept of the seven liberal arts as the basis of the educational experience that had been transmitted to medieval Europe through scholars such as Cicero, Varro, St Augustine, Martianus Capella, Cassiodorus and Isidore

---

44. See the comments of J. McConica, "The social relations of Tudor Oxford", *TRHS*, 5th ser. **27**, 1977, p. 132.
45. J. M. Fletcher, "Change and resistance to change: a consideration of the development of English and German universities during the sixteenth century", *History of Universities* **1**, 1981, pp. 10, 12, 13; also L. Jardine, "Humanism and the sixteenth-century Cambridge arts course", *History of Education* **4**, 1975, pp. 16–31. See also Cobban, *Medieval English universities*, pp. 250–4.
46. *Camb. Docs*, I, p. 361; D. R. Leader, "Professorships and academic reform at Cambridge: 1488–1520", *Sixteenth Century Journal* **14**, 1983, p. 218.
47. See the discussion by J. McConica, "Humanism and Aristotle in Tudor Oxford", *EHR* **94**, 1979, pp. 291–317.

of Seville. Cicero's ideal of the learned man, the *doctus orator*, was one who combined a deep knowledge of all the branches of learning with a broad experience of the practical problems of life. It was a type of education that aimed to make a man learned, humane and just, and qualified to take a leading role in society.[48] This educational ideal that was echoed by the Christian humanists of the twelfth century could not be accommodated by universities that had evolved as responses to the need to provide a utilitarian brand of education to meet the professional, governmental, and ecclesiastical requirements of society.

One point of considerable interest is that the utilitarian emphasis in the arts course did not support the notion of a rigid division between the arts and sciences. While the polarity between classical and Christian learning was an ever-present reality and gave rise to many exacting difficulties, near-insoluble problems and much fierce intellectual debate, English scholars were shielded from the modern idea of a cultural divide that seeks to separate the arts from the sciences. The combination of arts with scientific and mathematical subjects in the course leading to the MA is a convincing negation of such an artificial dichotomy. Moreover, the primacy of logic for so long in the arts course at Oxford and Cambridge, and indeed at Paris, and its equally important application to the higher faculty studies of theology, law and medicine, meant that the analytical talent was deemed to be the most valuable asset that a university scholar could have in the quest for a penetrative understanding of the problems and mysteries of the world. The contemplative or meditative approach to truth found a full expression outside the English universities in, for example, the forms of mysticism prevalent in England in the fourteenth and early-fifteenth centuries and also, to some extent, in the monastic orders. Within the universities, however, rational enquiry, as embodied in logical analyses, reigned supreme as the fundamental building-block of intellectual life in all its manifestations.

A training in arts was the groundwork for most areas of further study. The degree of MA was necessary for all secular scholars who wished to proceed to theology. This consideration did not apply to the

---

48. For Cicero's educational philosophy see, for example, A. Gwynn, *Roman education from Cicero to Quintilian* (Oxford, Clarendon Press, 1926), pp. 57–8, 100–1, 118–22; see also P. A. Olson, *The journey to wisdom: self-education in patristic and medieval literature* (Lincoln, Nebr., University of Nebraska Press, 1995), p. 14.

friars at Oxford and Cambridge. The most prominent of the mendicant orders, the Dominicans and Franciscans, were supported by a hierarchy of schools ranging from elementary to advanced levels and embracing a spread of subjects in arts, philosophy and theology. It could be said that the orders harboured what were tantamount to decentralized universities that were wholly adequate for the educational needs of many of their members. The ablest scholars, however, aspired to study for theology degrees at Oxford and Cambridge under their own mendicant masters. The mendicant orders would only allow their students to associate with the faculty of theology, contending that their students were already well trained in arts and furthermore that they should not be exposed to the alleged profanities that were inherent in the teaching of the secular masters. The claim of the friars to be exempt from taking the degree of MA before entering upon the study of theology was a much-contested issue, but eventually it was accepted by secular masters at both universities.[49] This privilege was also extended to monks at Cambridge. Monks at Oxford, however, were denied the same automatic exemption, although some monks, without an arts degree, were granted graces or dispensations to proceed to theology.[50]

Theology in the English universities was based largely upon the study of the Bible and the *Sentences* of Peter Lombard along with numerous glosses and commentaries on these texts, the works of the early Church Fathers, including Jerome, Augustine and Gregory, sermon collections, treatises on preaching, *florilegia* or excerpts of biblical and patristic passages, and books of *exempla* or short stories for use in sermons. Until modified to some degree by the advent of humanism, theology at Oxford and Cambridge took the form of scholastic theology. This was characterized by the application of logical analyses to theological and to selected philosophical propositions that had theological implications. The philosophical questions were often derived from Aristotle's

49. See Leader, *The university to 1546*, pp. 54–8, 171. For the series of disputes between the friars and the secular masters at Oxford see Rashdall, *Universities*, III, pp. 66–76; Rashdall, "The friars preachers versus the university to AD 1311–1313", in *Collectanea* **II**, M. Burrows (ed.), Oxford Historical Society **16** (Oxford, Clarendon Press, 1890), pp. 193–273; Leff, *Paris and Oxford Universities in the thirteenth and fourteenth centuries*, pp. 103–6. For disputes between friars and secular masters at Cambridge see, for example, Hackett, *The original statutes of Cambridge University*, pp. 241–4.
50. Aston, Duncan & Evans, "The medieval alumni of the University of Cambridge", p. 60, *n.* 141.

philosophy or from the opinions of a multitude of Aristotelian commentators. In this manner, theology, philosophy and logic were intimately intertwined.

For most of the thirteenth century Oxford theologians seem to have followed in the wake of Paris. By the 1280s, however, Oxford masters were beginning to make contributions to theological controversy on a par with those of their Parisian colleagues. It is perhaps fair to argue that Oxford's original theological era was launched with the realist philosophy of Duns Scotus towards the end of the century, was continued along very different nominalist lines with William of Ockham, and reached a zenith in the first half of the fourteenth century. Indeed, the originality of the thought of Scotus and Ockham was scarcely equalled anywhere in contemporary European universities.[51] This level of innovatory theological scholarship was not sustained after the university was embroiled in the throes of Wyclifism in the late-fourteenth century. In the fifteenth century Oxford masters of theology were prone to adopt conservative attitudes, and to regard the perpetuation of sound and established theological scholarship as more important than the subtleties and potential dangers of unrestrained originality. A renewed emphasis upon unvarnished biblical instruction, a strong commitment to preaching, more reliance upon the work of the early Church Fathers and less upon the highly-wrought speculative learning of the fourteenth century, and an openness to new ideas filtering through from the Italian Renaissance, these are some of the features of Oxford theology in the fifteenth century.[52]

While less is known about theology at Cambridge than at Oxford, it needs to be stressed that before c.1359 only Paris, Oxford and Cambridge had the right to confer degrees in theology.[53] This fact alone would seem to testify to the European regard for the Cambridge

---

51. See Catto, "Theology and theologians 1220–1320", in *HUO*, I, pp. 471–517.
52. J. I. Catto, "Theology after Wycliffism", in *HUO*, II, pp. 263–80.
53. It seems that Florence University had acquired this right by 1359: see Rashdall, *Universities*, II, p. 50, *n*. 1. Bologna had the right to grant degrees in theology only from the inception of its faculty of theology in 1364. The university that was established by Pope Innocent IV in the Roman curia in 1245 conferred degrees in theology of a rather unusual kind. They were given largely to members of religious orders, mostly Dominicans, and the Pope claimed the right to dispense with residential or study requirements: *ibid.*, II, p. 30.

faculty of theology. The prominence of theology at Cambridge, especially in the thirteenth and fourteenth centuries, is to be attributed in
large measure to the friars who dominated the faculty before their grip
lessened in the fifteenth century.[54] A significant proportion of the friars
in the theology faculty had come from the Continent attracted, in
part, by the university's capacity to grant theological degrees. This
international mix in the faculty of theology was a welcome feature in
a centre of learning that recruited relatively few foreign scholars who
were not members of the mendicant orders. It may be remarked that
Cambridge theologians were vigorously attuned to the religious con-
troversies of their time, whether it was the Great Schism, Wyclifism
and Lollardy, or the celebrated attack by William of St Amour on the
mendicants.[55] The activities of the Cambridge faculty of theology mir-
rored those of Oxford, although in a seemingly more subdued manner.
Speculative theology, biblical scholarship and an emphasis upon the
practicalities of preaching were the central ingredients of Cambridge
theology in the medieval period. It has to be said, however, that much
research needs to be done before anything like a fully rounded appraisal
of Cambridge theology can be made.

Whereas a degree in arts was a prerequisite for theology, it was not a
necessity for a law course, although many law students, if they did not
possess an arts degree, would have spent one or two years in arts as a
sensible basis for their legal studies. Exceptions do occur, and the fellows
of King's College, Cambridge, were actually forbidden by statute to
proceed to canon or civil law unless they had taken the degree of MA
and had completed their necessary regency in arts, the obligatory time
to be spent teaching in the arts faculty upon reaching the position of a
qualified master.[56] It was certainly an advantage for an aspiring law student to have some experience of arts because a grounding in grammar,
rhetoric and above all in logic were all suitable tools for a legal training.

The faculties of civil and canon law at Oxford and Cambridge were
in theory separate, but in practice they were interlinked. This arose
from the fact that some study in civil law was required for a degree in

54. Aston, Duncan & Evans, "The medieval alumni of the University of Cambridge",
    pp. 59–63.
55. Leader, *The university to 1546*, pp. 182–3.
56. *Camb. Docs*, II, p. 483.

canon law, and a candidate for a degree in civil law was obliged to have studied a measure of canon law.[57] In the thirteenth and early-fourteenth centuries it appears that the faculty of canon law was the more dominant of the two faculties at Oxford and Cambridge. With the increased demand for civil lawyers, however, arising from such movements as the Hundred Years War and European Conciliarism, the faculties of civil law became important areas of study in their own right. This developing interest in civil law was reflected in the emergence of colleges with strong legal concentrations, at Cambridge especially the King's Hall and Trinity Hall, and at Oxford New College and All Souls.[58] It was not uncommon for students to take a bachelor's degree in both civil and canon law, although to become a doctor of both laws (*doctor utriusque iuris*) was a more taxing achievement. The combination of degrees in civil and canon law was a useful one for a scholar because it increased the options for different types of employment. Even in England, where the common law prevailed, a qualification in civil law was a marketable asset. In this regard, it is well to remember that a knowledge of civil law was necessary for any scholar who wished to make a career as a practitioner in the ecclesiastical courts.[59]

The principal text for the course in civil law was the sixth-century codification of the Roman law by the Emperor Justinian. This had been restored and commented on by Italian jurists from the eleventh century onwards. The main parts of the *Corpus* of Justinian were the *Codex* (Code), a set of laws, the *Digest*, a compendium of the opinions of Italian jurists, the *Institutes*, a textbook, and the *Novellae*, Justinian's legal enactments after 534. Along with these basic texts were studied the glosses and commentaries on aspects of the Roman law by a host of European jurists, generally known as the Glossators and the later Post-Glossators or Commentators.[60] The Post-Glossators had many original

---

57. See the requirements at Oxford in L. E. Boyle, "Canon law before 1380", in *HUO*, I, pp. 539, 542, 543; for Cambridge see Leader, *The university to 1546*, p. 194; also p. 196 for graces relating to law degrees.
58. Cobban, "Theology and law in the medieval colleges of Oxford and Cambridge", *BJRL* **65**, 1982, pp. 61–5, 68–70, 77.
59. For many aspects of civil lawyers in England, including career opportunities, see C. T. Allmand, "The civil lawyers", in *Profession, vocation and culture in later-medieval England*, C. H. Clough (ed.) (Liverpool, Liverpool University Press, 1982), pp. 155–80.
60. On the revival of Roman law, the Glossators, and Post-Glossators, see W. Ullmann, *The medieval idea of law* (London, Methuen, 1946), pp. xv–xxxix, 1–6.

ideas on the nature and function of law in society, and their works must have been very stimulating for fledgling lawyers just as they are for modern scholars. Two of the most favoured of the Post-Glossators for English university consumption were the Italian jurists, Baldus of Ubaldis and Bartolus of Sassoferrato.[61] The central texts for canon law in the thirteenth century were Gratian's *Decretum* and the *Decretals* of Gregory IX of 1234. With the passage of time, there were added the *Liber sextus* (the *Sext*) of Boniface VIII of 1298 and the *Clementinae* (*Clementines*) of Clement V, issued by John XXII in 1317. As in the case of civil law, a galaxy of glosses and commentaries on the canon law were studied in conjunction with the set texts. An important indigenous source on English canon law was William Lyndwood's *Provinciale seu constitutiones Angliae* of the early-fifteenth century. This remained a widely read textbook through to the Reformation, although it may not have been part of the official curriculum at Oxford and Cambridge.[62]

Medicine, the last of the superior faculties, was by far the smallest of the five faculties at each of the English universities. Medical study or physic at Oxford and Cambridge was little geared to empirical medical practice. Rather it was taught as an intellectual and discursive discipline. The end product was to equip a graduate to teach the subject and not necessarily to function as a medical practitioner.[63] As an intellectual pursuit, university medicine, as any other discipline, was based upon the study of authoritative texts. In this respect, the Aristotelian texts on logic and the natural sciences of the arts course were essential for the speculative or philosophical nature of medical study. Of the scientific subjects, astronomy and astrology were deemed to be of importance, as previously mentioned, for the alleged influence of the planets on human health. The close nexus between arts and medicine meant that medical students were required to have a prior arts training, either a degree or at least two or so years in arts. Some of the abler scholars

---

61. E. Leedham-Green, *A concise history of the University of Cambridge* (Cambridge, Cambridge University Press, 1996), p. 20.
62. For a detailed discussion of the texts used for civil and canon law at Oxford see Boyle, "Canon law before 1380", and J. L. Barton, "The study of civil law before 1380", in *HUO*, I, pp. 531–64, 519–30. See also Barton, "The legal faculties of late-medieval Oxford", in *HUO*, II, pp. 281–313. For Cambridge see Leader, *The university to 1546*, pp. 192–201.
63. See the discussion on medicine at Oxford by F. M. Getz, "The faculty of medicine before 1500", in *HUO*, II, pp. 373–405.

combined degrees in medicine with degrees in arts, in theology and occasionally in law, and a few of them had double doctorates in medicine and theology.[64] This is in direct contrast with the situation at Paris and Bologna where efforts were made to preserve the standing of medicine by preventing medical students from studying for other degrees after obtaining a qualification in medicine.[65] In England, the medical student proceeded from a preparatory course in arts to study the inherited canon of Greek and Arabic medicine in Latin translation, accompanied by the appropriate commentaries.[66] Medicine or physic at the English universities had to compete with the variety of practitioners who plied their trade outside the universities, whether surgeons, barbers, apothecaries and those who were not members of any guild. In the late-medieval period Oxford and Cambridge tried to establish that a university licence was the only legitimate means by which medicine could be practised. The need for regulation was recognized by Henry V who, in 1421, enacted that only medical graduates of Oxford and Cambridge could practise medicine, although surgeons were given the right to control their professional activities within the kingdom.[67]

Teaching at Oxford and Cambridge, as in all continental universities, was based primarily upon the twin devices of the lecture and the disputation. Lectures in all faculties were divided into ordinary and extraordinary or cursory lectures. These distinctions depended upon the status of the lecturers in the academic hierarchy, the mode of lecturing and the subject matter of the lecture.[68] Ordinary lectures, the official statutory lectures, were the province of the regent masters. They were delivered on days that were designated for lectures (*dies legibilis*), at fixed hours, usually in the morning, and they were of at least one hour's

---

64. *ibid.*, p. 382.
65. V. L. Bullough, *The development of medicine as a profession* (Basel, S. Karger, 1966), p. 81.
66. For the key medical texts and other works used see Getz, "The faculty of medicine before 1500", pp. 373–405.
67. Bullough, *The development of medicine as a profession*, pp. 105–6.
68. For ordinary and extraordinary lectures in arts at Oxford see, for example, J. A. Weisheipl, "Curriculum of the faculty of arts at Oxford in the early-fourteenth century", *Medieval Studies* **26**, 1964, pp. 143–85. See also L. E. Boyle, "The curriculum of the faculty of canon law at Oxford in the first half of the fourteenth century", in *Oxford studies presented to Daniel Callus*, pp. 135–62. On ordinary and extraordinary lectures at Cambridge see Hackett, *The original statutes of Cambridge University*, pp. 133–8.

4. An initial from a legal text of *c.*1330, probably from Oxford, that illustrates a teaching master lecturing to students who are seated on benches and who have their own copy of the text.

duration.[69] Bachelors in the different faculties, who had to give lectures as part of their training, were not permitted to do so at the times when ordinary lectures were held. Within the context of the ordinary lecture the position of the regent master was paramount and, unless suspected of heresy, the teaching master was not subject to evaluation by academic peers or by any external body. After giving a thorough exposition of the work under review, the regent master would then deliver rulings on the complex questions (*quaestiones*) arising from the text or from the

69. Hackett, *The original statutes of Cambridge University*, pp. 135–6; Gibson, *Statuta antiqua*, pp. lxxxi.

glosses or commentaries upon it. One of the perennial problems con-
fronting regent masters was the extent to which they should take into
account the associated glosses and commentaries when lecturing upon
a set text. It is understandable that students were keen to encompass
the glossatorial literature because of the potential challenges it might
harbour for the established text. This would make for more lively sessions in the lecture hall. Clearly, regent masters had to steer a difficult
balance between rendering a faithful exposition of the text and allocat-
ing time to the opinions of the commentators.

It sometimes happened that when a skilful master tried to resolve
quaestiones, the problems generated by the text, using relevant glosses
and commentaries, new lines of enquiry would be opened up that
might transcend the parameters of the authoritative text. In this way,
original ideas could flow even within the conservative format that
was geared to the transmission of an inherited pattern of approved
knowledge.[70] Evidently, the scholastic system gave scope for considerable
disagreements to arise between teaching masters, and it also allowed
individual masters to disengage to some extent from tradition while
paying lip service to the authoritative texts. In this sense, there is perhaps
an analogy with Marxism as the central ideology of the former Soviet
Union. As long as a formal acknowledgement was made to Marxist–
Leninist doctrine, Soviet academics could, within cautious limits, present
what were recognizably their own scholarly opinions. The situation
was similar for medieval scholars, although they were dealing, not with
a wholly unitary ideology, but with a range of hallowed texts in each
discipline. The medieval universities were essentially teaching institutions and not research centres in the modern sense. Nevertheless, by
exploiting the flexibility inherent in the system of lectures and related
quaestiones a teaching master could arrive at intellectual positions that
went beyond the confines of received wisdom and were tantamount
to an advance in the understanding of the subject.

The official or ordinary lectures were concerned with the set texts
of the curriculum in each faculty. They had to be attended in order
to acquire a degree, although dispensations or graces were commonly
given to students in arts or scholars in the superior faculties who had
not met the full statutory requirements. Ordinary lectures were supple-

70. See Fletcher, "The faculty of arts", in *HUO*, I, pp. 375–6.

mented by extraordinary lectures. These were given by teaching masters on texts that were not part of the official curriculum.[71] Masters were not obliged to wear their formal habit when delivering extraordinary lectures. This type of lecture could be staged either on days not assigned to ordinary lectures (*dies non legibilis*), or on days specifically set aside for extraordinary lectures, or on days in which ordinary lectures were held (*dies legibilis*) but at some point after their conclusion. The importance of the system of extraordinary lectures is that this was a mechanism whereby new works or older texts that had never been included in the official syllabus could be brought to the attention of students. The availability of a range of fresh material served as an invigorating counterpoint to the authoritative texts of the ordinary lectures. Moreover, a text that had been the subject of extraordinary lectures and, with the passage of time, was deemed to be of proven value might qualify as a work to be treated in ordinary lectures. The process also worked in reverse. A good example comes from the faculty of canon law at Oxford. Gratian's *Decretum*, which had been an exceedingly important ordinary text, had become an extraordinary book by the early-fourteenth century. By contrast, the *Decretals* of Gregory IX of 1234, which had started life as an extraordinary text, had been elevated to the ranks of the ordinary works by 1333.[72]

It seems that bachelors in arts and in the superior faculties may sometimes have given extraordinary lectures in place of regent masters.[73] Whatever the extent of this practice, the term more commonly applied to the lectures of the bachelors was "cursory", and the cursory lectures usually refer to those delivered by bachelors studying for the degree of MA and by bachelors in the superior faculties preparing for the higher degree in theology, civil law, canon law or medicine. These lectures were given under the supervision of a master or doctor, and they were an essential part of the training of a bachelor prior to becoming a fully-fledged teaching master in the appropriate faculty. What was designed as a form of practical training for an apprentice regent master

71. On extraordinary lectures see Hackett, *The original statutes of Cambridge University*, p. 135.
72. Boyle, "The curriculum of the faculty of canon law at Oxford in the first half of the fourteenth century", pp. 148–9.
73. *ibid.*, p. 148; also Hackett, *The original statutes of the University of Cambridge*, pp. 133, 138.

was also of benefit for the student. As the name implies, cursory lectures were of a less learned and less complicated character than the ordinary lectures of the teaching masters. They seem to have consisted primarily of a literal exposition or outline of the main points of a text with only the minimum of commentary. In this way, cursory lectures gave students the opportunity to learn the salient features of a text as a basis for further and more complex study. This service for students was all the more valuable in view of the costly nature of texts and the scarcity of library provision.

The complementary method of university instruction was provided by the disputation. As part of their responsibilities, regent masters in the English universities were required to mount public disputations on assigned "disputable days" (*dies disputabilis*).[74] As with lectures, disputations were also divided into ordinary and extraordinary categories. An ordinary disputation was a public and formal occasion. It was conducted along strict procedural lines, utilized Aristotelian logic and was adversarial in character. Although there were many variations and changes over time, the typical disputation was directed by a regent master and involved several disputants. One or two of these, usually bachelors, assumed the role of principal respondents or defenders of the opinion debated, and another, often the presiding regent master, took the position of opponent and marshalled arguments against the proposition. Other disputants participated in lesser roles. When the disputation had ended, it was the task of the regent master to sum up and to give a ruling or determination on the question disputed, either immediately or within several days. Ordinary disputations were attended by bachelors of the faculty, sometimes by other masters, and, in arts, by undergraduates who were expected to play a minor role.[75] Two of the most favoured types of ordinary disputations in the faculty of arts were those dealing with logical matters and called *de sophismatibus* or *de problemate*,

---

74. For disputations at Oxford see Weisheipl, "Curriculum of the faculty of arts at Oxford in the early-fourteenth century", pp. 176–85. For disputations at Cambridge see Hackett, *The original statutes of Cambridge University*, pp. 138–42. A lot of detailed information on the different types of disputation is given by A. G. Little & F. Pelster, *Oxford theology and the theologians c.AD 1282–1302*, Oxford Historical Society **96** (Oxford, Clarendon Press, 1934), pp. 29–56.

75. Fletcher, "The faculty of arts", pp. 387–8; Little & Pelster, *Oxford theology and the theologians*, p. 37 imply that regent masters at Oxford were reluctant to attend the ordinary disputations of another master.

and those titled *de quaestione* that related to areas of quadrivial study.[76] Disputations were often captured in a literary form, and the redaction of disputed questions (*quaestiones disputatae*) became an important contemporary source of study that helped students to develop intellectual rigour, to avoid illogicalities and to be consistently relevant.

The term extraordinary disputation was an umbrella one and denoted any disputation that did not measure up to the criteria for an ordinary disputation. For instance, any regent master could hold a disputation for the sole benefit of the teacher's own students. This was a private disputation (*disputatio privata*) as opposed to a public and formal exercise.[77] Another form of extraordinary disputation was that held on the occasion of the admission of new masters and doctors to their degrees. These were sometimes called "solemn disputations".[78] One of the most exciting types of disputation was that known as the *disputatio de quolibet* or *quodlibet* (the disputation on anything).[79] Such disputations were general debates when those present could raise any point for discussion. There was no fixed agenda, and the subjects debated might refer to contemporary ecclesiastical or political affairs or to intellectual issues of a contentious and radical nature. These open debates, that reached their fullest maturity in theological faculties but were also staged in law, medicine and arts, gave a welcome opportunity for scholars to express their opinions with a freedom that was not always possible within the restraints of the more formal atmosphere of the ordinary lectures and disputations. The loose structure of the *quodlibet* encouraged a wide participation, and so it proved to be a useful training ground for the cut and thrust of logical argument among scholars of differing intellectual attainments. It is not surprising that the *quodlibet* was a seedbed for new and challenging ideas. Although disputations of this kind were likely to attract lively audiences, they were held sparingly throughout the year. Quodlibetical disputations were being staged in theology at

---

76. Weisheipl, "Curriculum of the faculty of arts at Oxford in the early-fourteenth century", p. 154.
77. Little & Pelster, *Oxford theology and the theologians*, p. 37.
78. *ibid.*, pp. 37–52.
79. For an account of disputations *de quolibet* see Leff, *Paris and Oxford Universities in the thirteenth and fourteenth centuries*, pp. 171–3; see also Lawn, *The rise and decline of the scholastic "quaestio disputata"*, pp. 15–17. For the different types of disputations in universities in Italy see A. Maierù, *University training in medieval Europe*, D. N. Pryds (trans. & ed.) (Leiden, New York & Cologne, Brill, 1994), pp. 62–9.

Cambridge by the early 1270s and at Oxford by the early 1280s, and in arts at Oxford in the fourteenth century.[80] The spontaneity of these disputations was probably at its height in the thirteenth century, but in the fourteenth century they declined in popularity as they became more organized and controlled in character.[81]

Not a great deal of evidence has survived concerning note-taking by students at lectures and disputations. There is enough, however, to convince that it was a general practice. In the university schools where lectures in the higher faculty studies of theology, law and medicine were held, it was usual to provide the scholars with desks as well as benches.[82] In the superior faculties scholars were commonly required to buy or to borrow copies of the central texts that were deployed in the lecture room.[83] These would rest on the desks, and the scholar would either make separate notes or gloss the margins of the text. For instance, a manuscript of *c*.1200 contains a student's notes on the opinions of John of Tynemouth and Simon of Sywell, two Oxford teachers of canon law who commented on aspects of Gratian's *Decretum*.[84] From the theology faculty at Oxford there has survived a notebook of a theological student of the early-thirteenth century. The notebook includes notes on Robert Grosseteste's lectures on the Psalms and notes on lectures on the Psalter.[85] In the lecture rooms of the arts faculties at Oxford and Cambridge it was apparently uncommon to find desks, only benches being provided for the students. Physically, this made note-taking more difficult. Nevertheless, students in arts did take notes. The case of Henry of Renham is instructive. In *c*.1300 Renham emended and made notes on a copy of Aristotle's *Libri naturales* while attending a course of lectures at Oxford on this topic.[86] Scholars not only made

---

80. Hackett, *The original statutes of Cambridge University*, p. 141, *n.* 2; Weisheipl, "Curriculum of the faculty of arts at Oxford in the early-fourteenth century", p. 183.
81. Lawn, *The rise and decline of the scholastic "quaestio disputata"*, pp. 16–17.
82. Pollard, "The *pecia* system in the medieval universities", in *Medieval scribes, manuscripts and libraries*, p. 150.
83. For Oxford see Gibson, *Statuta antiqua*, pp. 43, 44, 46. There appears to be no specific statute on this matter for Cambridge.
84. Boyle, "Canon law before 1380", p. 531.
85. Catto, "Theology and theologians 1220–1320", pp. 479–80.
86. Parkes, "The provision of books", in *HUO*, II, p. 424 and plate XI (between pp. 404 and 405) which shows Renham's lecture notes on the text of Aristotle's *Physics*; see also Emden, *BRUO*, III, p. 1565.

notes at lectures, they also took down the arguments of the main participants in disputations. Notes on lectures, disputations and sermons were sometimes fashioned into connected prose and arranged as booklets. Such booklets were useful aids for study, and some of them were copied and circulated among students who added them to their own store of academic material.[87] Notebooks of lecturers have also survived. These contain notes on a variety of academic exercises, drafts of the writer's own lectures or descriptions of disputations.[88]

In the thirteenth century English students had to rely largely upon lectures and disputations as their main form of instruction, with perhaps occasional private tuition from regent masters according to need. Early types of tutorial and lecturing facilities seem to have been established in the monastic colleges at Oxford in the fourteenth century.[89] The pioneering modes of monastic teaching that were supplementary to public university instruction were transplanted to the halls and hostels where they were further developed. When mandatory residence in a hall, hostel or college was decreed for all Cambridge scholars in the late-fourteenth century and for all Oxford scholars in c.1410 and reaffirmed in 1420, it was natural that internal teaching would eventually become the norm in the places where the academic population mainly lived.[90] Hall lectures probably date from the fourteenth century and they became common in the fifteenth century. They were generally given in the mornings and were followed in the afternoon by a *recitatio* or repetition, that is a revision exercise at which students were examined orally on the content of the day's lecture. This type of instruction was complemented by discussion groups and disputations.[91] As was shown in Chapter 1, the chance survival of the logic notebook of John Arundel, the principal of an Oxford hall in 1424, proves that Arundel acted as tutor to undergraduate commoners and managed their finances.[92] From the

87. Parkes, "The provision of books", p. 425.
88. *ibid.*, p. 454; Catto, "Theology after Wycliffism", in *HUO*, II, pp. 268–9.
89. For details see Cobban, "Decentralized teaching in the medieval English universities", pp. 193–4; Cobban, *Medieval English universities*, pp. 176–7.
90. For obligatory residence at Cambridge see *Camb. Docs*, I, p. 317 and at Oxford Gibson, *Statuta antiqua*, pp. 208, 226–7.
91. See the Oxford aularian statutes (*statuta aularia*) in Gibson, *Statuta antiqua*, especially pp. 579–80; see also Emden, *An Oxford hall*, p. 208.
92. See above, Chapter 1.

notebook, it is clear that Arundel had the assistance of at least three other tutors.[93] The evidence of Arundel's notebook demonstrates how far lectures and tutorial arrangements had become entrenched in one Oxford hall in 1424, and it has to be assumed that this was fairly typical of the larger halls of the period. The aularian or hall statutes of 1483–90 give many details of the lectures, revision exercises and disputations that were stipulated for halls towards the close of the fifteenth century. These presumably reflect the teaching practices that were growing up in halls over the whole of the century.[94] Concrete evidence has not yet been found concerning tutorial arrangements in the Cambridge hostels, but teaching developments similar to those in Oxford halls would almost certainly have occurred.

There were customary practices in most of the early English secular colleges whereby the senior fellows would encourage and teach the younger fellows. This embryonic tutorial system was formally established on a salaried basis at New College, Oxford, from 1379, money being set aside as payment for fellows or scholars who acted as tutors (*informatores*).[95] The tutorial system at New College was confined to fellows and scholars of the college. The earliest known evidence for tutorial arrangements involving undergraduate commoners in any secular college in the English universities occurs in the 1430s at the King's Hall, Cambridge. Here, fellows of the college acted as tutors to undergraduate commoners, called *pupilli*, for whose finances they were responsible.[96] A similar system in which fellows served as tutors to undergraduate commoners, again referred to as *pupilli*, is found in operation at Pembroke College, Cambridge, in 1476 and 1477.[97] At Oxford, William Waynflete, the founder of Magdalen College, made statutory arrangements in 1479/80 for the admission of up to 20 sons of nobles and other well-connected persons. They were to pay for board and lodging after the

93. Cobban, "John Arundel, the tutorial system, and the cost of undergraduate living in the medieval English universities", *BJRL* **77**, 1995, pp. 146–7.
94. Gibson, *Statuta antiqua*, pp. 579–80.
95. Cobban, *The King's Hall*, pp. 66–7; Cobban, "Colleges and halls 1380–1500", in *HUO*, II, pp. 596–8.
96. Cobban, *The King's Hall*, pp. 67–72; King's Hall accounts, IX, fols 29v, 44, 92v; XIII, fol. 19v; XV, fol. 118; XVI, fol. 115v; XIX, fols 17, 17v; XX, fol. 15v.
97. Pembroke College archives, Registrum Aa, y, column 2; Cobban, "Pembroke College: its educational significance in late-medieval Cambridge", *Transactions of the Cambridge Bibliographical Society* **10**, 1991, pp. 2–3.

manner of undergraduate commoners and they were to be under the direction of a tutor.[98]

The growth of tutorial facilities in a few of the colleges in the fifteenth century, and their firm entrenchment in virtually all of the colleges in the sixteenth century, was accompanied by the emergence of the college lectureship. In the fifteenth century an endowed lectureship was in force at Godshouse, later refounded as Christ's College, Cambridge, from 1439, and lectures were given at King's College from at least 1456.[99] An endowed lectureship was established at Queens' College, Cambridge, in 1470 and was operational by 1484–5, and at Magdalen College, Oxford, the statutes of 1479/80 made provision for three salaried lectureships, one in theology and the other two in natural and moral philosophy. These were complemented by lectures in logic and disputations in arts and theology.[100] In 1492 a lectureship in canon law at the King's Hall was endowed by the will of Robert Bellamy, a fellow of the college.[101] In the first half of the sixteenth century most of the English colleges, old as well as new, introduced collegiate lecturers for the benefit of undergraduate commoners who were in the process of migrating piecemeal from the halls and hostels to the colleges. This was tantamount to an academic revolution because the availability of lecturing and tutoring within the colleges meant that undergraduates had less need to rely upon the lectures of the regent masters in the university schools.

Attempts were made from the late-fifteenth through to the seventeenth centuries to regenerate university instruction by establishing a corps of salaried lecturers or professors, the terms being interchangeable in this period.[102] Salaried university lectureships had originated in the thirteenth century and are found in the universities of Palencia in Castile, Toulouse, Vercelli, Siena, Modena, Padua, Vicenza and, at the

98. *Statutes*, II, ch. 8, p. 60.
99. Cobban, *Medieval English universities*, pp. 196–8. For lectures in theology see King's College archives, mundum books, III, fols 23, 24v, 99, 99v; IV, fols 67v, 124v; VI, fol. 67; for lectures in civil law, III, fol. 100v; IV, fols 67v, 124v; VI, fol. 47; for lectures in canon law, III, fols 81v, 100v; IV, fols 67v, 124v; for lectures in astronomy and medicine, III, fols 81v, 100v.
100. For lectures at Queens' College see Queens' College archives, journale I, fols 23, 47, 51v, 57, 81, 97, 116, 131v, 141.
101. On the Bellamy lectureship see Cobban, *Medieval English universities*, pp. 200–1 and Cobban, *The King's Hall*, pp. 77–9, 80; King's Hall accounts, XX, fols 36v, 60v.
102. For details see Cobban, *Medieval English universities*, pp. 204–7.

end of the century, in Bologna.[103] From the late-fourteenth century salaried lectureships invaded the northern university scene and were important in the development of the German and Scottish universities. Salaried lectureships came very late to the English universities and, apart from earlier abortive ventures, the first successful endowed lectureships were launched at Cambridge in 1488.[104] The climax to the efforts made to revive university teaching in the sixteenth century came with the establishment at Oxford and Cambridge of Henry VIII's regius professorships of divinity, civil law, medicine (physic), Hebrew and Greek that were in place by at least 1542.[105] In the seventeenth century professorships were founded in geometry and astronomy at Oxford in 1619, chairs in history were instituted by William Camden at Oxford in 1622 and by Fulke Greville at Cambridge in 1627, and a professorship in Arabic was established at Oxford by Archbishop Laud.[106]

Despite these attempts to breathe renewed life into public university instruction, the colleges held their ground as the principal venues for undergraduate teaching. In the course of the sixteenth century the colleges became largely self-contained teaching corporations, although students were still officially supposed to attend university lectures. At Oxford, students were expected to hear public lectures until at least the mid-sixteenth century.[107] As late as 1562 the Cambridge chancellor, William Cecil, stipulated that university lectures were to be attended by all members of colleges.[108] There is no doubt, however, that the system of university instruction was heavily eclipsed by college teaching in the reign of Elizabeth, and the pattern was set for the English universities to be transformed into decentralized bodies based upon the collegiate unit. There is one qualification to be made. While university

---

103. Cobban, "Elective salaried lectureships in the universities of southern Europe in the pre-Reformation era", *BJRL* **67**, 1985, pp. 662–3.
104. *Camb. Docs*, I, p. 361.
105. F. D. Logan, "The origins of the so-called regius professorships: an aspect of the Renaissance in Oxford and Cambridge", in *Renaissance and renewal in Christian history*, D. Baker (ed.), Studies in Church History, 14 (Oxford, Basil Blackwell, 1977), pp. 271–8.
106. See K. Sharpe, "The foundation of the chairs of history at Oxford and Cambridge: an episode in Jacobean politics", *History of Universities* 2, 1982, pp. 127–52; Curtis, *Oxford and Cambridge in transition*, p. 102.
107. Pantin, *Oxford life in Oxford archives*, p. 36.
108. D. R. Leader, "Teaching in Tudor Cambridge", *History of Education* **13**, 1984, pp. 111–12.

lectures went into a progressive decline, it seems that university disputa-tions at both Oxford and Cambridge retained their importance right through to the seventeenth century. As evidence of this, members of colleges were urged to participate in them as a useful addition to their own college disputations.[109] This was one of the few reminders of a once vibrant system of university teaching that had fallen victim to the relentless march of collegiate teaching.

The contrast between the English students of the thirteenth century, who relied largely upon the twin props of university lectures and dis-putations for their educational development, and the students of the sixteenth century, who received most of their intellectual training from undergraduate to doctoral level within the walls of a single college, is the measure of the academic revolution that had occurred.

109. Leader, *The university to 1546*, pp. 106–7.

CHAPTER SIX

Urban relations, recreations and entertainments

Relations with the town

The emergence of the English universities made an immense contribution to the economic life of Oxford and Cambridge and the surrounding areas. As such, there was a general consensus that, from several points of view, they conferred obvious benefits on their urban communities. The presence of a large assemblage of masters and students created an academic enclave that was wholly dependent for its support upon the wide range of services that were provided by the citizenry. Of prime importance here was the availability of accommodation. Before the erection of purpose-made buildings, masters and students had to board and work in rented premises. This was clearly a boon to both individual and institutional landlords. In the pre-collegiate age the types of accommodation required were buildings suitable for use as lecture rooms, houses that could be converted for service as Oxford halls and Cambridge hostels. Before residence became obligatory in a hall, hostel or college, rented houses or parts of houses or single rooms were made available for masters or students who preferred to lodge in a more private and less communal manner.

Among the landlords in thirteenth-century Oxford were to be found burgesses and tradesmen, along with their wives or widows who sometimes acted as landladies. Religious houses, such as Oseney Abbey, the Priory of St Frideswide and St John's Hospital, owned a fair proportion of the halls before they passed into the possession of the university or its colleges. Another category of landlord comprised clerks and beneficed clergy living in the area who introduced scholars into their houses as paying boarders. A few of these houses subsequently became academic halls. For instance, the house of Walter, vicar of Charlbury, became Chimney Hall, that of William, vicar of Elsfield, was transformed into St George Hall, and that of Jordan, rector of Marsh Gibbon, emerged as St Catherine Hall.[1] A group of Oxford bedels in the mid-thirteenth century were men of considerable substance who owned several properties in the town and rented out accommodation to scholars. One or two of these properties were eventually converted into halls, among them Cat Hall and Bedel Hall, which also incorporated a school.[2]

At Cambridge, as at Oxford, religious houses were prominent as institutional landlords to several hostels including St Thomas' Hostel (one of several of that name), Crouched Hostel (Hostel of the Holy Cross), Ralph of Ekelington's Hostel and Wyestolke's Hostel. Barnwell Priory rented out Stone Hostel or Stone House (there are quite a few of that name), and in 1293 this was the subject of a dispute with the aspiring tenant, master Ralph of Leicester. St Giles Hostel also once belonged to Barnwell Priory. The nuns of St Radegund owned one of the two properties called St Gregory's Hostel. Among the individual ecclesiastics who served as landlords for scholars were Adam of Ayrmynne, Archdeacon of Norfolk, in respect of the Archdeacon's Hostel, and Roger of Haydon, a priest, who, in the mid-thirteenth century, donated to the university Long Entry Hostel and Haydon's Hostel John of Crauden, Prior of Ely, in the early-fourteenth century purchased a house in Cambridge, Crauden's Hostel, for monks from Ely studying in the university. In similar vein to Oxford, beneficed clergy in Cambridge are found as landlords to members of the university. For example, St Edward's Hostel at one time belonged to the vicar of St Edward's and was subsequently purchased by Henry VI from Trinity Hall in 1448.[3] As in Oxford, there were bedels who were property-holders

---

1. On Oxford religious houses, clerks and beneficed clergy as landlords see Emden, *An Oxford hall*, pp. 55–7.
2. For bedels as landlords to scholars see Catto, "Citizens, scholars and masters", in *HUO*, I, p. 165.
3. For details of the hostels mentioned above and many others see Stokes, *The medieval hostels of the University of Cambridge*, pp. 60–106.

in Cambridge, and in 1393 Physwick Hostel was bequeathed to Gonville College by the will of the bedel, William Fishwick.[4]

One of the more notorious burgesses who featured as a landlord to Cambridge scholars was John Bilneye.[5] Bilneye had been a clerk of the chapel royal, had become a fellow of the King's Hall in 1382 and, forsaking the academic life, entered Cambridge municipal politics. Having served as mayor of Cambridge several times in the early-fifteenth century and represented the borough in Parliament, Bilneye became involved in a bitter dispute with the university over the letting of a hostel, known as Bilneye's Hostel. On one occasion, when scholars expressed a wish to inhabit it, permission was refused on the grounds that Bilneye intended to live there himself. The university complained that this was contrary to the agreed procedures governing the renting of properties to scholars. At one point, a company of scholars marched on Bilneye's house and uttered death threats. In a schedule of 25 articles of complaint drawn up in 1420, the university accused Bilneye of perjury, of challenging the authority of the chancellor with a force of 100 armed men, of perpetuating a litany of misdeeds and of repeatedly acting in contravention of the law and of university statutes.[6] This was an extreme case, but it throws into strong relief the necessity of a regulatory body to maintain a just balance between the rights of landlords and the rights of scholars as tenants.

The regulating body in the English universities took the form of a joint committee of assessors or taxors comprising regent masters and burgesses whose function was to assess the rents of all accommodation leased by citizens for the use of scholars.[7] At Oxford, such a committee made a first definite appearance in the award of the papal legate for Oxford in 1214. It may, however, have been in operation before 1209. Originally, there were four masters and four burgesses, later reduced to two in each category. University taxors were among the oldest of all university officials and are found in most universities from an early stage in their development. At Cambridge, the system of assessors of

---

4. ibid., p. 95; Brooke, *A history of Gonville and Caius College*, p. 24.
5. On Bilneye's eventful career see Cobban, *Medieval English universities*, p. 272; also Emden, *BRUC*, p. 62.
6. Cooper, *Annals*, I, pp. 164–6.
7. On the system of university assessors or taxors see Hackett, *The original statutes of Cambridge University*, pp. 74–7, 153–6, 171–2; Rashdall, *Universities*, I, p. 191; III, pp. 47, 56, *n.* 1, 172; Emden, *An Oxford hall*, pp. 12–17, 118–19.

rents had been established by 1231, and it may well be that the principal aids to the English chancellors, the proctors, or rectors as they were called at Cambridge, were the original university assessors.[8] The regulation of rents by the taxors achieved two objectives. First, it provided a structure for the setting of fair rents, although the obstructive behaviour of the burgesses and their many complaints prevented the system from operating at Oxford with anything like smooth efficiency until the close of the thirteenth century. The burgesses had objected to the reassessment of rents after five years and argued for a seven-year period. Henry III intervened on behalf of the scholars and upheld the quinquennial period. Moreover, the burgesses contended that the taxors had jurisdiction only over the letting of entire houses and not over individual rooms. Again, Henry III clarified the issue by ruling that individual rooms, as well as houses, were liable to assessment by the taxors.[9] The second achievement of the system was that it helped to build up a collection of properties that were customarily identified with academic usage, whether as private lodgings, as halls or hostels or as lecture rooms. Superimposed upon these customary arrangements, more precise regulations were framed that were designed to secure properties for academic use for as long as possible while recognizing the rights of the landlord to regain control of rented premises under certain agreed conditions.

At Oxford, if a house or premises for lecture rooms had been rented to a scholar or master, the university was to retain an option on the property indefinitely unless the landlord wished to inhabit it at some future point, provided that due notice was given before a stipulated date. The landlord could also regain the property if an arrangement had been made to lease it to another for ten years or more.[10] The premium on accommodation that was reckoned to be suitable for lecture rooms or schools is embodied in the privileged status attached to such premises. It was enacted that if a building had at any time been used as a school and was not a dwelling-house, it must be surrendered willingly to any regent master who wished to convert it once again for the holding of

8. See the arguments of Hackett, *The original statutes of Cambridge University*, pp. 74–7, 153, 155.
9. For details of these disputes see Emden, *An Oxford hall*, pp. 14–15.
10. Gibson, *Statuta antiqua*, pp. lxxxiii–v, 79, 80; Emden, *An Oxford hall*, pp. 17, 25.

lectures. An exception was made in the case of members of the university who were accustomed to giving lectures in their own homes.[11]

There were similar arrangements at Cambridge for regulating the affairs between town landlords and masters and scholars. As at Oxford, special measures were taken to ensure that accommodation suitable for lecture rooms was retained for this purpose if at all possible. According to the statutes of the mid-thirteenth century, and repeated in those of the late-fourteenth century, no property that had been used as a school for ten years or more could be rented as living-quarters or for any other purpose unless the landlord had to live there out of genuine necessity.[12] Landlords were forbidden to charge a higher rent than that set by the taxors, and if they did so the chancellor could prevent masters and scholars from renting the premises. Similarly, masters and scholars were not allowed to gain an advantage in the competition for desirable accommodation by offering more than the prescribed rent, in effect a bribe.[13]

An early Cambridge statute of the late-thirteenth century provides a remedy against principals of hostels and landlords who had colluded jointly to bypass the system of university assessment in favour of reaching a private settlement. In these circumstances, the scholars who shared the hostel with such a principal were entitled to go to the chancellor to insist that their hostel be assessed.[14] On the one hand, this shows that the university authorities were concerned to regulate the business dealings of principals and landlords. On the other hand, there was concern to ensure that the rights of the inhabitants of hostels were safeguarded by proper residential contracts entered into with a reputable principal. Moreover, a principal who had not observed the legitimate procedures could not call upon the protection of the chancellor's court if the landlord indulged in unethical behaviour.

At Oxford and Cambridge principalships of halls and hostels were renewable annually. In order to secure official recognition of a principalship,

11. Gibson, *Statuta antiqua*, p. 79; Emden, *An Oxford hall*, p. 35.
12. Hackett, *The original statutes of Cambridge University*, pp. 171, 212–15; *Camb. Docs*, I, p. 350.
13. Hackett, *The original statutes of Cambridge University*, pp. 214, 215; *Camb. Docs*, I, pp. 350–1.
14. See Mullinger, *The University of Cambridge*, I, pp. 220, 639.

the Oxford principals had to attend the Church of St Mary the Virgin on 9 September each year to present their cautions or pledges as security for the rent to the chancellor or deputy chancellor on behalf of the landlord.[15] At Cambridge, the principals of hostels renewed their tenancies annually before the feast of the Nativity of our Lady on 8 September by offering a caution to the landlord or, if the landlord was not available, to the chancellor.[16] The caution might be a sum of money or a book or other valuable, or it might take the form of two sureties provided by acquaintances of the principal. There is no indication at either Oxford or Cambridge that principals were elected by scholars. The late-thirteenth-century Cambridge statute relating to hostels makes it clear that a potential principal had to apply directly to a landlord to be considered for the next vacancy. If the landlord turned down the request, the candidate could still hope to proceed by giving a caution to the chancellor who was empowered to nominate the contender to succeed a particular principal in office, even if the landlord and that principal objected.[17] There seems to be no evidence that the Oxford chancellor possessed such an overriding power. The responsibility for repairs to the Oxford halls lay with the landlord. If the landlord ignored the obligation after being informed three times about necessary repairs, the principal was entitled to have the repairs assessed by others and to have the work carried out at the landlord's expense. However, if the principal failed to give the landlord due warning of defects in the hall, the principal was supposed to bear the cost of the repairs.[18]

The system of joint assessment of rents by a committee of masters and burgesses that was present from an early stage in most European universities seems, in the English universities, to have settled down to work fairly well in the fourteenth and fifteenth centuries after weathering storms in the thirteenth century. It is probably true to say that, on balance, the system favoured the English universities more than the landlord population, although there were specific safeguards for landlords against the manipulations of unscrupulous scholars. The taxors administered a much-needed curb on excessive rents and restrained the malpractices of the more unruly landlords, a palpable exception being the case

---

15. Gibson, *Statuta antiqua*, p. 80; see also Emden, *An Oxford hall*, pp. 25–6.
16. Hackett, *The original statutes of Cambridge University*, pp. 172, 214, 215.
17. Mullinger, *The University of Cambridge*, I, pp. 219–20, 639.
18. Gibson, *Statuta antiqua*, p. 80; Emden, *An Oxford hall*, pp. 27–8.

of John Bilneye, who was well beyond the power of any university authority to call to account. The ultimate success of the system was the gradual accumulation of properties that came to be identified as primarily for university use, whether as private lodgings, halls, hostels or schools.

Apart from the stimulus given to landlordism, the presence of university communities in Oxford and Cambridge had a marked effect upon service occupations. Communal servants, including butlers, manciples, cooks, bakers, brewers, barbers, laundresses, book-bearers and gardeners were in much demand for halls, hostels and colleges. Master-builders and the hierarchy of tradesmen associated with the construction industry were hired either locally or from different parts of the country to execute the many building enterprises of the late-medieval period. This building activity transformed Oxford and Cambridge from universities that were geared to the uncertain nature of rented premises to centres of learning that drew confidence from the permanency of fine purpose-made structures. These ranged from the endowed colleges, with their increasingly elaborate gate-towers, imposing chapels, quadrangles and courts, to the solid buildings erected for the housing of lecture rooms for the various faculties and for early university libraries.[19] The specialist trades of parchment-dealers, bookbinders, illuminators and stationers were of some antiquity, and they were indispensable for the academic life of Oxford and Cambridge. Indeed, the greater part of their professional business came to be wedded to the service of the university community. As bodies of captive consumers, the English universities made an immense contribution towards enlarging the market economies of Oxford and Cambridge. Retailers of all manner of foodstuffs, ale and wine, drapers, cordwainers or shoemakers, tanners, skinners, smiths, tavern-keepers and millers are just some of the categories of

---

19. For building activities in the English universities see, for example, Harvey, "Architecture in Oxford 1350–1500", in *HUO*, II, pp. 747–68; Newman, "The physical setting: new building and adaptation", in *ibid.*, III, pp. 597–633; Colvin & Simmons, *All Souls: an Oxford college and its buildings*; Jackson-Stops, "The building of the medieval college", in *New College Oxford 1379–1979*, pp. 147–92; A. H. Smith, *New College and its buildings* (Oxford, Oxford University Press, 1952); S. Gillam, *The divinity school and Duke Humfrey's library at Oxford* (Oxford, Clarendon Press, 1988); Pantin, "The halls and schools of medieval Oxford: an attempt at reconstruction", in *Oxford studies presented to Daniel Callus*, pp. 31–100; Willis & Clark, *The architectural history of the University of Cambridge and the colleges of Cambridge and Eton*; J. Saltmarsh, *King's College and its chapel* (Cambridge, Jarrold, 1961).

tradespeople who benefited from the collective spending power of the university population.[20] Despite the obvious economic advantages to the citizenry, the daily presence of masters and scholars distributed throughout the towns of Oxford and Cambridge caused resentment to arise that flared into intermittent clashes between townspeople and university personnel.

There were two main reasons for this climate of hostility. Many citizens resented the clerical status of the scholars that set them apart as a privileged body within the town, exempted them from the normal procedures of borough jurisdiction and gave them the wide-ranging protection of the chancellor's court. The Oxford and Cambridge chancellors had, by the fourteenth century, through royal charters and papal awards accumulated impressive judicial powers.[21] With one or two exceptions, they had acquired jurisdiction over civil and criminal cases between scholars and citizens that had arisen from incidents within the university towns.[22] The chancellors had at their disposal an awesome collection of penalties that could be imposed upon masters, scholars and townspeople. The chancellors could levy fines, they could expel miscreants from the town and suburbs for short or long periods or for life, and they had the power of excommunication, subject to certain restrictions. As described in Chapter 4, the chancellors had the authority to investigate the morals of the citizenry, and prostitution and brothels were obvious concerns. Of major import also was the degree of involvement that the chancellors had in the economic and environmental affairs of Oxford and Cambridge.

In the course of the thirteenth century both universities were granted participatory rights, along with the mayor and other representatives of the town, over the conduct of the assize of bread and ale. After the Oxford riot of St Scholastica's Day of 1355, however, the Oxford chan-

---

20. On milling in the Cambridge area see Bennett, *Chaucer at Oxford and at Cambridge*, pp. 107–16, 122–3.
21. For royal charters of privileges granted to Oxford University see P. Kibre, *Scholarly privileges in the Middle Ages*, pp. 268–324; for Cambridge see Dyer, *The privileges of the University of Cambridge*, I, pp. 5–53. For examples of royal letters of protection for the chancellor and masters of Cambridge and for the guarantee of their privileges, see those of 24 March 1327 and 14 December 1335, Cambridge University Library, University Archives, Luard, nos 25, 28. For the powers of the English university chancellors see Cobban, *Medieval English universities*, pp. 64–72.
22. Criminal cases of murder and maiming were reserved for royal justice.

cellor was given full custody of the assize of bread, wine and ale, the supervision of weights and measures, as well as authority over disparate matters relative to the commercial life of the town. The Cambridge chancellor was given almost identical powers in 1382 following the riots in the town during the Peasants' Revolt of the previous year.[23] The mid-thirteenth-century statutes for Cambridge furnish details on how the university was to police trading in the town. On behalf of the chancellor, the two proctors or rectors were to ensure that bread and wine and necessary items of food were sold at a fair price, and that scholars and their servants were to be given preference over other buyers in all market transactions. They were to pay particular attention to monopolies or rings of tradesmen and their wives who entered into private agreements to withhold foodstuffs to create an artificial short-age so that scholars would later have to pay inflated prices. The rectors were bound to report the names of sellers who engaged in sharp practices to the chancellor who had powers to confiscate supplies of food and drink and to boycott cheating tradesmen, declaring their stalls to be out of bounds to members of the university.[24] It may seem obvious that the placing of curbs upon the malpractices of tradespeople of the town was for the general good of scholars and laity alike. How-ever, the municipal corporations of Oxford and Cambridge were made up largely of influential tradesmen who came to resent the amount of university intervention, whether justified or not, in their economic affairs.

Tensions also arose between town and gown over the involvement of both universities in environmental issues. By the mid-fourteenth cen-tury Oxford University had made many complaints about unhygienic practices within the town, and at various times had urged the town corporation to implement much-needed changes. In 1339 the univer-sity finally succeeded in pressurizing the municipal authorities into forcing the skinners to conduct their trade outside the walls of the

---

23. The royal charter of 1355 for Oxford University is printed by Salter, *The medieval archives of the University of Oxford*, I, pp. 152–7; the equivalent royal charter of 1382 for Cambridge University is printed by Dyer, *The privileges of the University of Cambridge*, I, pp. 82–4, and the summary in English is given by Cooper, *Annals*, I, pp. 124–5. Salter, *Medieval archives*, II, pp. 130–267 has printed the rolls of the courts held in Oxford in the first half of the fourteenth century that pertain to the assize of bread and ale. One roll for the assay of weights and measures is also printed.
24. Hackett, *The original statutes of the University of Cambridge*, pp. 156–7, 204, 205.

town. Among the reforms advanced by the university was the need to move the butchers' shambles to another part of the town and to ensure that townspeople did not keep livestock in their houses. The university also advocated the regular cleaning of the streets, a perennial issue, and entreated that only uncontaminated water ought to be used for baking and brewing. Conditions within the town prison caused concern, and the university argued for separate prison accommodation for women.[25] After the St Scholastica's Day riot of 1355 a royal charter transferred the supervision of street cleaning and of the upkeep of paving to the chancellor who was given power to punish townspeople who failed to carry out their designated roles in these matters.[26] This shift in environmental responsibility to the university suggests that the municipal corporation's record in street cleansing and repair had been somewhat deficient.

The situation appears to have been rather different at Cambridge because the university seems never to have been given overall charge of cleansing operations. Between 1391 and the sixteenth century the responsibility for public hygiene and the cleaning and paving of streets was carried out jointly by the chancellor and the mayor and bailiffs.[27] This co-operative arrangement had followed complaints made by the university to parliament to the effect that the municipal authorities had neglected their obligations in the field of public hygiene.[28] Co-operation between the chancellor and the mayor and bailiffs did not always work smoothly. As a result of a supplication from the Cambridge chancellor, Robert Wodelarke, the king in 1459 authorized Wodelarke to take stock of and to remedy such nuisances as dung, fetid water, garbage and the intestines and carcasses of animals that had been deposited in alleys, streets, ditches and rivers. The chancellor was also to seek out blocked gutters, watercourses and sewers.[29] The letters patent of Henry VI of 1459 that had empowered Wodelarke to carry out investigations into the state of the town had recited that section of the important statute enacted at the Cambridge Parliament of 1388 that was concerned with

---

25. For these proposed reforms see Catto, "Citizens, scholars and masters", in *HUO*, I, p. 166.
26. See the royal charter of 27 June 1355 in Salter, *Medieval archives*, I, pp. 152–7 at p. 155.
27. Cooper, *Annals*, I, p. 140.
28. *ibid.*, I, pp. 85, 102.
29. *ibid.*, I, p. 209.

the removal of unhygienic nuisances in London and other towns and boroughs within the realm. The environmental standards set out in this pioneering statute were here being highlighted to show the extent to which the mayor and bailiffs of Cambridge in 1459 had flagrantly fallen behind what were considered to be acceptable national standards in 1388. This statute is a significant landmark in the field of urban sanitary history.[30]

The privileged position of the scholars as clerks and the increasing powers of the university chancellors in the legal, social, economic and environmental life of the townspeople were severe restraints on the independence of the mayor, bailiffs and burgesses. In the eyes of their citizens, it seemed that the towns of Oxford and Cambridge were being largely taken over by the universities in their midst. This created a framework of resentment within which sporadic conflicts occurred. These sometimes led to serious injury or death.

A fracas at Oxford in 1248 resulted in the murder of a Scottish scholar, and a scholar and citizen were killed during an affray in 1297–8.[31] The most bloody conflict at Oxford was the riot of St Scholastica's Day of 1355.[32] This convulsion that lasted three days had its origins in a tavern brawl involving scholars and the taverner, and escalated into a series of street battles between scholars and townspeople. The ranks of the latter were augmented by groups of countrymen who, fired by anti-clerical passion, marched into the town and assisted in the killing or wounding of scholars, the mutilation of their bodies and the destruction of their books. The municipal authorities could claim that these extreme actions were in retaliation for the criminal behaviour of scholars who, at one point, armed with bows and arrows, had closed the gates of the town, started fires, robbed many houses and killed or wounded townspeople. Many more incidents are recorded in the two extant and

---

30. The statute is summarized in *ibid.*, I, pp. 132–6.
31. For the riot of 1248 see Kibre, *Scholarly privileges in the Middle Ages*, pp. 274–5 and p. 275, *n.* 34; Mallet, *A history of the University of Oxford*, I, p. 38. For details of the riots of 1297–8 and for ten associated documents see Salter, *Medieval archives*, I, pp. 43–81.
32. For the documentation relating to the St Scholastica's Day riot see J. E. T. Rogers (ed.), *Oxford city documents 1268–1665*, Oxford Historical Society **18** (Oxford, Clarendon Press, 1891), pp. 245–68 and Salter, *Medieval archives*, I, pp. 148–60. See also Rashdall, *Universities*, III, pp. 95–102; Pantin, *Oxford life in Oxford archives*, pp. 99–104; Kibre, *Scholarly privileges in the Middle Ages*, pp. 303–8; Mallet, *A history of the University of Oxford*, I, pp. 160–3.

differing versions of events, one written from the standpoint of the town, the other from that of the university. Given that propaganda and exaggeration were involved in these accounts, the whole truth may never be found. In the midst of these upheavals the university declared a cessation of lectures and most of the scholars fled into the surrounding area. A royal enquiry into the riot resulted in the imprisonment of several influential townsmen in the Tower of London. The university and the town were both ordered to surrender their privileges to the king. When they were returned, the privileges of the university had been enhanced and those of the town had been reduced. The settlement in favour of the university confirmed its commanding role in urban affairs for centuries to come. Conflicts continued to erupt between scholars and townspeople, but they were not comparable in scale to the St Scholastica's Day riot that had assumed the proportions of a miniature civil war.

At Cambridge, violent conflict was very much a fact of life for scholars and townspeople long before the riotous events that took place in the town in June during the Peasants' Revolt of 1381. In 1249 affrays erupted between scholars and citizens during which several persons were wounded or slain and many houses broken into and wrecked. The disorder was so unsettling that some students migrated to Oxford.[33] In 1260 townsmen joined in a conflict that arose between southern and northern scholars in which houses of both parties were sacked and some records of the university were burnt. At the conclusion of the affair, the king set up a commission for the trial of the offenders, and 16 townsmen were executed and many others on both sides were punished with varying degrees of severity. Some of the offenders fled to sanctuary, and 28 convicted southern scholars received a pardon from Henry III. A party of scholars left Cambridge to join groups of Oxford scholars at Northampton where an attempt was being made to establish a new university.[34] Henry III had given permission in 1261 for the settlement of a university at Northampton. This consent was revoked in 1264 because the scholars from Oxford and Cambridge had resisted the king during the seige of the town, an episode in the civil war

33. For the violent events of 1249 see Cooper, *Annals*, I, p. 45.
34. *ibid.*, I, p. 48 (Cooper is probably mistaken in giving the date of this affray as 1261 instead of 1260); Fuller, *The history of the University of Cambridge*, Prickett & Wright (eds), pp. 28–32.

between Henry III and the opposing baronial faction.[35] In April 1270 Henry III and the Lord Edward, the heir to the throne, visited Cambridge and were so perturbed by the frequent disputes and affrays between burgesses and scholars that Prince Edward agreed to act as a mediator. The royal intervention resulted in a composition whereby responsibility for keeping the peace was to rest with a joint committee of 10 burgesses, 7 from the town and 3 from the suburbs, and 13 scholars, 5 from the English counties, 3 from Scotland, 2 from Wales and 3 from Ireland.[36] This elaborate arrangement may have had some good effect in the remainder of the thirteenth century, but serious conflicts continued to plague relations between town and gown in the fourteenth century.

In 1304 hostilities once again broke out and townsmen attacked several hostels and assaulted the masters and scholars.[37] Major rioting took place in 1322 when the mayor and bailiffs incited townsmen to attack colleges, hostels and inns. The municipal rioters inflicted heavy injuries on scholars, imprisoned some of them, killed a parish priest, Walter of Skelton, seized books and other belongings, and destroyed documents relating to the privileges of the university. Edward II had to intervene to prevent the university from dispersing, and the mayor, four bailiffs and no fewer than 319 other persons were indicted for their criminal behaviour.[38] A violent series of events also occurred in 1371 when groups of scholars forcibly entered townsmens' houses and assaulted the owners. In that same year bailiffs, who had been sent by the mayor to apprehend malefactors and thieves, were beaten to within an inch of their lives by an armed band of scholars and others, including a rector.[39]

To some extent the rioting that broke out in Cambridge in June 1381 during the Peasants' Revolt was the cumulative outcome of almost two centuries of endemic struggle between scholars and citizens.[40] The

---

35. Cobban, *Medieval English universities*, p. 30.
36. Cooper, *Annals*, I, pp. 52–3.
37. *ibid.*, I, pp. 70–1.
38. *ibid.*, I, pp. 79–80.
39. *ibid.*, I, pp. 110–11.
40. For the following account of the rioting in Cambridge during the Peasants' Revolt of 1381 and its aftermath see *ibid.*, I, pp. 120–5; *Rotuli parliamentorum 1278–1503* (6 vols) (London, Record Commission, 1783), III, pp. 107–9; R. B. Dobson (ed.), *The Peasants' Revolt* (London, Macmillan, 1970), pp. 239–42; H. M. Cam, "The city of Cambridge", in *Victoria history of the county of Cambridge. Volume 3*, pp. 8–12.

mayor and burgesses took the opportunity in the course of the upris-
ing to ally with rebels from the county, whom they had invited into
Cambridge, to inflict heavy damage on university and college property.
The motives of the burgesses differed from those of their temporary
allies in some respects. The burgesses were primarily concerned, it seems,
to destroy the privileged position that the university had increasingly
come to occupy within the town. In the course of the disturbances,
they forced the university and its colleges to renounce all the privileges
that had been granted by the crown and to swear to uphold the ancient
custom of the borough. They were also required to end all legal cases
pending against the burgesses. The rebels from the county doubtless
saw the university as a bastion of privilege whose archives and legal documentation were symbolical expressions of a system that depressed the
unfree peasantry. Documents were legal chains. From different angles,
burgesses and rebels both had their own motives for the destruction
of university records.

Corpus Christi College suffered in this way when it was raided and
its archives removed or burnt. Similarly, some of the archives in the
university chest in St Mary's Church were burned as were charters of
privileges and other deeds surrendered to the burgesses and rebels by
the university and colleges. A university chest in the Carmelite friary was
also seized. Barnwell Priory was attacked by a combined force drawn
from the town and county, and indeed from other counties. The mob
was led by the mayor, and one of the objectives was to affirm the customary rights of driftway and pasture in the meadows that the Priory had
fenced off and planted with trees. Individuals, as well as corporate
bodies, were targets for assaults. As a commissioner for carrying out the
execrable Statute of Labourers, and as a hated poll-tax official, Roger
of Harleston's house was singled out for attack. The venom of the
townspeople was also directed against the university bedel, William
Wigmore (Wykmer). The many dealings that the townsmen had had
with this official had apparently made the bedel a figure of hatred in
their midst. Although Wigmore's house was destroyed, the insurgents
failed to catch the bedel and they were denied their declared aim of
decapitation.

The revolt in Cambridge was put down by the Bishop of Norwich
who entered the city with an armed band and defeated the rebels.
Those rebels who refused to repent were excommunicated. One burgess

was hanged, and the ex-mayor and bailiffs had to answer for their conduct before parliament. The concessions that the university had made under duress were quashed, and all previous privileges were restored with the addition that the custody of the assize of bread, wine and ale and the supervision of weights and measures were transferred from the town to the university. The settlement that followed the revolt in Cambridge gave the university a clear ascendancy in the affairs of the borough for several centuries, although disputes and the occasional riot still peppered the landscape.

Despite the many violent affrays and criminal behaviour caused by scholars and citizens, a tenuous framework of co-operation was preserved through all the vicissitudes of university and urban life. Most continental university towns had similar disruptive problems and many of them were far worse than those of Oxford and Cambridge. Disputes between scholars and townspeople were not the only source of conflict in the English universities. Discords arose between scholars of different colleges such as those that sullied relations between the King's Hall and Clare College at Cambridge in 1373.[41] There was a significant degree of inter-feuding between halls and hostels. For instance, one of the Oxford proctors, Thomas Reynold, was killed upon intervening in an affray between Peckwater Inn and St Edward Hall.[42] At Cambridge, St Nicholas' and St Clements' Hostels were renowned for their brawls with other hostels.[43] Moreover, there were frequent hostilities between northern and southern scholars at both universities right through to the sixteenth century. This climate of violence was further fuelled by the crimes of non-citizens who made temporary stays in Oxford and Cambridge and who engaged in disturbances and nefarious activities. In 1402, for example, there was a network of thieves operating in Oxford who specialized in robbing travellers passing through Oxford and the surrounding regions.[44] Within this broader perspective on violence the strife between scholars and citizens takes on a less exceptional character.

41. For the feud between the King's Hall and Clare College see Cooper, *Annals*, I, pp. 111–12.
42. W. A. Pantin, "Before Wolsey", in *Essays in British history presented to Sir Keith Feiling*, H. R. Trevor-Roper (ed.) (London, Macmillan, 1964), pp. 53–4.
43. Stokes, *The medieval hostels of the University of Cambridge*, pp. 40–1.
44. Catto, "Citizens, scholars and masters", p. 162.

Recreations and entertainments

From a cynical point of view it could be argued that the participation by scholars in brawls with townspeople or with each other was a form of recreational activity. Few licensed recreations were permitted by the university authorities or by the regimes of halls, hostels or colleges. There do not appear to have been organized sports at medieval Oxford and Cambridge, and there is no evidence of official inter-collegiate or inter-hall games. With the prospect of certain death, the student was expected to live a moral and sober life, and this is a common theme of contemporary sermons and educational treatises.[45] Lingering monastic influences pervaded the legislative codes governing English university life, and the denial of bodily pleasures was one of the principles that led to the adoption of repressive attitudes towards many forms of entertainment. Another factor that underlay this austere approach to amusements was the magnitude of the disciplinary problems that confronted the English universities right through to the sixteenth century. These problems ought not to be minimized, and it is understandable that strong action was taken to curb the more reckless student pastimes that could contribute to disorder or worse. It may be argued, however, that the response towards those diversions that were unlikely to give rise to serious strife was rather extreme and often provoked a reaction that was the opposite to that intended.

Notwithstanding the views held in some quarters that physical exercise was desirable for those following the academic life, the English universities did little to promote student health by organizing competitive games.[46] There are only occasional references to tolerated games or other types of exercise. The Oxford aularian statutes of 1483–90 encouraged principals of halls to send their students to some outdoor location for recreational purposes. The frequency of such outings is not

---

45. See, for example, the fifteenth-century Latin verse educational treatise by Goswin Kempgyn of Nussia, a master of arts of Erfurt University and law graduate of Cologne, that was written as a guiding handbook for new university entrants, M. Bernhard (ed.), *Goswin Kempgyn de Nussia trivita studentium: eine einführung in das universitätsstudium aus dem 15. jahrhundert*, Münchener Beiträge zur Mediävistik und Renaissance-Forschung **26** (Munich, Arbeo-Gesellschaft, 1976), especially the third tract, pp. 80–6.
46. See the views on the therapeutic value of physical exercise for students that are contained in the fourteenth-century treatise of a physician of Valencia printed by Thorndike, *University records and life in the Middle Ages*, pp. 154–60.

specified, but they were meant to be obligatory, except for reasonable cause.[47] On the other hand, these same statutes forbade handball and bracketed this with the more dangerous arts of two-handed swordplay and another type of fencing called "sword and buckler play", all of which were deemed likely to lead to a disturbance of the peace.[48] In the late-fifteenth and early-sixteenth centuries, however, handball had been accepted by at least two colleges. Corpus Christi College, Cambridge, had a court for handball by 1487, and the statutes of Corpus Christi College, Oxford, of 1517 allowed the playing of handball in the garden for the good of body and mind.[49] A fourteenth-century drawing shows fellows of New College engaged in a tilting match on horseback, archery and tennis were available at Pembroke College, Cambridge, in the 1530s, and Queens' College, Cambridge, and several of the Oxford colleges, including Cardinal College, Corpus, Lincoln and Oriel, built tennis courts at different points in the sixteenth century.[50] It is worth noting that this early form of tennis was often played with a gloved hand instead of a racket. As such, it was rather analogous to games of "fives".

While legitimate physical activities were extremely restricted within the university domain, scholars could scarcely be prevented from joining in the sports of the town and the neighbouring areas. Some would have taken part in bear-baiting and, at Oxford, there is the possibility that bull-baiting was staged on Bulstake Mead at Oseney Abbey. Both bear-baiting and bull-baiting were forbidden to members of Gonville and Caius College, Cambridge, in 1573–4 and to all scholars of Cambridge

47. Gibson, *Statuta antiqua*, p. 577; Emden, *An Oxford hall*, p. 205.
48. Gibson, *Statuta antiqua*, p. 576; Emden, *An Oxford hall*, pp. 204–5. "Sword and buckler play" was fashionable in London circles and was a type of fencing much used by highwaymen: Catto, "Citizens, scholars and masters", p. 183.
49. Leader, *The university to 1546*, p. 76; *Statutes*, II, ch. 10, p. 69; R. S. Rait, *Life in the medieval university* (Cambridge, Cambridge University Press, 1912), p. 72.
50. For New College fellows and sport on horseback see Gabriel, "The college system in the fourteenth-century universities", in *The forward movement of the fourteenth century*, p. 102. Nicholas Ridley, the master of Pembroke, practised archery and played tennis with a tutee, William Turner, in the 1530s; see Attwater, *Pembroke College Cambridge*, p. 36. For tennis at Queens' see Leader, *The university to 1546*, p. 76. For tennis courts at Oxford colleges in the sixteenth century see J. McConica, "Elizabethan Oxford: the collegiate society", in *HUO*, III, p. 650. See also J. G. Milne, *The early history of Corpus Christi College, Oxford* (Oxford, Basil Blackwell, 1946), p. 12; Green, *The commonwealth of Lincoln College*, p. 218; C. L. Shadwell & H. E. Salter (eds), *Oriel College records* (Oxford, Oxford University Press, 1926), pp. 214–15.

University in 1600–1.[51] Judging from earlier complaints about these sports, it is clear that scholars had been attending such spectacles for many years previously. Scholars would also have participated in the popular sport of hunting with dogs and hawking with birds of prey. Sometimes students carried country sports to excess as is illustrated from an example of a later date. At the beginning of the eighteenth century Edward, fourth Viscount Irwin of Temple Newsam, was a student at Christ's College, Cambridge, and would indulge in coursing, shooting and hunting at least 70 times a year, ostensibly for the promotion of good health. There were also ample opportunities for fishing in the districts bordering on Oxford and Cambridge, and dancing in the streets of the university towns was another form of distraction from the sobriety of the academic life. Chaucer indicated that Oxford had its own peculiar fashion of dancing as had many neighbouring villages in Oxfordshire and Berkshire.[52] Among the illegal country activities was poaching, and Oxford scholars certainly poached in the royal forests at Shotover and Woodstock.[53]

Less reputable outlets for youthful scholars were prostitution and excessive drinking. The extent of prostitution in Oxford and Cambridge was discussed in Chapter 4 and the details need not be repeated here. The reality that some scholars were involved as clients of prostitution or as pimps or both was wholly antithetical to the life of purity that the university authorities and college founders sought to impose upon celibate scholars. Women were seen as sinful beings from whom male academics had to be protected. The only concession that some colleges were prepared to make regarding contacts with women within their hallowed walls was to allow visiting facilities to female relatives and other women of approved character. At Corpus Christi College, Oxford, a college member was permitted a visit from a mother or sister, but

---

51. On the suggestion of bull-baiting at Oxford see Bennett, *Chaucer at Oxford and at Cambridge*, p. 54. For the attempted suppression of bear-baiting and bull-baiting by Gonville and Caius and by Cambridge University generally see A. H. Nelson (ed.), *Records of early English drama* (2 vols) (Toronto: Toronto University Press, 1989), I, pp. 267, 381.
52. For the case of Edward, fourth Viscount Irwin, I am indebted to Dr H. M. Jewell who derived this information from Temple Newsam correspondence in the Archives Department of the Leeds Central Library. For Chaucer and Oxford dancing see Bennett, *Chaucer at Oxford and at Cambridge*, p. 48.
53. Rashdall, *Universities*, III, p. 425.

only the president could receive a woman who was a non–relative.[54] At Peterhouse, very elaborate measures were taken to ensure that scholars and female visitors were given no opportunity to fall into sexual temptation. The female guest had to be received and entertained in the hall or in an alternative public area. The encounter was to be of minimal duration and a chaperon, either a scholar or a college servant, was to be present throughout.[55] Regulations regarding the admission of women as visitors were equally strict at Cardinal College, Oxford. According to the statutes of *c.*1525–7, only mothers and sisters and their servants were allowed access to the room of a college member. The penalty for breach of this prohibition was deprivation of commons for a month for the first offence, two months for the second, three months for the third and perpetual expulsion from the society for the fourth violation. The only exception to the rule was made in favour of the dean who was permitted to welcome any female guest, whether a relative or not.[56]

Extreme restrictions of this kind were paralleled in the halls and hostels, and they usually imposed a blanket ban on the admission of women to rooms.[57] Given the culture of celibacy and the distancing from women, it is at least understandable that some of the less inhibited scholars would seek solace in the arms of prostitutes. In a letter of *c.*1230, contained in an Oxford formulary, a bishop complained of those students who are nothing less than whoremongers and the equivalent of disreputable players.[58] This kind of complaint was still being echoed in the fifteenth century. Despite the best efforts of the English university authorities to drive it out, prostitution was a tenacious reality that survived to satisfy the deep-seated needs of at least a minority of scholars who were ordinarily deprived of the company of women in a natural setting.

---

54. *Statutes*, II, ch. 10, p. 79.
55. *Camb. Docs*, II, p. 30.
56. *Statutes*, II, ch. 11, p. 103.
57. Gibson, *Statuta antiqua*, pp. 81–2, 88.
58. Salter, Pantin & Richardson, *Formularies*, II, p. 348. Actors and entertainers of various types were commonly linked with prostitutes throughout medieval Europe, and in university towns it was believed in some quarters that students were closely involved with both professions to the clear detriment of the academic life. For the linkage between entertainers, actors and prostitutes see J. W. Baldwin, "The image of the jongleur in northern France around 1200", *Speculum* **72**, 1997, p. 639.

Apart from involvement in prostitution, drunkenness and violent behaviour loomed large among the common vices that besmirched the name of the student body. Drinking was a basic element of student life in Oxford and Cambridge and in all of the European universities. Most university events and each stage completed in a scholar's academic progress were usually marked by liberal measures of ale or wine. Moreover, away from the university precinct, some scholars spent many wasted hours carousing in the numerous taverns of Oxford and Cambridge. Here, it has to be remembered that medieval society was unacquainted with tea, coffee and tobacco, and ale and wine provided much of the lubricant of social intercourse. Unfortunately, excessive drinking sometimes led to a syndrome of violence, injury and death. The major confrontations between town and gown were discussed in the first section of this chapter. The Oxford coroners' rolls, however, give much information on the multitude of lesser but extremely grave incidents of violence that were perpetrated either by or against scholars. Some of these tragic happenings would have begun as high-spirited or mischievous recreational behaviour, often fuelled by alcohol, that got out of hand and ended in injury or death. Others were of a premeditated kind. Among the weapons in common use were knives, bows and arrows, staves, axes and swords. A few examples will give a flavour of the level of violence that stalked the streets of Oxford.

In 1303 three Irish scholars who lived in academic halls stabbed Adam of Sarum to death. Adam had been playing a ball game with others in the High Street when the Irish assailants struck with a mixture of fists and knives that had fatal consequences for Adam who died the following night. In 1441 Richard Adyson, a scholar, shot Thomas Cardiff, a chaplain, in the neck with an arrow and death ensued a few days later. Adam of Osegodby was a scholar who had a remarkably tempestuous career in which violence appears to have been the main form of recreation. In 1324 Adam, with the assistance of others, murdered Richard Overhe, a constable of the peace, and John of Staunford, a shopkeeper. The latter was killed by Adam with a piece of iron fixed to the end of a staff. Adam's career of violence came to an end in the same year when the riotous student was stabbed to death by a townsman.[59]

59. For these cases see H. E. Salter (ed.), *Records of medieval Oxford* (Oxford, Oxford Chronicle Co., 1912), pp. 11, 22, 23, 51.

Among other scholars who were murdered was Thomas Lynet who, in 1321, was killed by an arrow shot by Haimo of Lynford. The murderer fled with two companions to the wood of Shotover and there deterred pursuers by force of arms. In 1344 John of Snowdoune was similarly shot in the eye by an arrow, slain by Hugh Mymmes who managed to escape.[60] It is abundantly clear that when scholars made forays into the town in search of recreational adventure the results could be catastrophic. It is also clear that the university, college and hall prohibitions against wandering abroad at night and the carrying of weapons were well-founded in experience and designed in the scholars' best interests.[61] That these prohibitions were so often breached underlines the enormousness of the problem faced by the English universities in trying to establish an effective disciplinary control over their academic populations.

The prohibitions on recreations imposed by colleges and halls are a mixture of sensible provisions and those that seem to be excessively severe.[62] The primary concerns that underlay this strict regime were the need to maintain orderly conduct, to avoid nuisance to those intent on a studious life and to earn a good reputation for the college, hall or hostel in question. Most colleges forbade the keeping of animals and birds on the grounds that they created noise and were a distraction from study. Dogs and birds of prey, including hawks at New College and Magdalen and falcons at Peterhouse, were commonly proscribed by college statutes. Singing birds were also vetoed at Magdalen and Corpus Christi College, Oxford.[63] Ferrets were outlawed at New College, All Souls, and at Corpus Christi, Oxford, and at King's College, Cambridge.[64] The most noteworthy collection of barred animals and birds occurs in the statutes of King's College. The ban extended to dogs, ferrets, birds, monkeys, bears, wolves and stags, and it also specified

---

60. *ibid.*, pp. 21, 30–1.
61. See, for example, the table of fines to be imposed on masters and scholars who breached the disciplinary code regarding conduct outside the precincts of the Oxford halls, Emden, *An Oxford hall*, p. 199.
62. For recreations, forbidden or permitted, in continental universities see Rashdall, *Universities*, III, pp. 419–37.
63. For Peterhouse see *Camb. Docs*, II, p. 29; for New College, Magdalen and Corpus Christi see *Statutes*, I, ch. 5, p. 48; II, ch. 8, p. 42, ch. 10, p. 68.
64. For New College, All Souls and Corpus Christi see *Statutes*, I, ch. 5, p. 48, ch. 7, p. 44; II, ch. 10, p. 68; for King's College see *Camb. Docs*, II, p. 542.

nets for hawking or fishing.[65] Gambling, in all its forms, was prohibited by most colleges, whether with dice, knucklebones or cards. Gambling was condemned because it might interfere with studies, lead to rowdy behaviour and cause a scholar to run up crippling debts. The attitude of the English colleges towards chess was, however, more ambiguous and changed over time. In the fourteenth century chess was forbidden in the statutes of Queen's College, Oxford, of 1340, in the statutes of Peterhouse of 1344 and in those of New College of 1400. Whereas dice and other forms of gambling were suppressed at All Souls in 1443, the prohibition did not specifically embrace chess. Nor is chess mentioned among the proscribed entertainments at King's College, Cambridge, in the statutes of the early 1440s. Likewise, in the statutes of Magdalen College, Oxford, of 1479/80, in those of Christ's College, Cambridge, of 1505, and in those of Corpus Christi College, Oxford, of 1517 chess is not included as a vetoed activity.[66] This suggests that chess gained an increasing tolerance in the course of the fifteenth and early-sixteenth centuries, presumably because the intellectual qualities of the game gradually prevailed over its popular associations with the Devil.

In this matter of collegiate prohibitions there are two features in the statutes of Queen's College, Oxford, of 1340 that stand out from the norm. Whereas most colleges placed a ban on animals and birds because their presence might interfere with quiet study, at Queen's two additional objections were made. First, the feeding of animals by subsidized scholars was a waste of precious resources. Secondly, animals constituted a threat to the purity of the air, causing infection to arise among the fellows.[67] The statutes of Queen's also forbade the use of musical instruments by individual scholars because they were said to incite levity and arrogance in their owners and because their playing was bound to distract those studying within the college. The only exceptions allowed were the musical occasions that were mounted for the common benefit of all members of the college.[68] The prohibition

---

65. *ibid.*, II, p. 542.
66. *ibid.*, II, pp. 29–30 (Peterhouse), p. 542 (King's); III, pp. 197–8 (Christ's); *Statutes*, I, ch. 4, pp. 18–19 (Queen's), ch. 5, p. 48 (New College), ch. 7, pp. 44–5 (All Souls); II, ch. 8, p. 42 (Magdalen), ch. 10, p. 68 (Corpus Christi).
67. *Statutes*, I, ch. 4, pp. 18–19. The statutes of New College of 1400 also incorporate the point that it is unfitting for subsidized scholars to waste food on animals: *ibid.*, I, p. 48.
68. *ibid.*, I, ch. 4, p. 18.

of musical instruments is rather severe by English collegiate standards, but it is found here and there in colleges in continental Europe. For example, at the *Collegium Sapientiae* in Freiburg im Breisgau, founded in 1497, the playing of musical instruments was banned, only the clavichord being permitted.[69]

Despite the prohibitive regulations against recreational activity, European universities permitted periods of relaxation on the principal festivals of the ecclesiastical year or on the anniversaries of the patron saints of a faculty, a university nation or of a particular province from which students were recruited. On these occasions there would be church services, ceremonies, processions and a range of high-spirited diversions. For example, at the University of St Andrews the faculty of arts allowed undergraduates to indulge in cock-fighting at the time of Carnival before Lent, although in 1415 the period for this sport was limited to two or three days.[70] On the "Feast of the first snow" at Bologna university students of law, medicine and arts, in that order, would offer snowballs to the citizens in return for money, food or wine for their festivities later in the day.[71]

In the English universities the feast of St Nicholas on 6 December, Christmas and the feast of the Holy Innocents on 28 December were times of special merriment. In particular, this was the season for the temporary inversion of authority. Younger members of colleges and halls would elect a "lord of misrule" or a "mock king" or a "Christmas king" or a "king of the beans" who would hold sway over the festivities with the licence and indulgence of their seniors. A "king of the beans" was elected at Merton College, Oxford, as early as 19 November each year. On election day, the younger members would dress up in foreign garb and pretend to be messengers from a distant potentate from whom they would claim to have a letter ordering the masters of the college to elect a named senior fellow as "king of the beans".[72] It is interesting

---

69. Schwinges, "Student education, student life", in *A history of the university in Europe*, I, pp. 228–9.
70. A. I. Dunlop (ed.), *Acta facultatis artium Universitatis Sanctiandree 1413–1588* (Edinburgh & London, Oliver & Boyd, 1964), p. 4.
71. Schwinges, "Student education, student life", p. 230.
72. Salter, *Registrum annalium collegii Mertonensis 1483–1521*, pp. xviii–xix; E. K. Chambers, *The medieval stage* (2 vols) (Oxford, Oxford University Press, 1903), I, pp. 407–8; H. H. Henson, "The 'Rex Natalicus'", in C. R. L. Fletcher (ed.), *Collectanea*, Oxford Historical Society 5 (Oxford, Clarendon Press, 1885), I, pp. 41–2.

that the term "king of the beans" is still being used at Merton in the late-fifteenth century because, being strongly associated with French usage, it had rather gone out of fashion in England during the Hundred Years War.[73]

There was evidently considerable rivalry between different "mock kings" or "Christmas kings" as is clear from the spoof correspondence contained in an Oxford formulary. For instance, a spurious letter of 1432 claimed to have been sent by Balthasar, "king of kings and lord of lords", from the "palace" of Hinxey Hall to the "pretended" principal of Greek Hall.[74] Both of these halls were for legists, and the jocund tone of the letter and the studied insults give a flavour of the kind of jejune humour that amused the young medieval scholar. "Mock kings" or "Christmas kings" were featured in many of the English colleges, although from the evidence of surviving records they may have been a more common phenomenon at Oxford than at Cambridge. Indeed, the earliest instance of a "Christmas king" in a Cambridge college dates from 1539–40 at Christ's College.[75] Cambridge students, however, seem not to have been satisfied with the few occasions when "mock kings" were permitted to surface. In the fourteenth century, particularly on Ash Wednesdays, bands of students were wont to appoint their own alternative or mock university officials and to progress, with bells and trumpets, through the town with a captain, a mock chancellor, mock proctors and mock bedels. The university authorities legislated to attempt to suppress such unofficial parades in the later part of the century.[76]

Another form of inversion of authority that was practised in a few colleges was that akin to the ecclesiastical ritual of the "boy-bishop". "Boy-bishops" are found in the statutes of New College, Oxford, of 1400 where it is decreed that they were to officiate at services on the feast of the Holy Innocents. In the statutes of King's College, Cambridge, of the early 1440s "boy-bishops" are given the authority to preside over the feast of St Nicholas.[77] Entries for "boy-bishops" occur regularly in

73. S. Billington, *Mock kings in medieval society and Renaissance drama* (Oxford, Clarendon Press, 1991), p. 32.
74. Salter, Pantin & Richardson, *Formularies*, II, p. 438.
75. Nelson, *Records of early English drama*, I, p. 117; II, p. 731.
76. *ibid.*, II, pp. 730–1, 841; Cooper, *Annals*, I, p. 110.
77. *Statutes*, I, ch. 5, p. 69; *Camb. Docs*, II, p. 569. On "boy-bishops" see K. Young, *The drama of the medieval church* (2 vols) (Oxford, Clarendon Press, 1933), I, pp. 106–11.

the King's College accounts from 1450–1 to 1534–5, and in 1505–6 there is a list of items given to the "boy" that includes a scarlet robe and hood, a white coat, a scarlet gown and hood, a pair of gloves, gold rings, a golden brooch and a jewelled mitre.[78] "Boy-bishops" are also recorded in the accounts of Magdalen College, Oxford, from the late-fifteenth century.[79] "Boy-bishops" have not been detected in the copious accounts of the King's Hall, Cambridge. In 1386–7, however, there are payments to a "king" and a "bishop" of nearby All Saints parish church and to a "king" and a "bishop" of Great St Mary's Church. The latter had been appropriated to the college in 1343 and later served as the university church.[80] In both cases, the payments to the "kings" were made on the feast of St Edmund, and those to the "bishops" were handed over on the feast of St Nicholas. It seems likely that these "mock kings" were either "boy-kings" or "parish kings". Similarly, the "bishops" were probably "boy-bishops" or just conceivably "parish bishops". The "mock king" of Great St Mary's had a female servant, and this would have enhanced the pretentiousness of the position. "Boy-bishops" were suppressed in England in 1541. Although some were revived in Queen Mary's reign, they finally disappeared under Elizabeth.

In the fourteenth and fifteenth centuries several of the English colleges are known to have paid for minstrel entertainments. While the bulk of the evidence for minstrel activity in university colleges survives from the second half of the fifteenth century, a notable exception is provided by the King's Hall where plentiful references to a wide variety of minstrel entertainers are found in the annual accounts between 1342–3 and the final extant account of 1543–4. This material proves that rudimentary types of secular entertainment were being presented in at least one English college from the first half of the fourteenth century. The prominence of the minstrel revels at the King's Hall almost certainly reflects the organic connections that this college had with the royal household and court.

78. Extracts from the King's College accounts relating to "boy-bishops" are printed by Nelson, *Records of early English drama*, I, pp. 32–108. The entry for the inventory pertaining to the "boy-bishop" of 1505–6 is printed, pp. 79–80.
79. See extracts from the Magdalen accounts in Chambers, *The medieval stage*, II, pp. 248–70. See also for "boy-bishops" at Magdalen, R. S. Stanier, *Magdalen School*, 2nd edn (Oxford, Basil Blackwell, 1958), pp. 47–8.
80. King's Hall accounts, III, fols 58v, 61.

Apart from regular entertainments by individual or small bands of itinerant minstrels, the King's Hall played host to a rich diversity of specific groups of performers.[81] These included the folk players of All Saints parish, Cambridge, the king's household minstrels, the queen's minstrels, the troupes of minstrels of the Earl of Salisbury, the Duke of Norfolk and the Duke of Exeter, and, in 1342, even a group maintained by Richard of Goldynton, a King's Hall commoner and the future chancellor of Cambridge University. On occasion, the college was expensively entertained by specific acts, for example by the king's conjurer (*prestigiator regis*) in 1532–3 and two years later by "braunden the kyngs jogular".[82] The revels at the King's Hall were at their most lavish at Christmas and on Holy Innocents' Day. At this latter feast university officials, townsmen, often including the mayor, college tenants and their wives, friars and other guests were invited to share the festivities with the fellows and commoners. The scale of the entertainment at this feast may be gauged from the total bill of £2 2s 9d in 1468–9 for performers, guests and for the porterage of organs to the college.[83] An impressive feature of the entries for minstrels in the accounts of the King's Hall is the range of the terms employed. These include *ioculator, iugulator, me(i)ne(i)strallus, mimus, histrio, lusor, ludens, tripudians, fistulator, buccinator, tubicens, wayt* and *pleyar*. There is considerable uncertainty about the precise meanings of these terms. It is not known how many are interchangeable and how many may denote a specific type of dramatic performance. *Fistulator* (piper), *buccinator* and *tubicens* (trumpeters) were clearly performers of a specialist nature, and others such as *lusor* and *ludens* may well have been actors. The *wayts* and *histriones ville* were probably minstrels in the service of the municipal corporation of Cambridge, although *wayts* were also retained by the university.

From the extant records it appears that the King's Hall was the leading Cambridge college for minstrel entertainments before the mid-fifteenth century, after which it was paralleled in this respect by the frequency of minstrel performances at King's College. From 1388–9 Peterhouse had fairly regular visits from minstrels, and they are recorded at Corpus Christi College, Cambridge, in 1380–1 and 1398–9 and are

---

81. For this paragraph see the longer discussion, with detailed notes, by Cobban, *The King's Hall*, pp. 222–7.
82. King's Hall accounts, XXIV, fol. 117v; XXV, fol. 1v.
83. *ibid.*, XIV, fol. 6.

quite frequent in the second half of the fifteenth century.[84] The evidence for minstrels in Oxford colleges dates mainly from the late-fifteenth century, but earlier minstrel entertainments may be hidden from view because of lost or imperfect documentation.[85] An interesting series of entries in the King's College accounts of the second half of the fifteenth century are those for "disguisings" or masques that utilized costumes, music and perhaps painted scenery.[86] It is possible that plays were performed in King's College from 1465–6 and at the King's Hall in 1503–4, 1507–8 and 1508–9, if the enigmatic term *ludus* may be interpreted as a kind of ensemble playing.[87]

At Oxford, religious dramas were staged at Magdalen College from 1486. Fully-fledged plays were mounted at Cardinal College in 1530 and at Brasenose in *c.*1542.[88] The first definite evidence for the performance of a Latin classical play in an English college belongs to 1510–11 when a comedy of Terence was staged at the King's Hall.[89] Another play of Terence was performed in this royal college in 1516–17. On this occasion, the vice-master of the college, master Thorpe, directed the play, the actors being recruited from Thorpe's pupils.[90] Queens' College, Cambridge, performed a play by Plautus in 1522–3, and plays began to be staged at St John's College, Cambridge, from at least 1524–5. A production of Aristophanes' *Plutus* was mounted in the original Greek at St John's in 1536. Christ's College, Cambridge, performed annual plays from 1530–1 at the latest, and by the mid-sixteenth century the English colleges were noted venues for classical drama.[91] The university authorities were at first predictably wary about allowing dramatic productions in colleges, halls and hostels. They feared the alleged corrupting

---

84. See the extracts from the accounts of these Cambridge colleges up to 1500 in Nelson, *Records of early English drama*, I, pp. 3–76; see also G. C. Moore-Smith (ed.), "The academic drama at Cambridge: extracts from college records", in *Malone Society Collections* 2, pt 2 (Oxford, Oxford University Press, 1923), pp. 150–230.

85. For evidence of minstrels in Oxford colleges see R. E. Alton (ed.), "The academic drama in Oxford: extracts from the records of four colleges", in *Malone Society Collections* 5 (Oxford, Oxford University Press, 1960), pp. 29–95.

86. Nelson, *Records of early English drama*, I, pp. 36, 38, 39, 47, 49, 63, 64, 68.

87. For *ludi* at the King's Hall see King's Hall accounts, XX, fols 69v, 164, 196.

88. Chambers, *The medieval stage*, II, p. 195.

89. King's Hall accounts, XXI, fol. 137.

90. *ibid.*, XXVI, fol. 180v.

91. Nelson, *Records of early English drama*, II, pp. 711–12; Chambers, *The medieval stage*, II, p. 195. For early plays in English colleges see F. S. Boas, *University drama in the Tudor age* (Oxford, Clarendon Press, 1914), ch. 1.

influences associated with acting and also the unsavoury nature of the content of some of the classical plays. However, the impact of humanist learning gradually wore down resistance and led to a relaxing of attitudes. The educational value of classical drama came to be generally admitted as suitable for a university audience. In particular, the enacting of classical plays was seen to provide a useful practical training in the art of rhetoric.

In keeping with the strictures on women within a university context, female parts had to be undertaken by male students. It is ironic that cross-dressing for scholars for dramatic purposes came to be sanctioned by authorities who had for so long been obsessively opposed to a feminine influence in university life. Not all scholars were prepared to acquiesce in the practice, some on biblical grounds, and as late as the seventeenth century there are instances of scholars who refused to take women's roles.[92]

In conclusion, it is unfortunate that the recreational activities surrounding the initiation of freshmen at the English universities in the medieval period are largely hidden. At universities all over Europe new students were subjected to varying degrees of humiliating and sadistic treatment at the hands of their older peers, accompanied by all manner of unruly behaviour, excess drinking and horse-play. In the anonymous *Manuale scholarium*, a late-fifteenth century treatise featuring a dialogue between two students at Heidelberg University, some of the more barbaric aspects of initiation rites in the German universities are dramatically enacted. Here, the freshman is regarded as a foul-smelling wild beast with horns who has to undergo a series of crude, cleansing rituals before being considered suitable for admission to the fellowship of scholars. After these indignities, the traumatized victim had to provide a banquet for the company of tormentors.[93] In some of the French provincial universities student "abbots" were elected whose function was to hold regular courts in which freshmen were purged of alleged sins, their conduct was closely monitored and punishments were meted out in the form of a specified number of physical blows.[94] Nothing comparable to these practices has come to light for medieval English

---

92. See, for example, Nelson, *Records of early English drama*, I, pp. 543–4.
93. Seybolt, *The manuale scholarium*, pp. 24–33.
94. See, conveniently, Rashdall, *Universities*, III, pp. 383–4; Rait, *Life in the medieval university*, pp. 112–15.

freshmen. However, less barbarous though still unpleasant initiation ceremonies are recorded at Merton College, Oxford, and other colleges in the post-Reformation era. At Merton, freshmen were compelled to make mock speeches on certain occasions and were subject to "tucking", the cutting open of the chin with a thumb-nail, and the forced drinking of salted beer.[95] These customs presumably had their antecedents in the medieval period and were mercifully only pale dilutions of the more injurious continental practices.

95. Rashdall, *Universities*, III, p. 385.

CHAPTER SEVEN

Government and administration

The medieval English universities were privately financed corporations, deriving their resources in the main from teaching and
degree fees, fines, rents from urban property and the generous donations
of benefactors. As such, they were not obligated to the state in a financial
sense, although they relied upon consistent monarchical support for
their privileged status within the community. Problems arose, however,
with the external ecclesiastical powers that for a time seriously en-
croached upon the idea and reality of university autonomy.

In common with many universities in northern Europe, Oxford and
Cambridge, as institutions within the dioceses of Lincoln and Ely respectively, were, until the fifteenth century, subject to episcopal jurisdiction
and to the metropolitan jurisdiction of the Archbishop of Canterbury.
It is true that the exercise of ecclesiastical jurisdiction in the medieval
English universities was fairly low-key for lengthy stretches of time and
no great inroads were made upon the daily workings of university
government. Although the Bishops of Lincoln and Ely did not intervene
overmuch in the details of university administration, in the thirteenth
and fourteenth centuries they tended to adopt a firm paternalistic stance
towards the universities, regarding them as diocesan institutions that
were to be incorporated perpetually within the ecclesiastical hierarchy.
Such a view was incompatible with the aspirations of Oxford and Cambridge to be independent of episcopal dominion and to be recognized

213

as sovereign guilds regulated by their own statutes and privileges and governed by their own appointed officers.[1]

Originally, the chancellors of Oxford and Cambridge derived their authority as officials of the Bishops of Lincoln and Ely and were viewed as exercising delegated episcopal jurisdiction. Early in the thirteenth century, however, the position of the English chancellors was radically altered when they became the elected heads of their guilds of masters. Following on from this, the chancellors claimed to base their authority, not from a distant episcopal source, but from the academic guilds that had elected them. In this manner, the English chancellors were wholly identified with the interests of their magisterial guilds and they personified the drive for autonomous status. The intermittent conflicts that occurred between the universities and the episcopal powers centred principally upon the claim of the bishop to control the appointment of the chancellor by insisting upon episcopal confirmation of the chancellor-elect. Supplementary claims included the right of the Bishops of Lincoln and Ely to subject the universities to visitation and the right to hear appeals from the chancellor's court. These issues were fought out between the thirteenth and fifteenth centuries and the intensity of the conflict varied according to the character and attitudes of individual bishops and chancellors. In general, it may be said that the struggle was more bitterly fought at Oxford than at Cambridge where the issues were contested with less acrimony and easier compromise.

After many vicissitudes Cambridge University eventually gained a final exemption from all episcopal and archiepiscopal jurisdiction by a bull of Pope Eugenius IV in 1433, and Oxford acquired a similar exemption by a bull of Pope Sixtus IV in 1479.[2] Given these protracted struggles, it is clear that the masters' guilds of Oxford and Cambridge could not function as wholly independent corporations until their emancipation

1. For a detailed account of relations between the Universities of Oxford and Cambridge and their external ecclesiastical authorities see Cobban, *Medieval English universities*, pp. 274–99. On the struggle of universities in northern Europe to emancipate themselves from episcopal dominion see A. B. Cobban, "Episcopal control in the medieval universities of northern Europe", *Studies in Church History* 5, 1969, pp. 1–22.
2. For the bull of Eugenius IV of 18 September 1433 see the copy in Cambridge University archives, Luard, no. 114; see also *Calendar of entries in the papal registers relating to Great Britain and Ireland: papal letters. Volume 8 (1427–47)* (London, HMSO, 1909), pp. 484–5. The bull of Sixtus IV of 1479 is printed by J. Gutch (ed.), *Anthony Wood's history and antiquities of the University of Oxford* (2 vols in 3) (Oxford, Clarendon Press, 1792–6), I, pp. 632–5.

from the external ecclesiastical authorities had been effected. The record of the episcopate in England and throughout northern Europe *viv-à-vis* the place that universities ought to occupy in society was rather unenlightened before the fifteenth century when attitudes belatedly began to change. For long, bishops in northern Europe, with some exceptions, resisted the principle that the core of a university was its autonomy. Apparently, many bishops could not understand that the universities could not be treated as ecclesiastical "colonies", but were evolving organisms that needed to breathe the air of independence if they were to grow as influential intellectual centres.[3] It is especially surprising that Oxford's relations with the Bishop of Lincoln in the thirteenth and fourteenth centuries were frequently strained when it is considered that six or seven of the nine bishops who held the see between 1209 and 1362 had been masters at Oxford. However, it seems that once they ascended the episcopal throne, their previous teaching careers had little effect on modifying their determination to uphold diocesan rights to the full at the expense of the university. For example, Robert Grosseteste and Oliver Sutton had spent many years at Oxford University before becoming Bishops of Lincoln. They both proved to be remarkably vigorous in exercising the rights of their office over the university. Sutton's tenure of the see witnessed a series of bitter wrangles that, at one point, almost drove the university to disperse.[4] It is ironical that whereas ecclesiastics were among the most generous of benefactors to the English universities, their diocesan bishops sought for so long to impede their progress towards full autonomous status.

Despite the fact that before the fifteenth century there was a potential ecclesiastical brake upon their unfettered functioning, the English universities, in common with a wide spectrum of craft guilds, claimed to operate from the early-thirteenth century as self-contained, independent corporations with their own statutes, privileges, immunities, seals and elected officers. As such, they had complete control over the recruitment

3. Cobban, "Episcopal control in the medieval universities of northern Europe", pp. 1–22.
4. For Grosseteste's dealings with the university see C. H. Lawrence, "The university in state and church", in *HUO*, I, pp. 100–2. For Sutton and the University of Oxford see *ibid.*, pp. 106–11; R. M. T. Hill, "Oliver Sutton, Bishop of Lincoln, and the University of Oxford", *TRHS*, 4th ser. **31**, 1949, pp. 1–16; Hill (ed.), *The rolls and register of Bishop Oliver Sutton 1280–1299*, Lincoln Record Society **3**, 1952, pp. xiii–xxiii, lxiv–lxxvii, and Hill, *Oliver Sutton*, Lincoln Minster Pamphlets **4** (Lincoln, J. W. Ruddock, 1950), pp. 28–32.

of teaching staff and students, and all university personnel were subject to guild jurisdiction. In this way, the masters' guilds of Oxford and Cambridge sought to embody the intellectual, legal and political autonomy that are the necessary freedoms if universities are to realize their full capabilities. The politicization of the English universities was not really apparent until the sixteenth century when the Tudor government began to treat Oxford and Cambridge as an arm of the state and expected compliance to the royal will.[5] Before the sixteenth century, however, the masters' guilds, led by their elected chancellors, assumed full responsibility for university government and for the setting and maintenance of academic standards. They were not accountable in any specific sense to external bodies, and they were not subject to outside monitoring of academic progress and teaching quality. The medieval English universities were blessedly innocent of the modern obsession of attempting to measure the culturally unmeasurable by means of flawed and ultimately absurd performance indicators. They were threatened by no outside agency with a mission to impose a catalogue of norms and guidelines. Self-regulation and internal policing were the means by which the university authorities sought to control their regimes.

The English universities were well aware that they had to inspire confidence in their educational vocation and in the success with which it was carried out on behalf of the society that they served. If they failed to retain that confidence, their sources of private income and capital investment would be seriously diminished. This general and non-mechanistic type of accountability was the only sensible and effective control that was exercised. Where such amorphous and elusive subjects as education and scholarship are concerned, the value for money concept is rendered meaningless when translated crudely into rigidly defined objectives or targets. The only meaningful judgment is the general perception of the standing of a university on the part of those individuals and social groupings that have experienced its services, employed its graduates or benefited from its scholarship. Since generations of graduates of medieval Oxford and Cambridge appear to have sustained England's political, administrative, legal, ecclesiastical and educational systems with

---

5. See, for example, C. Cross, "Oxford and the Tudor state from the accession of Henry VIII to the death of Mary", in *HUO*, III, pp. 117–49.

a marked degree of success, it is a fair conclusion that the English universities were widely acknowledged as occupying a necessary and valuable place in society.[6]

That the government of the English universities should have rested in any hands other than those of the masters' guilds would have seemed a very singular proposition in the medieval period. Following the analogy of craft guilds, only those who were professionally qualified as academic masters were entitled to direct the affairs of a university. It was part of the natural order that only those who were directly responsible for the essential processes of teaching, learning, examining and the awarding of degrees were authorized to regulate such activities. Within this context, non-academic administrative staff might play a supportive role, but they were few in number and were assigned to a suitably subordinate position. There could be no possibility of power-sharing between academic and non-academic staff. There were no academic and administrative sectors as in a modern university, and no imposing structures for the housing of an administrative hierarchy. In the medieval period, the university was overwhelmingly an academic corporation.

At the pinnacle of English university government was the office of chancellor. By 1400 the chancellors of Oxford and Cambridge, as the elected heads of their academic guilds, had accumulated a remarkable array of powers. As discussed in Chapter 6, the chancellors came to exercise a commanding authority over the economic and environmental business of their towns, and they had a considerable control over those issues of morality that affected the daily lives of the citizenry. Moreover, the chancellors had jurisdiction over all university personnel, whether clerical, lay or members of the religious orders, and they also claimed to have cognizance of all "mixed" civil and criminal cases involving both scholars and citizens, although this gave rise to much legal dispute with the municipal authorities. An arresting feature of the English chancellorships is that they possessed quasi-archidiaconal functions, seemingly conferred upon them by their diocesan bishops. By virtue of these powers, the chancellors supervised, among other matters, the

---

6. For an analysis of the careers of medieval English graduates see Cobban, *Medieval English universities*, pp. 393–9; Aston, "Oxford's medieval alumni", pp. 27–32; Aston, Duncan & Evans, "The medieval alumni of the University of Cambridge", pp. 67–84; J. Dunbabin, "Careers and vocations", in *HUO*, I, p. 565–605.

5. A confirmation, probably of 1294, by Edward I of Henry III's writ to the sheriff of Cambridge University concerning the imprisonment of scholars who were troublesome disturbers of the peace. The sheriff was to act on the request of the chancellor. Co-operation between the chancellor and sheriff was one of the means by which the serious crime problem in Cambridge was to be addressed.

probate of wills of members of the university who had died within its precincts.[7] The range of penalties at the disposal of the English chancellors was impressive, and it is clear that they were formidable figures within both their own domain and in the town. In certain circumstances, the chancellors even had the power to imprison for up to a few days. Whereas the Paris chancellor had a university prison until this was forbidden in 1231, the English chancellors had to use prison accommodation made available either by the king or by the town. In this matter of imprisonment, the chancellors generally co-operated with the sheriffs of Oxford and Cambridge. In the case of Cambridge Henry III initiated in 1242 the machinery whereby the sheriff, at the instance of the chancellor, was to arrest or imprison rebellious and troublesome scholars.

7. For the Oxford chancellor's archidiaconal powers see Salter, *Registrum cancellarii oxoniensis*, I, pp. xv–xvii; for the similar powers of the Cambridge chancellor see Hackett, *The original statutes of Cambridge University*, pp. 108–9.

This provision was confirmed by Edward I, probably in 1294.[8] It seems clear that the powers of the English chancellors, that included a spiritual jurisdiction derived from their diocesan bishops, were more extensive than those wielded by any of their continental equivalents. For instance, neither the chancellor nor the rector of Paris, nor the chancellor of Montpellier, nor the student rectors of Bologna, could in any way match the chancellors of Oxford and Cambridge with respect to the remarkable extent of their authority.

Whereas the chancellor of Paris University was an external official set above the masters' guild and acted as the delegate of the Bishop of Paris, the English chancellors were the living embodiment of guild autonomy. From the second half of the fifteenth century, however, the chancellors became increasingly non-resident dignitaries who were often selected for the political influence that they could wield in government circles on behalf of their universities. Eventually, non-resident chancellors came to hold the office for life. John Russell, Lord Chancellor and Bishop of Lincoln, was the first Oxford chancellor to do so, being elected in 1483, and John Fisher, Bishop of Rochester, was the first to hold the Cambridge chancellorship for life following election to that position in 1504.[9] Although a non-resident chancellor with influence at the centre of political power could be of benefit to the academic world, the problem arose when the chancellorship was used by the crown as one of the agencies by which the English universities were subjected to state control. A similar fate had befallen Paris University when it lost its hard-won autonomous standing and was reduced to a marked degree of dependence upon the monarchy.[10] The emergence of non-resident chancellors in the English universities brought to prominence the office of vice-chancellor. The terminology pertaining to this office varied as between Oxford and Cambridge. The main point is, however, that from the late-fifteenth century vice-chancellors were

8. The varied powers of the English university chancellors are discussed by Cobban, *Medieval English universities*, pp. 64–72. For the writ of Henry III of 1242 to the sheriff of Cambridge see Cooper, *Annals*, I, p. 44.
9. For Russell see Emden, *BRUO*, III, pp. 1609–11 and for Fisher see Emden, *BRUC*, pp. 229–30. Mullinger, *The University of Cambridge*, I, pp. 423–629 provides much information on Fisher and Cambridge.
10. See, for example, Cobban, *The medieval universities: their development and organization*, pp. 94–5; Verger, *Les universités au moyen âge*, pp. 167–9.

acting, under delegated powers from the chancellors, as the *de facto* heads of their universities.

The English university chancellors could not have functioned without the unceasing support of their chief executive agents, the proctors, who were burdened with a remarkable range of responsibilities. Indeed, the proctors were the energetic wheels that drove the essential administrative processes of both universities.[11] The proctors were two in number at each university, and they were elected for a year at a time, renewable by re-election. Given the onerous nature of the office, few would have wished to serve beyond the minimum period.

The proctors were usually masters of arts, and at Oxford they were elected by an indirect procedure by the regents in arts.[12] In thirteenth-century Cambridge the regents in theology and canon law shared in the election alongside the regents in arts. In the fourteenth century, however, the voting constituency was normally confined to the regent masters in arts, non-regents in arts being called in to assist if there were insufficient teaching masters in the arts faculty or if an electoral deadlock had been reached.[13] The English office of proctor was almost certainly inspired by that of Paris University where the proctors were the heads of the four subdivisions or nations of the faculty of arts. A crucial difference between the Parisian and the English proctors is that those of Paris were primarily representatives of the faculty of arts whereas those of Oxford and Cambridge were the executive agents of the entire university. At Oxford, one of the proctors was chosen from the northern regent masters in arts, defined as north of the river Nene, and the other was selected from the southern masters. This geographical balance was designed to assuage to some extent the bitter strife between northern and southern scholars that was an endemic element of Oxford life. The north–south geographical basis of appointment was applied to many of the other administrative officers within Oxford,

---

11. For the statutory functions of the Oxford proctors see Gibson, *Statuta antiqua*, pp. lxxv–vi, 66, 67, 197–8. For other references to their duties in Oxford statutes see *ibid.*, pp. 28–30, 57–9, 68, 73, 88, 96, 107, 123–6, 182, 187, 195–6, 211–12. For the Cambridge proctors see *Camb. Docs*, I, pp. 340–49. A succinct account of the Oxford proctors from the medieval period to the twentieth century is given by Pantin, *Oxford life in Oxford archives*, pp. 76–84.
12. Gibson, *Statuta antiqua*, pp. xxxix, lxxvi, 64–6.
13. Hackett, *The original statutes of Cambridge University*, pp. 153–4, 204–5; *Camb. Docs*, I, pp. 338–9.

although exceptions were made in the cases of the chancellor, the registrar, the chaplains and the bedels.[14] It was customary for one of the proctors to be known as the senior proctor and the other as the junior proctor, a distinction that seemed to indicate their relative seniority as masters of arts.[15] At Cambridge, the title of senior proctor was given to the regent master who had gained the most votes in the election, and the candidate who came next in the election received the title of junior proctor.[16] There is no clear evidence that the Cambridge proctors were appointed on the same north–south basis as at Oxford, although Cambridge experienced similar rivalries and feuds between northern and southern scholars.

The enormous range of responsibilities that were discharged by the proctors is an overwhelming illustration of the fact that the administrative life of the English universities was very much the concern of the professional academics. In association with the chancellor, the proctors had an involvement in almost every aspect of university business. They had ultimate responsibility for the smooth workings of all facets of the teaching regime, including the arrangement of the timetable and the proper conduct of lectures, disputations and inceptions. They organized the liturgical functions within the university, administered oath-taking, made the arrangements for funerals, directed university ceremonies and had to ensure that academics of all ranks observed holy days and other feast occasions. The proctors were heavily involved in the enforcement of university discipline. They and their agents had to identify masters and scholars who had perpetrated criminal acts or who had contravened university statutes, and the names of offenders had to be reported to the chancellor for possible legal action in the chancellor's court. They also recorded the names of academics and townspeople who had been sentenced to prison, or who had been banished from the town, or who were known disturbers of the peace, murderers or who were otherwise of ill repute. As representatives of the chancellor, the proctors were concerned with the implementation of the regulations governing the economic affairs of the town. Among other matters, they were required to root out the economic malpractices of tradesmen and their

---

14. A. B. Emden, "Northerners and southerners in the organization of the University to 1509", in *Oxford studies presented to Daniel Callus*, pp. 2–4.
15. *ibid.*, p. 18.
16. *Camb. Docs*, I, p. 339.

wives and, as far as possible, to ensure that foodstuffs were sold at fair and not at artificially inflated prices. The names of cheating tradespeople were to be sent to the chancellor. The proctors also served as archivists, and they had custody of the charters, privileges and other muniments of the university that were stored in administrative chests.

The role of the proctors in summoning university assemblies seems to have differed at Oxford and Cambridge. At Oxford, the proctors normally consulted the chancellor before summoning the congregation of regents. The proctors alone, however, could summon the congregation of regents and the sovereign body, the congregation of regents and non-regents, if the chancellor refused to do so for no good reason. Likewise, there were occasions when the chancellor alone could summon university assemblies if the proctors proved to be unwilling. In this way, the Oxford chancellor and proctors acted as a check on each other, although co-operation was the norm. By contrast, the Cambridge chancellor appears to have summoned all university congregations without having to gain the prior agreement of the proctors.[17] A statute of 1276 gave the proctors the right to convoke the regents in exceptional circumstances as a remedy against a chancellor who had failed in some way to give the regents adequate protection.[18] Typically, however, the chancellor's sole prerogative right to summon congregations went unchallenged. From this, it is evident that the authority of the proctors in this matter of the summoning of university assemblies was markedly less at Cambridge than at Oxford.

The medieval English universities did not consider the employment of non-academic administrators to manage their finances. Such an important matter for the health of the masters' guilds had to be under the control of their own members. In practice, this substantial burden fell upon the redoubtable shoulders of the proctors, and was one of the most intricate and time-consuming of their many tasks. In this regard, the proctors were required to submit annual accounts of income and

17. For the Oxford and Cambridge proctors and university assemblies see Cobban, *Medieval English universities*, pp. 80–1; Hackett, *The original statutes of Cambridge University*, pp. 143–6.
18. This statute is discussed by W. Ullmann, "The decline of the chancellor's authority in medieval Cambridge: a rediscovered statute", *Historical Journal* **I**, 1958, pp. 176–82. See also the comments of Hackett, *The original statutes of Cambridge University*, p. 144.

expenditure. Among the sources of university income that were collected by the proctors were those that came under the umbrella heading of degree fees. These were usually referred to as "commons" for candidates who were about to take a master's or doctor's degree, and "semi-commons" for those taking a bachelor's degree in any faculty. These payments were graded according to the degree in question and also in relation to the amount that the candidates had been paying for their weekly commons in their university accommodation.[19] Fees of this type were quite modest and stand in stark contrast to the very heavy degree payments known as composition fees. Composition fees were those paid in place of giving a feast for the regent masters in the faculty in which the degree was taken.[20] The provision of a feast was a statutory obligation for admission to a degree. It seems that candidates for the degree of master of arts quite often opted for the banquet while composition fees were commonly paid by candidates for doctoral degrees.[21] One or two examples will illustrate the costly nature of composition fees. At Oxford, two secular masters paid £20 each upon admission to doctoral degrees in theology in 1469–70. For the same degree two friars expended £10 each in 1472–3, and one friar paid £10 in 1474–5. Four friars advanced a combined fee of £26 13s 4d in 1481–2, and one friar paid £6 13s 4d in 1496–7.[22] It is evident that it was most advantageous for the university to have such large cash payments in lieu of degree banquets.

The Cambridge proctors derived an important source of revenue from forfeited cautions (*cautiones*) or pledges. Candidates for a degree at Cambridge had to give a caution such as a book, an item of plate or an article of dress when they declared their intention of proceeding to a degree. The pledges were forfeited if the statutory academic exercises

---

19. Salter, *The medieval archives of the University of Oxford*, II, p. 275; Pantin & Mitchell, *The register of congregation 1448–1463*, p. xxiii. For the receipt of degree fees known as "commons" or "semi-commons" in the Oxford proctors' accounts see Salter, *The medieval archives*, II, pp. 294, 298, 306, 310, 314, 317, 321, 326, 330, 336, 341, 346, 350, 355. There are innumerable entries for degree fees or "commons" received by the Cambridge proctors throughout Leathes, *Grace Book A*.
20. Gibson, *Statuta antiqua*, pp. 244–5, 290–1.
21. Pantin & Mitchell, *The register of congregation*, pp. xxiii–iv.
22. Salter, *The medieval archives*, II, pp. 298, 306, 314, 330, 355. Composition fees tended to be smaller at Cambridge, although there were exceptions: see Leathes, *Grace Book A*, pp. 4, 5, 9, 18, 32, 84.

required for the degree were not performed.[23] This system did not operate at Oxford where candidates were not obliged to give cautions. Instead, they had to swear an oath that all the necessary steps and duties associated with obtaining the degree would be carried out.[24]

The proctors also added to university income through the garnering of fees for graces. Graces were dispensations from the full statutory requirements governing degrees. Not all of them had fees attached, but the Oxford proctors drew a significant revenue from graces in the fifteenth century. For instance, sums of about £35 were realized from this source in 1469–70 and in 1478–9.[25] Thomas Gascoigne, who was Oxford's chancellor in the early 1440s, made a written attack before c.1457 on those regent masters and proctors who granted too many dispensations from the statutes for purely financial reasons.[26] It is true that in the mid-fifteenth century Oxford University was seeking every conceivable way of raising revenue to finance the building of the divinity school and graces presented one such opportunity. From the available evidence, however, it is not possible to estimate the degree of academic corruption relating to the selling of graces. Study of the first extant proctors' book for Cambridge, *Grace Book A*, that covers the years from 1454 to 1488 suggests that the granting of graces for financial gain was only a limited practice at this period, although the frequency of monetary dispensations increased from the end of the fifteenth century.[27]

As privately financed corporations, bequests, whether in the form of loan-chests or of capital sums for building or other stipulated purposes, were vital transfusions for sustaining the vigorous life of Oxford and Cambridge. The proctors had the responsibility of processing corporate gifts, although they probably had no direct jurisdiction over benefactions to colleges. They were also responsible for the collection of rents from

23. Leathes, *Grace Book A*, p. ix. A list of books deposited as cautions between 1454 and 1488 is printed in *ibid.*, pp. x–xvi, and a similar list for the period from 1488 to 1511 is printed in Bateson, *Grace Book B Part I*, pp. viii–xiii. The monetary value of pledges for degrees in the superior faculties was considerably higher than for the lower arts degree.
24. Salter, *Medieval archives*, II, p. 275.
25. *ibid.*, II, pp. 298, 321.
26. T. Gascoigne, *Loci e libro veritatum*, J. E. T. Rogers (ed.) (Oxford, Clarendon Press, 1881), p. 3; Gibson, *Statuta antiqua*, p. xxvi, *n.* 1.
27. Leathes, *Grace Book A* and Bateson, *Grace Book B Part I*, p. xiii and throughout.

urban property, for enforcing the fines imposed by the chancellor's court and for the receipt of many other miscellaneous sums. As well as acting as receivers for university income, the proctors had to keep detailed accounts of expenditure. Money was spent on a vast variety of items that are far too numerous to specify here, and only a flavour of the multifarious areas of expenditure can be indicated.

The proctors' accounts record payments, for example, for building materials and construction, for the expenses and allowances of the chancellor, proctors and bedels, for entertainment for the auditors of the accounts, visiting royalty and other guests, for monetary aid for poor masters and scholars, for the regular cleaning of university schools and rushes or straw for their floors, for the clearing of drains, for the enrolment of privileges, for the writing of letters, for bearers of crosses in university processions, for bellropes, candles, chains for books, keys, seals and wax for seals.[28] It is manifest that overseeing university income and expenditure and causing everything to be recorded in intricate detail was an arduous task in itself. When combined with the many other activities that were heaped upon the proctors, there can be no doubt that they had to be extremely versatile, possessed of immense stamina, and that they formed, with the chancellor, the core of administrative government.

Given that the proctors at Oxford and Cambridge were regents in arts, it follows that many of them would have been quite young. Since it was common for a high proportion of teaching masters in arts to leave university to seek alternative employment or to migrate to a superior faculty while still in their twenties, the proctors would generally have been of that age. Despite their awesome responsibilities, the proctors do not appear to have received a statutory salary. They were, however, entitled to a share of the fines and fees collected, and they were allowed to keep some of the proceeds from the sale of confiscated weapons. They were fully reimbursed for expenses incurred in the prosecution of university business and, certainly at Oxford, an allowance was given for their night patrols of the town when enforcing the

---

28. These items of income and expenditure are derived from the 15 audited proctors' accounts for Oxford, extending from 1464 to 1496, and printed in Salter, *Medieval archives*, II, pp. 272–358, and from the unaudited Cambridge proctors' accounts that are almost continuous from 1454 and are printed in Leathes, *Grace Book A* (1454–88) and in Bateson, *Grace Book B Part I* (1488–1511).

peace.[29] The approximate personal income of the proctors is known in only two instances. In 1426–7 the Oxford junior proctor, John Arundel, achieved an income of about £10 6s 3d, not counting gifts in kind, and in 1474 the income of the Oxford proctor, Richard Bradley, was £5 17s 1d.[30] These are modest rewards indeed for the discharge of such pivotal university offices, and they probably indicate that teaching masters were often led to take on this burden through feelings of *noblesse oblige*.

An analysis of the extant proctors' accounts for Oxford and Cambridge of the fifteenth century reveals that the English universities, excluding the endowed colleges, could scarcely be described as opulent corporations. On the basis of the proctors' accounts, it seems that Oxford's average annual current income was somewhere in the region of £70. Using the same material, H. E. Salter gave the average as £58, and this figure was repeated by W. A. Pantin.[31] This appears to be inaccurate, and the higher average of £70 is probably more realistic, although this sum is the average of very marked annual fluctuations over the century. Current university income must be taken in conjunction with the university's capital assets of which the endowed loan-chests, excluding collegiate chests, formed the principal source. It has been reckoned, as a broad estimate, that by 1360 the capital value of the university's loan-chests was about £1,300.[32] As in the case of current income, there were wide fluctuations in annual expenditure in the fifteenth century. The average yearly outlay appears to have been about £61, although it is puzzling that Salter gives the average as less than £45.[33]

It is even more difficult to estimate Cambridge's annual income and expenditure in the fifteenth century. This is because the surviving proctors' accounts are not the final audited versions, and reliable figures for total income and expenditure may be calculated for just over half of the years of account. That is, of the 46 years of account between 1454–5 and 1499–1500, reasonably sound figures for total income are obtainable

29. Salter, *Medieval archives*, II, p. 283; Hackett, "The university as a corporate body", in *HUO*, I, p. 85.
30. For Arundel's income as proctor see A. B. Emden, "The remuneration of the medieval proctors of the University of Oxford", *Oxoniensia* **26–7**, 1961–2, pp. 202–6. For Bradley's income see Salter, *Medieval archives*, II, p. 283.
31. Salter, *Medieval archives*, II, pp. 298, 346; Pantin, *Oxford life in Oxford archives*, p. 80.
32. Aston & Faith, "The endowments of the university and colleges to *c*.1348", in *HUO*, I, p. 283.
33. Salter, *Medieval archives*, II, p. 272.

for only 26 years, and only 23 years yield usable figures for total expenditure. Bearing in mind these substantial limitations, it may be advanced that the average annual current income was about £27 and the average annual figure for current expenditure may have been approximately £21. Cambridge, as well as Oxford, had capital assets in the form of endowed loan-chests and, after all expenses had been deducted, the proctors often left useful annual reserves in the common chest of the university. For example, in 1492–3 the reserve in the common chest was just over £59 and in 1494–5 the surplus was slightly in excess of £54.[34]

The estimates for current income and expenditure of the English universities in the fifteenth century do not suggest conspicuous affluence. They seem to have achieved credit surpluses in most years, but they were heavily dependent on attracting external funding for building ventures and other exceptional purposes. In these circumstances, neither the chancellor nor the proctors nor anyone else could hope to engage in accurate forward planning.

While the chancellors and proctors comprised the executive heart of the medieval English universities, sovereignty came to reside in the congregation of regents and non-regents. No matter how powerful the chancellors appeared to be, standing as they did at the apex of university government, they were ultimately accountable to the sovereign body, from which, with the exception of their spiritual jurisdiction, they derived their authority. The chancellors, chosen normally from the doctors of theology and canon law, may have been the elected constitutional heads and chief executive agents of the masters' guilds, but, like the humblest scholar, they were wholly bound by the constraints of university law. The non-regents, as part of the sovereign assembly, form an interesting category in the English university context. The non-regents were masters who had ceased to teach either because they were pursuing a course of further study or because they had left the university. In the latter eventuality, they still retained the title of non-regent and could return to university teaching at a future date. In the thirteenth century the congregation of regents had been the sovereign body at both Oxford and Cambridge, to which the non-regents were admitted on exceptional occasions.[35] By the end of the thirteenth century, however,

34. Bateson, *Grace Book B Part I*, pp. 56, 78.
35. For Oxford see Hackett, "The university as a corporate body", *HUO*, I, pp. 55–61; for Cambridge see Hackett, *The original statutes of Cambridge University*, pp. 240–1.

the Oxford non-regents had acquired, in practice, the status of co-legislators with the regents, and this right was made official in *c*.1303.[36] The Cambridge non-regents had been granted a similar status by 1304.[37] The congregation of regents at Oxford and Cambridge had now been replaced by the congregation of regents and non-regents as the highest legislative assembly in the university, with the power to enact, repeal and amend statutes.

The sovereign body at Oxford was also the highest university court of appeal. It had the right to hear appeals from the chancellor's court, although exceptions were made in the case of convictions for breaches of the peace for which appeals were not allowed.[38] At Cambridge, however, even after the congregation of regents and non-regents had been established as the supreme legislature, the congregation of regents retained its position as the highest court of appeal with the authority to decide appeals from the chancellor's court.[39] Whereas the non-regents came to occupy a fairly important role in English university government, they never acquired a comparable status at Paris. Non-regents were admitted to the Parisian sovereign assembly only by invitation of the rector on rare occasions, and they do not appear to have become a necessary constituent of that supreme body.[40]

Because of the impracticability of frequent summonings of the sovereign assemblies at Oxford and Cambridge, the congregation of regents became the body that carried out the routine functions of university government. They dealt with such matters as graces for degrees and dispensations from the statutes, loan-chests, accommodation, the election of university officers including the chancellor, proctors and bedels, the auditing of accounts, peace-keeping, building activity and many other administrative concerns.[41] There may have been some potential overlap between the functions of the proctors and the matters that came before

36. Gibson, *Statuta antiqua*, p. 109.
37. *Camb. Docs*, I, p. 308; Hackett, *The original statutes of Cambridge University*, pp. 241, 244.
38. Gibson, *Statuta antiqua*, pp. lxxx, 87, 125–6, 333–4.
39. Hackett, *The original statutes of Cambridge University*, p. 151.
40. P. Kibre, *The nations in the medieval universities* (Cambridge, Mass., Medieval Academy of America, 1948), p. 102. Rashdall probably exaggerated the extent to which the non-regents at Paris were associated with the sovereign body of regents: Rashdall, *Universities*, I, p. 410.
41. For a detailed view of the business conducted by the Oxford congregation of regents see the only surviving register of congregation before the sixteenth century, Pantin & Mitchell, *The register of congregation 1448–1463*.

the assembly of regents, although the degree to which this gave rise to conflict or ill-feeling is unknown. While the congregation of regents could not usurp the prerogatives of the sovereign body by assuming statute-making powers, at both Oxford and Cambridge the assembly of regents claimed the right to interpret the statutes.[42] Through membership of the supreme legislative body and of the congregation of regents, the teaching masters, in association with the executive committees of chancellors and proctors, had a high stake in university government and administration. Since arts was by far the largest of the faculties in the English universities, as it was at Paris, the regent masters in arts had, *ipso facto*, a dominant position in the congregation of regents. Given the youthfulness of many of the teachers in arts, commonly in their early or mid-twenties, the character of university government, must have been coloured to some extent by youthful vigour and youthful inexperience. Many of these regents in arts did not contemplate a long-term career in university teaching, and this may have encouraged in some a cavalier attitude towards university decision-making.

Arising from the preponderance of masters of arts among the regents, a rather odd development occurred at Oxford, though not at Cambridge. This was the emergence of a third assembly, that of the artists, named the Black Congregation because of the colour of their habits. The congregation of artists claimed to have a customary right of prior deliberation on proposed legislation that was scheduled for discussion by the sovereign assembly.[43] Moreover, the artists claimed the right to veto any item on its agenda.[44] The raucous demands of the assembly of artists were not always accepted, and in 1357 the non-regents combined with the regents in the superior faculties of theology and civil law to reject the alleged power of veto.[45] The Black Congregation declined in importance in the late-fifteenth century, and it disappeared from view in the sixteenth century. It had always been something of an anomaly. Although its existence was a rationalization of the numerical superiority of the regents in arts, they already had a natural majority in

---

42. On this point see, for Oxford, Gibson, *Statuta antiqua*, p. xxiii; for Cambridge see Hackett, *The original statutes of Cambridge University*, pp. 235–6.
43. For the congregation of artists, the Black Congregation, see Gibson, *Statuta antiqua*, pp. xxiii–iv, xxvi–xxxii; Pantin & Mitchell, *The register of congregation*, pp. 57–8, 227–8.
44. Gibson, *Statuta antiqua*, p. 179.
45. *ibid.*, p. 156.

the congregation of regents, and to try to gain a further advantage by means of the Black Congregation was bound to cause resentments and tensions within the body politic of the university.

Apart from the democratic involvement of the teaching masters in the governmental assemblies and the possibility of election to the offices of chancellor or proctor or taxor, they also had the opportunity to engage in a variety of administrative tasks. Previous chapters have shown that teaching masters might become principals of halls and hostels, they could serve as keepers of university or college loan-chests or of administrative chests that housed muniments, vestments or seals, and they could be hired to write letters on behalf of the university. If they were college fellows, they would probably be drawn into collegiate government or administration. A few privileged regent masters might receive an invitation to represent the king or pope diplomatically on the international stage. On the judicial front, there were opportunities for bachelors of civil and canon law at Oxford to deputize for the chancellor or vice-chancellor in weekly courts for the hearing of minor cases that had to be decided expeditiously within three days. This provided good work experience for the bachelor judges, although cases involving regent masters were reserved for the chancellor's court.[46]

The nations at Oxford, which were subdivisions of the faculty of arts, made little constructive contribution to university government.[47] Quite the reverse. In imitation of Paris, the Oxford nations were groupings of masters, although undergraduates may have been informally associated. The Oxford nations were divided into a northern grouping, comprising English masters from north of the river Nene and masters from Scotland, and a southern grouping, made up of English masters from south of the Nene and masters from Wales, Ireland and from overseas. In a large cosmopolitan university such as Paris, there was a manifest rationale for nation divisions in so far as they helped to inculcate a sense of belonging among masters of a similar regional identity. In the more insular University of Oxford, however, this need was circumscribed, and the nations in the thirteenth century did not serve any sharply defined purpose. They failed to develop much in the way of

46. *ibid.*, pp. lxxviii, 90.
47. For the nations in the English universities see Cobban, *Medieval English universities*, pp. 103–6; Kibre, *The nations in the medieval universities*, pp. 160–1, 166–7.

corporate organization, and they appear to have contributed little to the educational life of the university. Indeed, they were mainly characterized by turbulent behaviour and inter-nation feuding that sometimes simulated a miniature civil war. The gang-warfare activities of the nations reached such a pitch that in 1274 the university tried to abolish them through amalgamation. It is not known if nations were ever formally realized at Cambridge, although north–south divisions were certainly a destabilizing feature of the university scene.

English university government and administration was largely an academic monopoly, as was entirely consonant with the idea of a university as a self-regulating guild. The multiplicity of functions involved, however, necessitated the employment of a few non-academic administrators. The office of bedel was one of the oldest in the English universities, and bedels were the administrative assistants of the chancellor and proctors.[48] They publicized the times of the meetings of the chancellor's court, announced the decrees of the chancellor and of the sovereign assembly, they helped the proctors with the collection of fees and fines, and they had to be present in full ceremonial dress at inceptions, masses, funerals, processions and at congregations where they acted as ushers. The bedels read out proclamations and the texts of new statutes in the schools, and announced the timetable for disputations. They served writs, and kept lists of scholars who had received the teaching licence. The bedels also supervised the conduct of the university schools, paying particular attention to their cleanliness and seating arrangements. These officials were sometimes required to write out the agreements that were made between the university and the town, and on occasion they acted as mediators in disputes. Along with other officials, the bedels were ordered to seek out and destroy false weights and measures. There are instances where bedels are found as members of university delegations to the king or to parliament. The bedels were commonly quite prominent figures in the town. They tended to own urban property, were sometimes landlords to students and they could

48. For the Oxford bedels see Gibson, *Statuta antiqua*, pp. lxxvii–viii, 68–70; Salter, *Registrum cancellarii oxoniensis*, I, pp. xlv–vii; Hackett, "The university as a corporate body", pp. 86–7; Pantin & Mitchell, *The register of congregation*, pp. 424–5. For the Cambridge bedels see H. P. Stokes, *The esquire bedells of the University of Cambridge from the 13th century to the 20th century*, Cambridge Antiquarian Society, Octavo Publications **45**, 1911; Hackett, *The original statutes of Cambridge University*, pp. 159–62, 206–9, 281–5; *Camb. Docs*, I, pp. 353–6, 359.

6. The Cambridge vice-chancellor, all three bedels and others supervising the destruction of false weights and measures. The bedels are carrying their maces as symbols of their office. The illustration probably dates from *c*.1587.

act as agents for colleges, halls and hostels in the matter of property transactions. In the medieval period, Oxford had six bedels, three superior and three inferior, and Cambridge had two. All of the bedels were accredited to particular faculties.[49] So far as is known, the office of bedel in the English universities was not open to purchase as it was in some of the universities in France. For instance, in 1463 a bedel at Avignon bought the office for 200 guilders.[50]

As university government became more sophisticated in the later-medieval period, the demands of record-keeping and official correspondence justified the appointment of a registrar or secretary who was in

49. At Oxford each of the faculties of arts, theology and law (civil and canon law combined) was served by one superior and one inferior bedel. At Cambridge there were two statutory bedels before 1500, one serving the faculty of arts and the other the faculties of theology and canon law. In 1549 a third Cambridge bedel was officially recognized by statute.
50. See A. Gieysztor, "Management and resources", in *A history of the university in Europe*, I, p. 126.

harness at Oxford by 1447.[51] Before this time, the formal writing business of the university had been carried out by different hands. The proctors had been responsible for a variety of writing commitments, there was a clerk attached to the chancellor's office, regent masters were sometimes employed on an *ad hoc* basis to help with the drafting of letters and occasionally the bedels drew up written documents. In the course of the fifteenth century there was clearly a need at Oxford to make much of the recording of business and official epistolary work the prime responsibility of one non-academic salaried official. Because of the legal technicalities involved, the registrar had to be an MA, learned in rhetoric and a public notary.[52] To this new office belonged the drafting and registration of university letters, the recording of the proceedings of the university assemblies and all public acts of the chancellor, the drawing up of indentures and acquittances, the registration of graces, the listing of the names of graduates with the dates of their degrees and the fees paid, and the listing of sermons given as part of examinations. It also fell to the registrar to enter annually in the chancellor's register the names of the principals of halls, and to make a fair copy of the rolls of the proctors' annual accounts. In this way, the registrar helped to relieve the chancellor and proctors of some of the more mechanical burdens of their offices. The office of registrar at Cambridge cannot be traced before 1506. In that year, one of the bedels was made registrar, called registrary at Cambridge, and a bedel held the position through to the seventeenth century.[53] Prior to 1506 the university engaged a variety of letter writers ranging from the Italian humanist scholar, Caius Auberinus, to a master from Clare College.[54]

Of the remaining non-academic administrators mention should be made of the university chaplain. Both Oxford and Cambridge had employed a chaplain from the thirteenth century for the celebration of

51. Pantin & Mitchell, *The register of congregation*, pp. xi–xii, 427–8. The duties of the Oxford registrar are set out in a fifteenth-century statute of uncertain date: see Gibson, *Statuta antiqua*, pp. 285–6.
52. Gibson, *Statuta antiqua*, p. 285.
53. Peek & Hall, *The archives of the University of Cambridge*, pp. 7, 28.
54. For Caius Auberinus as a university letter-writer see Leathes, *Grace Book A*, pp. 185, 198 and Bateson, *Grace Book B Part I*, pp. 10, 29, 50, 63, 64, 87, 88, 96, 104, 119–21, 136–8, 171–3, 183–4, 193–5. For the master from Clare College as a letter-writer see *ibid.*, p. 175.

the statutory masses and for conducting the services for benefactors and the funerals of deceased university members.[55] In the fifteenth century the office of librarian was added to the duties of the chaplain at both universities.[56] Finally, the office of university stationer was of some antiquity at Oxford, as indeed it was at many continental universities. There were four official stationers at Oxford by 1346. They were elected each year by the congregation of regents, and they were subject to the chancellor's jurisdiction. Their responsibilities embraced the valuation of manuscripts and books and other items that had been given as pledges for sums borrowed from loan-chests. They were empowered to sell forfeited pledges on behalf of the university. The stationers were further charged with keeping an adequate supply of accurate exemplars or approved copies of texts, lectures and disputations for use in the university schools or for private study. As official university stationers, they probably had a watching brief over the conduct of the book trade in Oxford and its specialist workers such as the makers of parchment and paper, illuminators, binders and copyists.[57] Likewise, Cambridge had its official stationers who acted as agents for the university and whose functions were presumably similar to those of Oxford, although relatively little is known about them.[58]

In conclusion, it may be said that, as communities of scholars, the medieval English universities were organized and governed primarily in the interests of their academic members. They were free from the restraints of external paymasters and undue political pressure became a reality only in the Tudor period. Their organizational structures were cast in a democratic mould. Although the executive committees of chancellors and proctors were undoubtedly powerful, the system had built-in checks and balances and ultimate accountability lay with the sovereign assembly of regents and non-regents. The ordinary teaching masters had ample opportunities to make their voices heard in the university congregations. If they were teaching masters in arts at Oxford, they

55. For the Oxford chaplain see Hackett, "The university as a corporate body", p. 87 and Salter, *Medieval archives*, II, p. 286. For the Cambridge chaplain see H. P. Stokes, *The chaplains and the chapel of the University of Cambridge 1256–1568*, Cambridge Antiquarian Society, Octavo Publications **41**, 1906.
56. Gibson, *Statuta antiqua*, p. 217; J. P. C. Roach, "The university of Cambridge", in *Victoria history of the county of Cambridge. Volume 3*, p. 313.
57. For the Oxford stationers see Gibson, *Statuta antiqua*, pp. 183–6, 211.
58. See the brief remarks of Leathes, *Grace Book A*, pp. xliii–iv.

had a further vehicle for the expression of opinions in the form of the congregation of artists. Even the non-regents had a place on the supreme legislative assemblies of Oxford and Cambridge. Moreover, there was a variety of ways in which regent masters could make a contribution to the administrative life of both universities and to their colleges, halls and hostels. There was no question, at least before the Tudor era, of the exclusion of teaching staff from self-perpetuating and unrepresentative university bodies. The frequency of elections for university officials ensured a regular turnover of personnel and prevented the entrenchment of oligarchical structures. Much of this was to change in the course of the sixteenth century when the Tudor government tried, with some degree of success, to reduce the English universities to a constricting measure of state control.

Before 1500 non-academic administrative staff were thin on the ground. The few administrators who were hired were very pointedly regarded as university servants. Indeed, the bedels were often known as "public" or "common" servants. In no way were administrative staff permitted to share in policy-making. Their task was to serve, not to manage. Their worth was recognized through the conferment of the status of "privileged person". They could never, however, occupy more than a subordinate place within academic guilds whose *raison d'être* was teaching and scholarship. The idea of a professional administrative class for university support-services was scarcely adumbrated in the medieval period. The teaching masters were prepared to make considerable sacrifices in terms of time and energy so that all of the essential processes of university life would remain under their control. The medieval English universities set their own fees, attracted their own private income and endowments, gave their teaching staff a strong sense of corporate belonging through democratic procedures and fought to retain as much autonomy as possible from predatory external powers. There is much here that may have a bearing upon how best to organize universities in the modern age.

Bibliography

Original sources

Oxford University

All Souls College archives, bursars' books for 1450–1, *c*.1495, and 1497–8, Bodleian MSS D. D. b. 29.

Exeter College archives, rectors' accounts, late-fourteenth and fifteenth centuries.

Expenses of John Arundel, principal of an Oxford hall in 1424, North Devon Record Office, MS B1/3960.

Expenses of John Hychcok, bachelor of St Mary Hall, Oxford, of *c*.1460, Bodleian MS Lat. misc. d. 83, fol. 1.

Expenses of Thomas Jolyffe, principal of Glasen Hall, Oxford, of *c*.1460, Bodleian MS Digby 26, fol. 140v.

Lincoln College archives, bursars' books, I, II (the earliest surviving account dates from 1455–6).

Merton College archives, bursars' rolls, fourteenth and fifteenth centuries.

New College archives, bursars' rolls, 1376–1499, 7711(1)–7459(136). The reference numbers are rather oddly sequenced.

Oriel College archives, treasurers' accounts, I(1409–15), II(1450–82).

Queen's College archives, long rolls (transcripts), I–VI, fourteenth and fifteenth centuries.

University College archives, bursars' rolls, 1385–6 – *c*.1494–5.

Cambridge University

Bull of Eugenius IV of 18 September 1433, Cambridge University archives, Luard, no. 114.

Charter of Edward I, probably of 1294, Cambridge University archives, Luard, no. 11.

Charter of Edward III of 24 March 1327, Cambridge University archives, Luard, no. 25.

Charter of Edward III of 14 December 1335, Cambridge University archives, Luard, no. 28.

Christ's College archives, college accounts, B. 1. 1. (1530–45).

Corpus Christi College archives, college accounts, 1376–1485.

Gonville College archives, computus books, *c*.1423–5, 1523, Gonville & Caius MS 365.

James Duport's "Rules to be observed by young pupils and schollers in the University", Trinity College Library, MS O. 10A. 33.

King's College archives, mundum books, I–IX (1447–1507).

Liber procuratoris antiquus (Old Proctor's Book), Cambridge University archives, Coll Admin 3.

Pembroke College archives, *Registrum A* and *Registrum Aa*.

Peterhouse archives, computus rolls, late-fourteenth and fifteenth centuries.

Queens' College archives, journale I (1484–1518).

St Catharine's College muniments, XL/10 (original statutes).

Trinity College archives, King's Hall accounts, 26 volumes (1337–1544).

Public Record Office

PRO Exchequer accounts, King's Remembrancer, E101/348/12/16/17.

Printed sources

Alton, R. E. (ed.), "The academic drama in Oxford: extracts from the records of four colleges", in *Malone Society Collections* **5** (Oxford, Oxford University Press, 1960), pp. 29–95.

Anstey, H. (ed.), *Munimenta academica: documents illustrative of academical life and studies at Oxford* (2 vols) (London, Longman, 1868).

Anstey, H. (ed.), *Epistolae academicae oxoniensis* (2 vols), Oxford Historical Society **35, 36** (Oxford, Clarendon Press, 1898).

Bateson, M. (ed.), *Grace Book B Part I*, Cambridge Antiquarian Society, Luard Memorial Series, II (Cambridge, Cambridge University Press, 1903).

Bateson, M. (ed.), *Grace Book B Part II*, Cambridge Antiquarian Society, Luard Memorial Series, III (Cambridge, Cambridge University Press, 1905).

Bernhard, M. (ed.), *Goswin Kempgyn de Nussia trivita studentium: eine einführung in das universitätsstudium aus dem 15. jahrhundert*, Münchener Beiträge zur Mediävistik und Renaissance-Forschung **26** (Munich, Arbeo-Gesellschaft, 1976).

Caius, J., *Historiae Cantabrigiensis academiae ab urbe condita, liber primus* (London, Day, 1574),

Calendar of entries in the papal registers, relating to Great Britain and Ireland. Volume 8 (1427–47) (London, HMSO, 1909).

Calendar of inquisitions post mortem. Volume 8 (London, Fisher Unwin, 1913).

Cooper, C. H. (ed.), *Annals of Cambridge* (4 vols) (Cambridge, Warwick & Co., 1842–53).

Davis, N. (ed.), *Paston letters and papers of the fifteenth century* (2 vols) (Oxford, Clarendon Press, 1971–6).

Denifle, H. & E. Chatelain (eds), *Chartularium universitatis Parisiensis* (4 vols) (Paris, Delalain, 1889–97).

Dobson, R. B. (ed.), *The Peasants' Revolt* (London, Macmillan, 1970).

Dunlop, A. I. (ed.), *Acta facultatis artium Universitatis Sanctiandree 1413–1588* (Edinburgh & London, Oliver & Boyd, 1964).

Dyer, G. (ed.), *The privileges of the University of Cambridge* (2 vols) (London, Longman, 1824).

Fournier, M. (ed.), *Les statuts et privilèges des universités françaises depuis leur fondation jusqu'en 1789* (3 vols) (Paris, Larose & Forcel, 1890–2).

Gibson, S. (ed.), *Statuta antiqua universitatis oxoniensis* (Oxford, Clarendon Press, 1931).

Gutch, J. (ed.), *Anthony Wood's history and antiquities of the University of Oxford* (2 vols in 3) (Oxford, Clarendon Press, 1792–6).

Highfield, J. R. L. (ed.), *The early rolls of Merton College Oxford* (Oxford, Clarendon Press, 1964).

Leach, A. F. (ed.), *Educational charters and documents 598 to 1909* (Cambridge, Cambridge University Press, 1911).

Leathes, S. M. (ed.), *Grace Book A*, Cambridge Antiquarian Society, Luard Memorial Series, I (Cambridge, Cambridge University Press, 1897).

McGarry, D. D. (trans.), *The Metalogicon of John of Salisbury* (Berkeley, Calif., University of California Press, 1955).

MacLagan, M. (ed.), *Philobiblon of Richard de Bury* (Oxford, Basil Blackwell, 1960).

Malagola, C. (ed.), *Statuti delle università et dei collegi dello studio bolognese* (Bologna, N. Zanichelli, 1888).

Moore-Smith, G. C. (ed.), "The academic drama at Cambridge: extracts from college records", in *Malone Society Collections* **2**, pt 2 (Oxford, Oxford University Press, 1923), pp. 150–230.

Nelson, A. H. (ed.), *Records of early English drama* (2 vols) (Toronto, Toronto University Press, 1989).

Pantin, W. A. (ed.), *Canterbury College Oxford* (3 vols), Oxford Historical Society, new ser. **6, 7, 8** (Oxford, Clarendon Press, 1946–50).

Pantin, W. A. & W. T. Mitchell (eds), *The register of congregation 1448–1463*, Oxford Historical Society, new ser. **22** (Oxford, Clarendon Press, 1972).

Philpott, H. (ed.), *Documents relating to St Catharine's College in the University of Cambridge* (Cambridge, Cambridge University Press, 1861).

Prickett, M. & T. Wright (eds), T. Fuller's *The history of the University of Cambridge* (Cambridge, Cambridge University Press, 1840).

Queen's Commissioners (ed.), *Documents relating to the university and colleges of Cambridge* (3 vols) (London, Longman, 1852).

Queen's Commissioners (ed.), *Statutes of the colleges of Oxford* (3 vols) (Oxford & London, Parker & Longmans, 1853).

Riley, H. T. (ed.), *Memorials of London and London life in the 13th, 14th and 15th centuries* (London, Longmans, 1888).

Rogers, J. E. T. (ed.), Thomas Gascoigne's *Loci e libro veritatum* (Oxford, Clarendon Press, 1881).

Rogers, J. E. T. (ed.), *Oxford city documents 1268–1665*, Oxford Historical Society **18** (Oxford, Clarendon Press, 1891).

Rotuli parliamentorum 1278–1503 (6 vols) (London, Record Commission, 1783).

Salter, H. E. (ed.), *Records of medieval Oxford* (Oxford, Oxford Chronicle Co., 1912).

Salter, H. E. (ed.), *The Oxford deeds of Balliol College* (Oxford, H. Hart, 1913).

Salter, H. E. (ed.), *The medieval archives of the University of Oxford* (2 vols), Oxford Historical Society **70, 73** (Oxford, Clarendon Press, 1917–19).

Salter, H. E. (ed.), *Registrum annalium collegii Mertonensis 1483–1521*, Oxford Historical Society **76** (Oxford, Clarendon Press, 1923).

Salter, H. E. (ed.), *Registrum cancellarii oxoniensis 1434–1469* (2 vols), Oxford Historical Society **93, 94** (Oxford, Clarendon Press, 1932).

Salter, H. E., W. A. Pantin & H. G. Richardson (eds), *Formularies which bear on the history of Oxford c.1204–1420* (2 vols), Oxford Historical Society, new ser. **4, 5** (Oxford, Clarendon Press, 1942).

Seybolt, R. F. (ed.), *The manuale scholarium* (Cambridge, Mass., Harvard University Press, 1921).

Shadwell, C. L. & H. E. Salter (eds), *Oriel College records* (Oxford, Oxford University Press, 1926).

Thorndike, L. (ed.), *University records and life in the Middle Ages* (New York, Octagon, 1971).

Secondary works

Allmand, C. T., "The civil lawyers", in C. H. Clough (ed.), *Profession, vocation and culture in later-medieval England* (Liverpool, Liverpool University press, 1982), pp. 155–80.

Aston, M., *Thomas Arundel* (Oxford, Clarendon Press, 1967).

Aston, T. H., "Oxford's medieval alumni", *Past & Present* **74**, 1977, pp. 3–40.

Aston, T. H., "The external administration and resources of Merton College to c.1348", in Catto (ed.), *HUO*, I, pp. 311–68.

Aston, T. H. & R. Faith, "The endowments of the university and colleges to c.1348", in Catto (ed.), *HUO*, I, pp. 265–309.

Aston, T. H., G. D. Duncan & T. A. R. Evans, "The medieval alumni of the University of Cambridge", *Past & Present* **86**, 1980, pp. 9–86.

Attwater, A., *Pembroke College, Cambridge: a short history* (Cambridge, Cambridge University Press, 1936.

Bagley, J. J., *Margaret of Anjou Queen of England* (London, Jenkins, 1948).

Baldwin, J. W., "The image of the jongleur in northern France around 1200", *Speculum* **72**, 1997, pp. 635–63.

Barton J. L., "The study of civil law before 1380", in Catto (ed.), *HUO*, I, pp. 519–30.

Barton, J. L., "The legal faculties of late-medieval Oxford", in Catto & Evans (eds), *HUO*, II, pp. 281–313.

Bataillon, L., B. Guyot & R. H. Rouse (eds), *La production du livre universitaire au moyen âge: exemplar et pecia* (Paris, CNRS, 1988).

Bean, J. M. W., "Plague, population and economic decline in England in the later Middle Ages", *Economic History Review*, 2nd ser. **15**, 1962–3, pp. 423–37.

Beaujouan, G., "The transformation of the quadrivium", in Benson, R. L. & G. Constable (eds), *Renaissance and renewal in the twelfth century* (Oxford, Clarendon Press, 1982), pp. 463–87.

Bennett, H. S., *The Pastons and their England* (Cambridge, Cambridge University Press, 1951).

Bennett, J. A. W., *Chaucer at Oxford and at Cambridge* (Oxford, Clarendon Press, 1974).

Billington, S., *Mock kings in medieval society and Renaissance drama* (Oxford, Clarendon Press, 1991).

Boas, F. S., *University drama in the Tudor age* (Oxford, Clarendon Press, 1914).

Boyle, L. E., "The curriculum of the faculty of canon law at Oxford in the first half of the fourteenth century", in *Oxford studies presented to Daniel Callus*, pp. 135–62.

Boyle, L. E., "Canon law before 1380", in Catto (ed.), *HUO*, I, pp. 531–64.

Brooke, C. N. L. *A history of Gonville and Caius College* (Woodbridge, Suffolk, Boydell Press, 1985).

Brooke, C. N. L., "The churches of medieval Cambridge", in D. Beales & G. Best (eds), *History, society and the churches: essays in honour of Owen Chadwick* (Cambridge, Cambridge University Press, 1985), pp. 49–76.

Brooke, C. N. L. & J. R. L. Highfield, *Oxford and Cambridge* (Cambridge, Cambridge University Press, 1988).

Brundage, J. A., "The Cambridge faculty of canon law and the ecclesiastical courts of Ely", in Zutshi (ed.), *Medieval Cambridge*, pp. 21–45.

Bullough, V. L., *The development of medicine as a profession* (Basel, S. Karger, 1966).

Bury, J. P. T., "Corpus Christi College", in Roach (ed.), *Victoria history of the county of Cambridge. Volume 3*, pp. 371–6.

Butcher, A. F., "The economy of Exeter College, 1400–1500", *Oxoniensia* **44**, 1979, pp. 38–54.

Buxton, J. & P. Williams (eds), *New College Oxford 1379–1979* (Oxford, Warden and fellows of New College, 1979).

Cam, H. M., "The city of Cambridge", in Roach (ed.), *Victoria history of the county of Cambridge. Volume 3*, pp. 1–149.

Catto, J. I. (ed.), *The early Oxford schools*, vol. 1 of *The history of the University of Oxford* (Oxford, Clarendon Press, 1984).

Catto, J. I., "Citizens, scholars and masters", in Catto (ed.), *HUO*, I, pp. 151–92.

Catto, J. I., "Theology and theologians 1220–1320", in Catto (ed.), *HUO*, I, pp. 471–517.

Catto, J. I., "Theology after Wycliffism", in Catto & Evans (eds), *HUO*, II, pp. 263–80.

Catto, J. I., "Wyclif and Wycliffism at Oxford 1356–1430", in Catto & Evans (eds), *HUO*, II, pp. 175–261.

Catto, J. I. & T. A. R. Evans (eds), *Late medieval Oxford*, vol. 2 of *The history of the University of Oxford* (Oxford, Clarendon Press, 1992).

Chambers, E. K., *The medieval stage* (2 vols) (Oxford, Oxford University Press, 1903).

Chandler, R., *The life of William Waynflete, Bishop of Winchester* (London, White & Cochrane, 1811).

Cheney, C. R., *Notaries public in England in the thirteenth and fourteenth centuries* (Oxford, Clarendon Press, 1972).

Chibnall, A. C., *Richard de Badew and the University of Cambridge 1315–1340* (Cambridge, Cambridge University Press, 1963).

Clanchy, M. T., "*Moderni* in education and government in England", *Speculum* **50**, 1975, pp. 671–88.

Clough, C. H., "Cardinal Albornoz, the Spanish College in Bologna, and the Italian Renaissance", *Studia Albornotiana* **12**, 1972, pp. 227–38.

Cobban, A. B., *The King's Hall within the University of Cambridge in the later Middle Ages* (Cambridge, Cambridge University Press, 1969).

Cobban, A. B., "Episcopal control in the medieval universities of northern Europe", *Studies in Church History* **5**, 1969, pp. 1–22.

Cobban, A. B., "Medieval student power", *Past & Present* **53**, 1971, pp. 28–66.

Cobban, A. B., "Origins: Robert Wodelarke and St Catharine's", in E. E. Rich (ed.), *St Catharine's College 1473–1973* (Leeds, Maney, 1973), pp. 1–32.

Cobban, A. B., "Decentralized teaching in the medieval English universities", *History of Education* **5**, 1976, pp. 193–206.

Cobban, A. B., "The medieval Cambridge colleges: a quantitative study of higher degrees to *c*.1500", *History of Education* **9**, 1980, pp. 1–12.

Cobban, A. B., "Theology and law in the medieval colleges of Oxford and Cambridge", *BJRL* **65**, 1982, pp. 57–77.

Cobban, A. B., "Elective salaried lectureships in the universities of southern Europe in the pre-Reformation era", *BJRL* **67**, 1985, pp. 662–87.

Cobban, A. B., *The medieval English universities: Oxford and Cambridge to c.1500* (Berkeley, Calif. & Aldershot, England, University of California Press & Scolar Press, 1988).

Cobban, A. B., "The role of colleges in the medieval universities of northern Europe, with special reference to England and France", *BJRL* **71**, 1989, pp. 49–70.

Cobban, A. B., "Colleges and halls 1380–1500", in Catto & Evans (eds), *HUO*, II, pp. 581–633.

Cobban, A. B., "Medieval universities in contemporary society", in L. Smith & B. Ward (eds), *Intellectual life in the Middle Ages: essays presented to Margaret Gibson* (London & Rio Grande, Ohio, Hambledon Press, 1992).

Cobban, A. B., "Commoners in medieval Cambridge colleges", in Zutshi (ed.), *Medieval Cambridge*, pp. 47–64.

Cobban, A. B., "John Arundel, the tutorial system, and the cost of undergraduate living in the medieval English universities", *BJRL* **77**, 1995, pp. 143–159.

Colish, M. L., *Medieval foundations of the western intellectual tradition 400–1400* (New Haven, Conn. & London, Yale University Press, 1997).

Colvin, H. & J. S. G. Simmons, *All Souls: an Oxford college and its buildings* (Oxford, Oxford University Press, 1989).

Courtenay, W. J., "The effect of the Black Death on English higher education", *Speculum* **55**, 1980, pp. 696–714.

Courtenay, W. J., "The role of English thought in the transformation of university education in the late Middle Ages", in Kittelson & Transue (eds), *Rebirth, reform and resilience*, pp. 103–62.

Courtenay, W. J., *Schools and scholars in fourteenth-century England* (Princeton, NJ, Princeton University Press, 1987).

Courtenay, W. J., *Teaching careers at the University of Paris in the thirteenth and fourteenth centuries* (Notre Dame, Ind., University of Notre Dame Press, 1988).

Courtenay, W. J., "Inquiry and inquisition: academic freedom in medieval universities", *Church History* **58**, 1989, pp. 168–81.

Courtenay, W. J., "Theology and theologians from Ockham to Wyclif", in Catto & Evans (eds), *HUO*, II, pp. 1–34.

Cross, C., "Oxford and the Tudor state from the accession of Henry VIII to the death of Mary", in McConica (ed.), *HUO*, III, pp. 117–49.

Curtis, M. H., *Oxford and Cambridge in transition 1558–1642* (Oxford, Clarendon Press, 1959).

Davis, V., *William Waynflete: bishop and educationalist* (Woodbridge, Suffolk, Boydell Press, 1993).

Denholm-Young, N., "Magdalen College", in Salter & Lobel (eds), *Victoria history of the county of Oxford. Volume 3*, pp. 193–207.

Denton, J. H., *Robert Winchelsey and the crown 1294–1313* (Cambridge, Cambridge University Press, 1980).

D'Irsay, *Moyen âge et renaissance*, vol. 1 of *Histoire des universités françaises et étrangères des origines à nos jours* (Paris, Picard, 1933).

Dobson, R. B., "The religious orders 1370–1540", in Catto & Evans (eds), *HUO*, II, pp. 539–79.

Dunbabin, J., "Careers and vocations", in Catto (ed.), *HUO*, I, pp. 565–605.

Ellis, D. M. B. & L. F. Salzman, "Religious Houses", in L. F. Salzman (ed.), *Victoria history of the county of Cambridge and the Isle of Ely. Volume 2* (London, Oxford University Press, 1948), pp. 197–318.

Emden, A. B., *An Oxford hall in medieval times* (Oxford, Clarendon Press, 1927).

Emden, A. B., *A biographical register of the University of Oxford to AD 1500* (3 vols) (Oxford, Clarendon Press, 1957–9).

Emden, A. B., "The remuneration of the medieval proctors of the University of Oxford", *Oxoniensia* **26–7**, 1961–2, pp. 202–6.

Emden, A. B., *A biographical register of the University of Cambridge to 1500* (Cambridge, Cambridge University Press, 1963).

Emden, A. B., "Northerners and southerners in the organization of the University to 1509", in *Oxford studies presented to Daniel Callus*, Oxford Historical Society, new ser. **16** (Oxford, Clarendon Press, 1964), pp. 1–30.

Emden, A. B., *A biographical register of the University of Oxford AD 1501 to 1540* (Oxford, Clarendon Press, 1974).

Evans, T. A. R., "The number, origins and careers of scholars", in Catto & Evans (eds), *HUO*, II, pp. 485–538.

Evans, T. A. R. & R. Faith, "College estates and university finances 1350–1500", in Catto & Evans (eds), *HUO*, II, pp. 635–707.

Feingold, M., *The mathematicians' apprenticeship: science, universities and society in England 1560–1640* (Cambridge, Cambridge University Press, 1984).

Fletcher, J. M., "Wealth and poverty in the medieval German universities", in J. R. Hale, J. R. L. Highfield & B. Smalley (eds), *Europe in the late Middle Ages* (London, Faber & Faber, 1965), pp. 410–36.

Fletcher, J. M., "The teaching of arts at Oxford, 1400–1520", *Paedagogica Historica* **7**, 1967, pp. 417–54.

Fletcher, J. M., "Change and resistance to change: a consideration of the development of English and German universities during the sixteenth century", *History of Universities* **1**, 1981, pp. 1–36.

Fletcher, J. M., "The faculty of arts", in Catto (ed.), *HUO*, I, pp. 369–99.

Fletcher, J. M., "The history of academic colleges", in D. Maffei & H. de Ridder Symoens (eds), *I collegi universitari in Europa tra il xiv e il xviii secolo* (Milan, Giuffrè, 1991), pp. 13–22.

Fletcher, J. M., "Developments in the faculty of arts 1370–1520", in Catto & Evans (eds), *HUO*, II, pp. 315–45.

Fletcher, J. M. & C. A. Upton, "Expenses at admission and determination in fifteenth-century Oxford: new evidence", *EHR* **100**, 1985, pp. 331–7.

Fletcher, J. M. & C. A. Upton, "The cost of undergraduate study at Oxford in the fifteenth century: the evidence of the Merton College 'founder's kin'", *History of Education* **14**, 1985, pp. 1–20.

Fletcher, J. M. & C. A. Upton, "'Monastic enclave' or 'open society'? A consideration of the role of women in the life of an Oxford college community in the early Tudor period", *History of Education* **16**, 1987, pp. 1–9.

Forde, S., "The educational organization of the Augustinian Canons in England and Wales, and their university life at Oxford, 1325–1448", *History of Universities* **13**, 1994, pp. 21–60.

Gabriel, A. L., "The practice of charity at the University of Paris during the Middle Ages", *Traditio* **5**, 1947, pp. 335–9.

Gabriel, A. L., *Student life in Ave Maria College, medieval Paris* (Notre Dame, Ind., University of Notre Dame Press, 1955).

Gabriel, A. L., *Skara House at the medieval University of Paris* (Notre Dame, Ind., University of Notre Dame Press, 1960).

Gabriel, A. L., "The college system in the fourteenth-century universities", in F. L. Utley (ed.), *The forward movement of the fourteenth century* (Columbus, Ohio State University Press, 1961), pp. 79–124.

Gabriel, A. L., *Garlandia: studies in the history of the medieval university* (Frankfurt, Knecht, 1969).

Gabriel, A. L. (ed.), *The economic and material frame of the medieval university* (Notre Dame, Ind., University of Notre Dame Press, 1977).

Gabriel, A. L., *The Paris Studium: Robert of Sorbonne and his legacy* (Notre Dame, Ind. & Frankfurt, Knecht, 1992).

Garrod, H. W., "Merton College", in Salter & Lobel (eds), *Victoria history of the county of Oxford. Volume 3*, pp. 95–106.

Gasquet, F. A., *The Black Death of 1348 and 1349*, 2nd edn (London, Bell, 1908).

Getz, F. M., "The faculty of medicine before 1500", in Catto & Evans (eds), *HUO*, II, pp. 373–405.

Gieysztor, A., "Management and resources", in Ridder-Symoens (ed.), *A history of the university in Europe*, I, pp. 108–43.

Gillam, S., *The divinity school and Duke Humfrey's library at Oxford* (Oxford, Clarendon Press, 1988).

Gimpel, J., *The medieval machine: the industrial revolution of the Middle Ages*, 2nd edn (Aldershot, Wildwood House, 1988).

Gottfried, R. S., *The Black Death* (London, R. Hale, 1983).

Greatrex, J., "Monk students from Norwich Cathedral Priory at Oxford and Cambridge, *c.*1300 to 1530", *EHR* **106**, 1991, pp. 555–83.

Green, V. H. H., *Oxford University* (London, Batsford, 1974).

Green, V. H. H., *The commonwealth of Lincoln College 1427–1977* (Oxford, Oxford University Press, 1979).

Griffiths, R. A., *The reign of King Henry VI* (London & Tonbridge, Kent, E. Benn, 1981).

Gwynn, A., *Roman education from Cicero to Quintilian* (Oxford, Clarendon Press, 1926).

Hackett, M. B., *The original statutes of Cambridge University: the text and its history* (Cambridge, Cambridge University Press, 1970).

Hackett, M. B., "The university as a corporate body", in Catto (ed.), *HUO*, I, pp. 37–95.

Hajnal, I., *L'enseignement de l'écriture aux universités médiévales*, 2nd edn (Budapest, Académie des Sciences de Hongrie, 1959).

Hall, C. P., "The gild of Corpus Christi and the foundation of Corpus Christi College: an investigation of the documents", in Zutshi (ed.), *Medieval Cambridge*, pp. 65–91.

Hammer, C. J., Jr, "Oxford town and Oxford University", in McConica (ed.), *HUO*, III, pp. 69–116.

Hanham, A., *The Celys and their world* (Cambridge, Cambridge University Press, 1985).

Haren, M., *Medieval thought: the western intellectual tradition from antiquity to the thirteenth century* (London, Macmillan, 1985).

Hargreaves-Mawdsley, W. N., *A history of academical dress in Europe until the end of the eighteenth century* (Oxford, Clarendon Press, 1963).

Harrison, F. Ll., "Music at Oxford before 1500", in Catto & Evans (eds), *HUO*, II, pp. 347–71.

Harrison, W. J., "Clare College", in Roach (ed.), *Victoria history of the county of Cambridge. Volume 3*, pp. 340–6.

Harvey, B. F., "The monks of Westminster and the University of Oxford", in F. R. H. Du Bouley & C. M. Barron (eds), *The reign of Richard II* (London, Athlone Press, 1971).

Harvey, J. H., "Architecture in Oxford 1350–1500", in Catto & Evans (eds), *HUO*, II, pp. 747–68.

Harvey, P. D. A., *A medieval Oxfordshire village, Cuxham 1240 to 1400* (Oxford, Oxford University Press, 1965).

Haskins, C. H., *Studies in medieval culture* (Oxford, Clarendon Press, 1929).

Hays, R. W., "Welsh students at Oxford and Cambridge Universities in the Middle Ages", *Welsh Historical Review* **4**, 1968–9, pp. 325–61.

Henson, H. H., "The 'Rex Natalicus'", in C. R. L. Fletcher (ed.), *Collectanea*, Oxford Historical Society **5** (Oxford, Clarendon Press, 1885), I, pp. 39–49.

Hill, R. M. T., "Oliver Sutton, Bishop of Lincoln, and the University of Oxford", *TRHS* 4th ser. **31**, 1949, pp. 1–16.

Hill, R. M. T., *Oliver Sutton*, Lincoln Minster Pamphlets **4** (Lincoln, J. W. Ruddock, 1950), pp. 3–36.

Hill, R. M. T. (ed.), *The rolls and register of Bishop Oliver Sutton 1280–1299*, Lincoln Record Society **3**, 1952.

Hodgkin, R. H., *Six centuries of an Oxford college: a history of the Queen's College 1340–1940* (Oxford, Basil Blackwell, 1949).

Hodgkin, R. H., "Queen's College", in Salter & Lobel (eds), *Victoria history of the county of Oxford. Volume 3*, pp. 132–43.

Hussey, M., *Chaucer's world: a pictorial companion* (Cambridge, Cambridge University Press, 1967).

Isewijn, J. & J. Paquet (eds), *The universities in the late Middle Ages* (Louvain, Belgium, Louvain University Press, 1978).

Jackson-Stops, G., "The building of the medieval college", in Buxton & Williams (eds), *New College Oxford 1379–1979*, pp. 147–92.

Jacob, E. F., "English university clerks in the later Middle Ages: the problem of maintenance", *BJRL* **29**, 1946, pp. 304–25.

Jacob, E. F., "Petitions for benefices from English universities during the Great Schism", *TRHS* 4th ser. **27**, 1949, pp. 41–59.

Jacob, E. F., *Essays in the conciliar epoch*, 2nd edn (Manchester, Manchester University Press, 1953).

Jardine, L., "Humanism and the sixteenth-century arts course", *History of Education* **4**, 1975, pp. 16–31.

Jenkinson, H., "Mary de Sancto Paulo, foundress of Pembroke College, Cambridge", *Archaeologia* **66**, 1914–15, pp. 410–46.

Jones, A. H. M., "New College", in Salter & Lobel (eds), *Victoria history of the county of Oxford. Volume 3*, pp. 144–62.

Jones, J., *Balliol College: a history, 1263–1939* (Oxford, Oxford University Press, 1988).

Kagan, R. L., "Universities in Castile 1500–1700", *Past & Present* **49**, 1970, pp. 44–71.

Kagan, R. L., *Students and society in early modern Spain* (Baltimore, Md., The Johns Hopkins University Press, 1974).

Kaluza, Z., "Nicolas d'Autrécourt: ami de la vérité", in Académie des Inscriptions et Belles-Lettres (ed.), *Histoire littéraire de la France*, 42 (Paris, A. Bontemps, 1995), pp. 1–232.

Ker, N. R., "Oxford college libraries before 1500", in Isewijn & Paquet (eds), *The universities in the late Middle Ages*, pp. 293–311.

Ker, N. R., "The books of philosophy distributed at Merton College in 1372 and 1375", in A. G. Watson (ed.), *Books, collectors and libraries: studies in the medieval heritage* (London & Ronceverte, West Virginia, Hambledon Press, 1995), pp. 331–78.

Kibre, P., *The nations in the medieval universities* (Cambridge, Mass., Medieval Academy of America, 1948).

Kibre, P., *Scholarly privileges in the Middle Ages* (London, W. Clowes for the Medieval Academy of America, 1961).

Kittelson, J. M. & P. T. Transue (eds), *Rebirth, reform and resilience: universities in transition 1300–1700* (Columbus, Ohio State University Press, 1984).

Knowles, D., *The evolution of medieval thought*, 2nd edn, D. E. Luscombe & C. N. L. Brooke (eds) (Harlow, England, Longman, 1988).

Laffan, R. G. D., "Queens' College", in Roach (ed.), *Victoria history of the county of Cambridge. Volume 3*, pp. 408–15.

Lawn, B., *The rise and decline of the scholastic "quaestio disputata"* (Leiden, Belgium, New York & Cologne, Brill, 1993).

Lawrence, C. H., "The university in state and church", in Catto (ed.), *HUO*, I, pp. 97–150.

Leader, D. R., "Professorships and academic reform at Cambridge: 1488–1520", *Sixteenth Century Journal* **14**, 1983, pp. 215–27.

Leader, D. R., "Teaching in Tudor Cambridge", *History of Education* **13**, 1984, pp. 105–19.

Leader, D. R., *The university to 1546*, vol. 1 of *The history of the University of Cambridge* (Cambridge, Cambridge University Press, 1988).

Leedham-Green, E., *A concise history of the University of Cambridge* (Cambridge, Cambridge University Press, 1996).

Leff, G., *Paris and Oxford Universities in the thirteenth and fourteenth centuries* (New York, John Wiley, 1968).

Lesne, E., "Les écoles de la fin du viiie siècle à la fin du xiie", in *Histoire de la propriété ecclésiastique en France* (Lille, Facultés Catholiques de Lille, 1940).

Lewry, P. O., "Grammar, logic and rhetoric 1220–1320", in Catto (ed.), *HUO*, I, pp. 401–33.

Leyser, H., *Medieval women: a social history of women in England 450–1500* (London, Weidenfeld & Nicolson, 1995).

Little, A. G., *The grey friars in Oxford* (Oxford, Clarendon Press, 1892).

Little A. G. & F. Pelster, *Oxford theology and the theologians c.AD 1282–1302*, Oxford Historical Society **96** (Oxford, Clarendon Press, 1934).

Lloyd, A. H., *The early history of Christ's College, Cambridge* (Cambridge, Cambridge University Press, 1934).

Logan, F. D., "The origins of the so-called regius professorships: an aspect of the Renaissance in Oxford and Cambridge", in D. Baker (ed.), *Renaissance and renewal in Christian history*, Studies in Church History **14** (Oxford, Basil Blackwell, 1977), pp. 271–8.

Lovatt, R., "Two collegiate loan-chests in late-medieval Cambridge", in Zutshi (ed.), *Medieval Cambridge*, pp. 129–65.

Lytle, G. F., *Oxford students and English society c.1300–c.1510* (PhD thesis, Department of History, Princeton University, 1975).

Lytle, G. F., "Patronage patterns and Oxford colleges c.1300–c.1530", in Stone (ed.), *The university in society*, I, pp. 111–49.

Lytle, G. F., "The social origins of Oxford students in the late Middle Ages: New College, *c*.1380–*c*.1510", in Isewijn & Paquet (eds), *The universities in the late Middle Ages*, pp. 426–54.

Lytle, G. F., "Patronage and the election of Winchester scholars during the late Middle Ages and Renaissance", in R. Custance (ed.), *Winchester College: sixth-centenary essays* (Oxford, Oxford University Press, 1982), pp. 167–88.

McConica, J., *English humanists and Reformation politics* (Oxford, Clarendon Press, 1965).

McConica, J., "The social relations of Tudor Oxford", *TRHS* 5th ser. **27**, 1977, pp. 115–34.

McConica, J., "Humanism and Aristotle in Tudor Oxford", *EHR* **94**, 1979, pp. 291–317.

McConica, J. (ed.), *The collegiate university*, vol. 3 of *The history of the University of Oxford* (Oxford, Clarendon Press, 1986).

McConica, J., "Elizabethan Oxford: the collegiate society", in McConica (ed.), *HUO*, III, pp. 645–732.

McConica, J., "Studies and faculties: introduction", in McConica (ed.), *HUO*, III, pp. 151–6.

McConica, J., "The rise of the undergraduate college", in McConica (ed.), *HUO*, III, pp. 1–68.

McGarry, D. D., "Educational theory in the *Metalogicon* of John of Salisbury", *Speculum* **23**, 1948, pp. 659–75.

Magrath, J. R. M., *The Queen's College* (2 vols) (Oxford, Clarendon Press, 1921).

Maierù, A., *University training in medieval Europe*, D. N. Pryds (trans. & ed.) (New York, Leiden & Cologne, Brill, 1994).

Mallet, C. E., *A history of the University of Oxford* (3 vols) (London, Methuen, 1924–7).

Marti, B. M., *The Spanish College at Bologna in the fourteenth century* (Philadelphia, University of Pennsylvania Press, 1966).

Miller, E., *Portrait of a college* (Cambridge, Cambridge University Press, 1961).

Milne, J., *The early history of Corpus Christi College, Oxford* (Oxford, Basil Blackwell, 1946).

Minns, E., "Pembroke College", in Roach (ed.), *Victoria history of the county of Cambridge. Volume 3*, pp. 346–55.

Moran, J. A. H., *The growth of English schooling 1340–1548* (Princeton, NJ, Princeton University Press, 1985).

Mullinger, J. B., *The University of Cambridge* (3 vols) (Cambridge, Cambridge University Press, 1873–1911).

Murphy, J. J., "Rhetoric in fourteenth-century Oxford", *Medium Aevum* **34**, 1965, pp. 1–20.

Newman, J., "The physical setting: new building and adaptation", in McConica (ed.), *HUO*, III, pp. 597–633.

North, J., "The quadrivium", in Ridder-Symoens (ed.), *A history of the university in Europe*, I, pp. 337–59.

Olson, P. A., *The journey to wisdom: self-education in patristic and medieval literature* (Lincoln, Nebr., University of Nebraska Press, 1995).

Orme, N., *English schools in the Middle Ages* (London, Methuen, 1973).

Orme, N., *Education and society in medieval and renaissance England* (London & Ronceverte, West Virginia, Hambledon, 1989).

Oschinsky, D., *Walter of Henley and other treatises of estate management and accounting* (Oxford, Clarendon Press, 1971).

Oswald, A. "University College", in Salter & Lobel (eds), *Victoria history of the county of Oxford. Volume 3*, pp. 61–81.

Pantin, W. A., "Oriel College", in Salter & Lobel (eds), *Victoria history of the county of Oxford. Volume 3*, pp. 119–29.

Pantin, W. A., "Before Wolsey", in H. R. Trevor-Roper (ed.), *Essays in British History presented to Sir Keith Feiling* (London, Macmillan, 1964), pp. 29–59.

Pantin, W. A., "The halls and schools of medieval Oxford: an attempt at reconstruction", in *Oxford studies presented to Daniel Callus*, Oxford Historical Society, new ser. **16** (Oxford, Clarendon Press, 1964), pp. 31–100.

Pantin, W. A., *Oxford life in Oxford archives* (Oxford, Clarendon Press, 1972).

Paquet, J., "Recherches sur l'universitaire 'pauvre' au moyen âge", *Revue belge de philologie et d'histoire* **66**, 1978, pp. 301–53.

Paquet, J., "Coût des études, pauvreté et labeur: fonctions et métiers d'étudiants au moyen âge", *History of Universities* **2**, 1982, pp. 15–52.

Paquet, J., *Les matricules universitaires* (Turnhout, Belgium, Brepols, 1992).

Paré, G., A. Brunet & P. Tremblay, *La renaissance du xiiᵉ siècle: les écoles et l'enseignement* (Paris, Vrin, 1933).

Parker, J., *The early history of Oxford 727–1100* (Oxford, Clarendon Press, 1885).

Parkes, M. B., "The provision of books", in Catto & Evans (eds), *HUO*, II, pp. 407–83.

Peek, H. E. & C. P. Hall, *The archives of the University of Cambridge* (Cambridge, Cambridge University Press, 1962).

Pegues, F., "Royal support of students in the thirteenth century", *Speculum* **31**, 1956, pp. 454–62.

Pollard, G., "Medieval loan-chests at Cambridge", *BIHR* **17**, 1939–40, pp. 113–29.

Pollard, G., "The *pecia* system in the medieval universities", in M. B. Parkes & A. G. Watson (eds), *Medieval scribes, manuscripts and libraries: essays presented to N. R. Ker* (London, Scolar, 1978).

Pollard, G., "The loan-chests", in Pantin & Mitchell (eds), *The register of congregation 1448–1463*, pp. 418–20.

Post, G., "Masters' salaries and student-fees in the medieval universities", *Speculum* **7**, 1932, pp. 181–98.

Powicke, F. M., *The medieval books of Merton College* (Oxford, Clarendon Press, 1931).

Rait, R. S., *Life in the medieval university* (Cambridge, Cambridge University Press, 1912).

Rashdall, H., "The friars preachers versus the university AD 1311–1313", in M. Burrows (ed.), *Collectanea* **II**, Oxford Historical Society **16** (Oxford, Clarendon Press, 1890), pp. 193–273.

Rashdall, H., *The universities of Europe in the Middle Ages* (3 vols), 2nd edn, F. M. Powicke & A. B. Emden (eds) (Oxford, Oxford University Press, 1936).

Reitzel, J. M., *The foundation of the earliest secular colleges within the Universities of Paris and Oxford* (PhD thesis, Department of History, Brown University, Rhode Island, 1971).

Richardson, H. G., "An Oxford teacher of the fifteenth century", *BJRL* **23**, 1939, pp. 436–57.

Richardson, H. G., "Business training in medieval Oxford", *American Historical Review* **46**, 1940–1, pp. 259–80.

Ridder-Symoens, H. de (ed.), *Universities in the Middle Ages*, vol. 1 of *A history of the university in Europe* (Cambridge, Cambridge University Press, 1992).

Roach, J. P. C. (ed.), *Victoria history of the county of Cambridge and the Isle of Ely. Volume 3* (London, Oxford University Press, 1959).

Roach, J. P. C., "The University of Cambridge", in Roach (ed.), *Victoria history of the county of Cambridge. Volume 3*, pp. 150–333.

Rosenthal, J. T., "The universities and the medieval English nobility", *History of Education Quarterly* **9**, 1969, pp. 415–37.

Rosenthal, J. T., *The purchase of paradise* (London, Routledge & Kegan Paul, 1972).

Roth, C., *The Jews of medieval Oxford*, Oxford Historical Society, new ser. **9** (Oxford, Clarendon Press, 1987).

Rothblatt, S., "London: a metropolitan university?", in T. Bender (ed.), *The university and the city: from medieval origins to the present* (New York & Oxford, Oxford University Press, 1988), pp. 119–49.

Rouse Ball, W. W., *The King's Scholars and King's Hall* (privately printed, 1917).

Rubin, M., *Charity and community in medieval Cambridge* (Cambridge, Cambridge University Press, 1987).

Russell, E., "The influx of commoners into the University of Oxford before 1581: an optical illusion?", *EHR* **92**, 1977, pp. 721–45.

Salter, H., *Medieval Oxford*, Oxford Historical Society **100** (Oxford, Clarendon Press, 1936).

Salter, H. E. & M. Lobel (eds), *Victoria history of the county of Oxford. Volume 3* (London, Oxford University Press, 1954).

Saltmarsh, J., "King's College", in Roach (ed.), *Victoria history of the county of Cambridge. Volume 3*, pp. 376–407.

Saltmarsh, J., *King's College and its chapel* (Cambridge, Jarrold, 1961).

Sanderson, M., *The universities in the nineteenth century* (London & Boston, Routledge & Kegan Paul, 1975).

Schwinges, R. C., "Admission", in Ridder-Symoens (ed.), *A history of the university in Europe*, I, pp. 171–94.

Schwinges, R. C., "Student education, student life", in Ridder-Symoens (ed.), *A history of the university in Europe*, I, pp. 195–243.

Searle, W. G., *History of the Queens' College of St Margaret and St Bernard in the University of Cambridge, 1446–1662* (2 vols) (Cambridge, Cambridge Antiquarian Society, 1867–71).

Sharpe, K., "The foundation of the chairs of history at Oxford and Cambridge: an episode in Jacobean politics", *History of Universities* **2**, 1982, pp. 127–52.

Siraisi, N., "The faculty of medicine", in Ridder-Symoens (ed.), *A history of the university in Europe*, I, pp. 360–87.

Smith, A. H., *New College and its buildings* (Oxford, Oxford University Press, 1952).

Smith, C. E., *The University of Toulouse in the Middle Ages* (Milwaukee, Wis., Marquette University Press, 1958).

Somers, M. H., *Irish scholars in the universities at Paris and Oxford before 1500* (PhD thesis, Department of History, City University of New York, 1979).

Southern, R. W., "Exeter College", in Salter & Lobel (eds), *Victoria history of the county of Oxford. Volume 3*, pp. 107–18.

Southern, R. W., "From schools to university", in Catto (ed.), *HUO*, I, pp. 171–94.

Squibb, G. D., *Founder's kin: privilege and pedigree* (Oxford, Clarendon Press, 1972).

Stamp, A. E., *Michaelhouse* (privately printed, 1924).

Stanier, R. S., *Magdalen School*, 2nd edn (Oxford, Basil Blackwell, 1958).

Stevenson, W. H. & H. E. Salter, *The early history of St John's College, Oxford*, Oxford Historical Society, new ser. **1** (Oxford, Clarendon Press, 1939).

Stokes, H. P., *The chaplains and the chapel of the University of Cambridge 1256–1568*, Cambridge Antiquarian Society, Octavo Publications **41**, 1906.

Stokes, H. P., "Early university property", *Proceedings of the Cambridge Antiquarian Society* **13**, 1908–9, new ser. **7**, pp. 164–84.

Stokes, H. P., *The esquire bedells of the University of Cambridge from the 13th century to the 20th century*, Cambridge Antiquarian Society, Octavo Publications **45**, 1911.

Stokes, H. P., *The medieval hostels of the University of Cambridge*, Cambridge Antiquarian Society, Octavo Publications **49**, 1924.

Stone, L., (ed.), *The university in society* (2 vols) (Princeton, NJ, Princeton University Press, 1975).

Stone, L., "The size and composition of the Oxford student body 1580–1910", in Stone (ed.), *The university in society*, I, pp. 3–110.

Storey, R. L., "The foundation and the medieval college 1379–1530", in Buxton & Williams (eds), *New College Oxford 1379–1979*, pp. 3–43.

Streeter, B. H., *The chained library* (London, Macmillan, 1931).

Swanson, R. N., *Church and society in late-medieval England* (Oxford, Basil Blackwell, 1989).

Twigg, J., *A history of Queens' College, Cambridge, 1448–1986* (Woodbridge, Suffolk, Boydell Press, 1987).

Ullmann, W., *The medieval idea of law* (London, Methuen, 1946).

Ullmann, W., "The decline of the chancellor's authority in medieval Cambridge: a rediscovered statute", *Historical Journal* **1**, 1958, pp. 176–82.

Underhill, F. A., "Elizabeth de Burgh: connoisseur and patron", in J. H. McCash (ed.), *The cultural patronage of medieval women* (Athens, Ga., University of Georgia Press, 1996), pp. 266–87.

Venn, J., "Monks in college", *Caian* **3**, 1893–4, pp. 25–34.

Venn, J., *Biographical history of Gonville and Caius College 1349–1897* (3 vols) (Cambridge, Cambridge University Press, 1897–1901).

Venn, J., *Early collegiate life* (Cambridge, Heffer, 1913).

Verger, J., *Les universités au moyen âge* (Vendôme, Presses universitaires de France, 1973).

Verger, J., "Le coût des grades: droits et frais d'examen dans les universités du Midi au moyen âge", in Gabriel (ed.), *The economic and material frame of the medieval university*. pp. 19–36.

Verger, J., "Teachers", in Ridder-Symoens (ed.), *A history of the university in Europe*, I, pp. 144–68.

Verger, J., "Les écoles cathédrales méridionales. Etat de la question", *Cahiers de Fanjeaux* **30**, 1995, pp. 245–68.

Walker, T. A., *A biographical register of Peterhouse men, part i. 1284–1574* (Cambridge, Cambridge University Press, 1927).

Ward, J. C., *English noblewomen in the later Middle Ages* (Harlow, England, Longman, 1992).

Watt, D. E. R., *A biographical dictionary of Scottish graduates to AD 1410* (Oxford, Clarendon Press, 1977).

Weisheipl, J. A., "Curriculum of the faculty of arts at Oxford in the early-fourteenth century", *Medieval Studies* **26**, 1964, pp. 143–85.

Weisheipl, J. A., "Ockham and the Mertonians", in Catto (ed.), *HUO*, I, pp. 607–58.

Weiss, R., *Humanism in England during the fifteenth century*, 2nd edn (Oxford, Basil Blackwell, 1957).

Willis, R. & J. W. Clark, *The architectural history of the University of Cambridge and the colleges of Cambridge and Eton* (4 vols) (Cambridge, Cambridge University Press, 1886).

Winstanley, D. A., *Unreformed Cambridge* (Cambridge, Cambridge University Press, 1935).

Young, K., *The drama of the medieval church* (2 vols) (Oxford, Clarendon Press, 1933).

Ziegler, P., *The Black Death* (New York, Harper & Row, 1969).

Zutshi, P. (ed.), *Medieval Cambridge: essays on the pre-Reformation university* (Woodbridge, Suffolk, Boydell Press, 1993).

Index

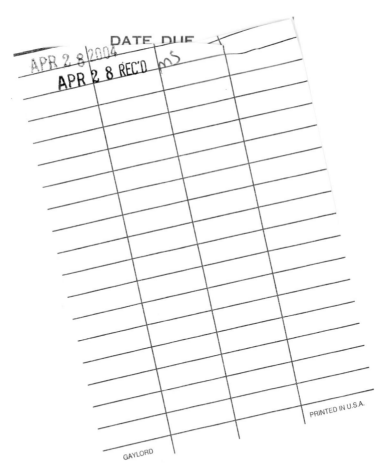

DATE DUE

APR 2 8 2004

APR 2 8 REC'D

GAYLORD   PRINTED IN U.S.A.